Something Old/Something New

Marriage and Family Ministry
in a
Postmodern Culture

RAY S. ANDERSON

Wipf & Stock
PUBLISHERS
Eugene, Oregon

SOMETHING OLD, SOMETHING NEW
Marriage and Family Ministry in a Postmodern Culture

ISBN: 978-1-55635-474-8

In Memory Of
my colleague and friend

Dennis B. Guernsey

Contents

Preface

When my faculty colleague, Dennis Guernsey, came to me twenty-seven years ago to suggest that we create and team-teach a course on Theology of the Family, he challenged me to find within the theological literature any significant treatment of marriage and family from a theological perspective. I discovered that I could name very few, and even those were buried within the larger corpus (the word is 'corpse' Dennis retorted!) of systematic theology and not very accessible to pastors and practitioners of family education and ministry. "We need your help," Dennis said, "Let's work together to create a course that has serious theological as well as sociological and psychological content."

And so we did and, after a few years of teaching the course we published our book, *On Being Family: A Social Theology of the Family* (Eerdmans, 1985). We continued to team-teach the course until Dennis left to join the faculty at Seattle Pacific University in Seattle where he developed a program in Marriage and Family modeled after the one he had developed at Fuller Theological Seminary.

Teaching with Dennis was both an adventure and a challenge. His experience as a family counselor and his creative mind not only brought rich learning to the classroom from his research in the discipline of family psychology but also practical insights from his counseling practice. Before completing his doctoral work in family sociology at the University of Southern California, he earned a theological degree at Dallas Theological Seminary, that gave him ready access to the Greek New Testament from which he shared helpful biblical insights on the texts related to marriage and family. His lively mind was accompanied by a transparent vulnerability. When he came to class he was occasionally (often?) unprepared to lecture and instead of concealing this, he was not comfortable until he found some way to share this fact with the students and then he was off and running with material that was not only anecdotal but profound. If I came to a lecture not fully prepared, the last thing that I wanted was for the class to discover this. Dennis was not as skilled in deception! Nor was he especially good at tying up loose ends administratively. He excelled in creativity, but admitted that he needed others to 'clean up after him.' Hundreds of students who took our marriage and family course were later to recall somewhat fondly (I hope!) what they called the 'Ray and Dennis Show.'

What follows in this book represents the culmination of a quarter of a century of teaching a course on Theology of the Family. As such, it is more of an academic work than a manual that attempts to lay out patterns and practices; that is, it is intended not so much as a 'how to' book but a 'what is' book. At the same time, it has a praxis orientation rather than a purely theoretical bent. It is meant to inspire and edify as well as to inform. At the inception of our journey, postmodernity was barely visible on the horizon. In the last decade, it has become an unavoidable part of our contemporary culture. While this is not a work on postmodernity itself, it has become part of the culture and context in which marriage and family ministry exists. I have found it interesting to discover that the basic insights and instincts that informed our original work anticipated and prepared the way for a more biblical understanding of how God's design for marriage and family points toward authenticity of community and the narrative of life lived under the mandate of what is real as well as what is true.

The death of Dennis in 1996 due to a brain tumor was a great loss to the academic community, and one that left me with a deep sadness along with an abiding gratitude for sharing in his life. In writing this book, I remembered once more my debt to him and hope that what I have written will be faithful to his vision and our mutual commitment to marriage and family ministry.

Chapter 1

The Cross Currents of Modernity

A few years ago, one of my students shared with me a painful story. His sister was in a long-term lesbian relationship that, in and of itself, had caused a great deal of conflict and some alienation between his sister and his parents, as well as with other family members. Recently, he related, his sister announced to her mother that she and her partner were going to 'start a family.' Her partner was going to have a child through artificial insemination. "You are going to become a grandmother," she told her mother! Instead of excitement and joy over the prospects, her mother expressed consternation and confusion. "How can this child be my grandchild," she responded? "The child will have no father, you have no husband, and you cannot be a family living with another woman." As my student related the story he expressed his own confusion and uncertainty. "My older brother and his wife adopted a child," he said, "and my mother immediately accepted that child as her grandchild even though there is no biological connection. Is the difference just due to the fact that the lesbian relationship cancels out the possibility of family? Are my parents just caught in their own tradition and unable to accept modern versions of what a family is?"

I remembered that it was during a conference on the family our seminary sponsored that one of the main speakers, a Roman Catholic priest, announced that he had to leave the conference early as he had an appointment to meet with an adoption agency concerning the adoption of a child. "I am going home to start a family," he said! Well, he was already a 'father' so to speak! Are we caught in the cross currents of modernity, not knowing which way to turn?

What is 'Modern' after all?

Historians generally date the birth of the modern mind to the Enlightenment of the eighteenth century, but its foundation was laid two hundred years before in the Renaissance, which elevated Man to the center of reality. New ways of thinking about the world developed, spurred by Francis Bacon's advances in scientific method, and Rene Descartes's search for an indubitable foundation for human knowledge. The human person was defined as an autonomous rational subject, and the work of men like Isaac Newton gave rise to a mechanistic perception of the cosmos open to human investigation and discovery, and ultimately to human control. Scientific knowledge gave birth to technology that resulted in advances in quality of life and economic growth. Belief in the supernatural was replaced with naturalism. The social implications of modernism included an expanding secularism, for to foster the freedom of human reason, the binding force of ecclesiastical authority had to be broken. The social historian, Arnold Toynbee, writing in 1939, suggested that the modern age ended in 1914, and that the new era that emerged from the rubble of WWI should be described as 'Post-Modern.' The term was later used in the arts, particularly to describe a school of architecture, before being applied to philosophical and literary trends, and finally to a general cultural phenomenon that began to blossom in the late '60s and early '70s.

The Emergence of a Postmodern View of Reality

The structure of the family in every society has always been a reflection of the cultural ethos and traditions of that society. In the face of what appeared to be relativism and pluralism, a Christian approach in the modern era has tended to appeal to a version of the family that transcends cultural and social forms. Biblical texts were chosen that lent support to definitions of family based on a Western/European, often bourgeois, view of the family. The ideal family was narrowly construed as the nuclear unit of husband, wife and one or more children living for the most part with parents and separate from other extended family members. Armed with what was considered to be a 'biblical' and therefore, morally correct concept of the family, missionaries moved aggressively into other cultures, often deploring their forms of family life as unbiblical and therefore immoral. Where polygamous marriage traditions existed, for example, some missionaries refused to baptize males until they abandoned all of their wives except one, regardless of the social and moral consequences thrust upon these abandoned wives.

A student newly arrived on our campus from Africa was asked by a colleague of mine whether his family was here with him. The student replied, "Oh no, they had to remain back in Africa." 'I'm so sorry," my colleague responded, "it must be difficult to be here for such a long time without your family." "Not really," he replied, "my wife and children are here with me!" Somewhat chagrined, my colleague realized that he was speaking a different cultural language when it came to family, though the conversation took place in English.

Only recently have some theologians awakened to the fact that their construct of a biblical version of the family was essentially a reflection of what has now become known as the 'modern' period of western intellectual and ethical thought, baptized as the Christian norm. In brief, the modern mind set was optimistic, always looking for progress as knowledge increased--for knowledge was good. The modern mind set valued objective certainty, based on rational--rather than religious or mystical--means of attaining truth. The modern mind set looked for a totality and unity in all knowledge, believing that all rational minds operating independently would come to similar conclusions about what is universally true and good. In contrast, a postmodern worldview, celebrates diversity, which can result in moral relativism and a demand for tolerance. The claims for universal truth and norms are now considered by some postmodernists as arrogant, imperialistic and have a 'secretly terroristic function.' That is, claims to hold to an absolute truth can lead to suppression and even aggression against those who hold to a different truth.

From a Christian perspective we can agree that postmodernism rightly rejects the myth that all knowledge is objective. We are involved as moral and personal agents in all that we know, and as Blaise Pascal pointed out well before the onset of the postmodern mind set, "The heart has its reasons which reason cannot know." A modern view of reality based solely on objective human thought is not Christian, and we should be prepared to make this concession.

Second, Christians can agree with postmoderns in acknowledging the importance of communities in our perception of truth. None of us is an autonomous individual, cut off from the influences of social traditions. We belong to communities that help shape our perception of reality. The distrust of reason as the sole basis for truth means that truth must be experienced to be believed, and it is in the church as the community of believers that the truth of the gospel is experienced and lived out.

Thirdly, postmodernism rightly emphasizes the significance of narrative and story. Though there is skepticism and even hostility toward meta-narratives in our postmodern world, that condition cannot last. Human beings cannot live without the meaning and purpose that such stories give.

A Christian Assessment

How do we assess this shift in our culture? We might begin by recognizing three areas of common ground that we as Christians share with our postmodern neighbors. **First**, we can applaud the postmodern attack on the hubris of contemporary modernism, which has for at least the last two centuries exalted reason and deified science. Christians ought to agree with the postmodernists that human knowledge is not indubitably certain, entirely objective, and necessarily good, though we must recognize that we have at times conformed too closely to the modernist spirit of our age. The postmodernists have helped us to appreciate that neither reason nor empirical sense perception can function as unassailable foundations for our knowledge. Nothing can be more basic to our epistemology than our faith that God is. Secular modernism is not Christian, and we can rejoice in its overthrow.

Second, we who are ministers of the gospel can agree with postmoderns in acknowledging the importance of communities in our knowing. None of us is an autonomous individual, cut off from the influences of social traditions. We belong to communities that help shape our perception of reality. This can function for good or ill, but we should rejoice in the opportunity this provides to help mold the thinking of people in the context of the church. **Third**, we must confess that our postmodern neighbors are right in asserting that universal claims to truth can be used to oppress and to exclude others. There is far too much in the history of the church that could be marshaled as evidence in support of this assertion. How many Anabaptists were burned by the Reformers because of their refusal to conform to the established version of the gospel?

But however much we may appreciate the elements of truth in the postmodern critique of the modern, we must still be cautious in aligning ourselves too closely with it. For on its most significant point the essence of modernism has not been abandoned: in postmodernism, God is still dead. This necessarily has two devastating consequences. First, since God is dead, the postmoderns also declare the death of truth. But a declaration of the death of truth is ultimately self-defeating. In denying others the right to a 'meta-narrative' which would provide a comprehensive perspective on reality, they surreptitiously introduce their own--the 'meta-narrative' of postmodernism itself. The denial of truth is at the same time a claim to truth, and is self-defeating. Second, since God is dead, the postmoderns, like the moderns, are left only with the self, but the disconnecting of the self from God is ultimately self-destroying. Without an anchor in reality, the postmoderns believe the self can be created and recreated at will. But what is the real me? What is the enduring center that does the creating? The greatest challenge is in establishing the notion of truth. In the modern world the gospel was attacked by those who claimed it was not true. In a postmodern world it is attacked simply because it claims to be true. To a culture lost at sea we broadcast a message of hope. Postmodernity may be as secular as the modernity it rejects. When we look behind both modernity and postmodernity we discover a more creative and biblical kind of modernity that is actually 'pre-modern' and thus more hopeful as well as more human. We need to explore this kind of modernity more fully.[1]

Biblical Modernity Contrasted with Secular Modernity

The common belief that what we call modernity is a recent phenomenon is challenged by Brigette and Peter Berger: "Our own version of modernization theory puts much greater stress on ideas, values and structures of consciousness as factors in social change as the result of the interaction of institutions and consciousness."[2] The Bergers also suggest that modernization as a dynamic of consciousness, "may go back as far as the origins of the Judeo-Christian religious world view." What the Bergers have suggested about the roots of modernization and the Judeo-Christian worldview is insightful. In following their thesis we could advance a theology of modernity that is anchored in the creative tension between covenant and creation. When the divine covenant was introduced in its most dramatic and liberating form through the exodus event, it gave Moses a theological hermeneutic by which he could interpret the redemptive purpose of God with respect to the original and existing social, political and religious forms of human life and worldview. The themes of liberation, humanization and re-socialization are derived from the redemptive effect of the covenant upon the existing world order. In this way we can look past the modernist/postmodernist debate and view modernity as creative grace with respect to the deterministic structure of the world as fallen from grace.

Liberation from natural/biological determinism

The fall of humanity threw persons back into the sixth day, where nature determines destiny (as with all non-human creatures). The seventh day was a gracious gift of the Creator that 'modernized' the first six days by bringing the creative power of renewal, rest and hope to the humans who were originally taken from the dust. The first humans experienced liberation from natural and biological determinism in the form of the relentless power of the created order over the freedom of those created in the image and likeness of God. No longer were humans subject to their physical or temporal nature, as were other creatures. While still under the effects of the fall, the sabbath brought the promise of release from this determinism, even as a temporary liberation.

Liberation from technological fatalism

The 'tool making' capacity was originally given to the first humans in order that the element of play and creativity might be introduced into the task of 'tilling the garden.' The first tool was thus a venture of the human spirit rather than a routinization of labor. With the fall, the technological innovation of the tool became fatal for the human spirit. The seventh day as introduced through the covenant of grace released the grip of the tool upon humans and liberated humanity from the fatal consequence of being only the productive end of technological innovation. Technology is not itself a cause nor a product of modernity. Modernity created technology and only modernity as a restoration and revitalization of the human spirit as rooted in God's grace can liberate humans from technological fatalism.

Humanization: desacralization of social structures

The original creation was 'made out of nothing,' and was not an emanation from a deity. The first humans were not 'small gods' but were created 'in the image and likeness of God.' The distinction between the sacred and the profane was absolute and essential to the humanity of the first humans. In determining to 'be like God,' humans became less human, as all forms of idolatry demonstrate. It is not modernity that dehumanizes; the dehumanization of humanity is as old as the first attempt to fashion God in the image of creatures rather than to worship the Creator (Romans 1). The covenant humanized humanity by demolishing the sacred rituals, incantations, and myths by which human social life was viewed as 'impregnated' with the arbitrary and inscrutable passions of the gods--a common theme among the Greeks, for example. Biblical modernity restores humanity by removing all that is viewed as sacred in the world as belonging to God, the God who loves, upholds, and graciously reveals himself to those same humans.

Humanization: destabilization of traditional Centers of moral authority

After the fall, moral authority tended to become identified with genealogical, tribal, familial, political and cultural traditions. The covenant 'destabilized' existing social and political structures that assumed moral power over people through the natural order. To attack these structures of moral authority was to risk persecution and even death, as Jesus ultimately discovered. To heal on the Sabbath was just one example of 'modernity' when the value of health and wholeness is given moral status over and against the law. Humanization of humanity will always be viewed as a de-stabilizing force. Socrates was given the death sentence because he was charged with 'subverting the youth of Athens' by challenging them to question conventional wisdom for the sake of truth.

Re-Socialization: realignment of kinship bonds

The social structures of natural kinship give 'rights' of the firstborn over subsequent sons (males!), and privilege and power to the sons over the daughters, and the elders over the younger. The covenant intercepted these kinship and familial alignments and assignments. Abraham leaves his father and ancestral home to seek a new home and to establish, with Sarah, a new 'family of God.' It is Isaac (the second son), not Ishmael, Jacob (the second born) not Esau, who impose modernity upon the existing structure of kinship and familial 'rights.'

Re-Socialization: assimilation of cultural diversity

The covenant, while revealed through the 'seed of Abraham'--Isaac--is for the purpose of providing a blessing for 'all the families of the earth.' Esau is rejected as the bearer of the covenant seed, but receives the blessing of Abraham and is assimilated into the promise without being absorbed into the tribe of Isaac. Modernity is multi-cultural in texture because it is authentically human at its core. There is a 'core social paradigm' which underlies all human cultures.

Re-Socialization: redefinition of moral responsibility

The divine covenant is unilateral in its inception, and bilateral in its expectations. That is, the covenant was established only from God's side, but required reciprocity on the part of humans. Having instituted the covenant solely out of the motivation of love, God exposed the law of love as the basis for moral responsibility toward God and the neighbor. With the fall came shifting of the blame (The woman whom you gave me!--The serpent beguiled me!), and the evasion of personal moral responsibility. Modernity calls forth the human out of the 'victim defense,' into the bright light of divine judgment where the reality of sin becomes the way forward to moral repentance and responsibility, demolishing the 'walls of partition' that divide and demean humanity.

Stability and Change: The Crisis of Modernity

Brigette and Peter Berger, in their book, *The War over the Family* (Anchor

Press, 1983), reported that 1980 was to be the 'year of the family' and to be celebrated by a White House Conference. Here the question of definition preoccupied the conference, with a change made from speaking about the family to speaking about families. The Bergers report that ". . . the shift reveals itself as anything but innocent: it gave governmental recognition to precisely the kind of moral relativism that has infuriated and mobilized large numbers of Americans."[3] The Roman Catholic lay theologian, Stephen Clark, argues that a traditional definition of family requires that the father be viewed as having more value as well as authority in both marriage and family. He cites as an example, the writing of the medieval theologian, Thomas Aquinas who wrote: "Father and mother are loved as principles of our natural origin. Now the Father is principle in a more excellent way than the mother, because he is the active principle. Consequently, strictly speaking, the father is to be loved more."[4]

The Bergers say that the traditional view of family is: "a married couple and their minor children, living together in their own home, forming an intimate and protective environment, providing nurture and care to the individuals concerned." With the change to families as the working definition, the Bergers suggest that "demography is translated into a new morality." They then suggest that it is now important to find an "explanatory model that will include both change and continuity in the modern western family."[5]

The role of primary and secondary relationships in family life

Primary relationships as represented in the family unit are more likely to be intimate, personal and systematic. Secondary relationships, on the other hand tend to be functional, task oriented, and compartmentalized. When family dynamics give way to the pressure of secondary type relationships there is more of an emphasis on efficiency than effectiveness. For example, when a child comes home from school with a report from the teacher that some behavior problem occurred, parents who are heavily committed to tasks and roles outside of the parenting responsibility may, for the sake of efficiency, delay dealing with the child until a later time when the schedule permits. In this case, the more effective response would be to deal with the situation when it first arises. Coping strategies in the face of the fragmentation of primary relationships tend to be impersonal and functional.

Some of the factors and forces that affect the contemporary family are: 1) technological change--computers, television, electronic games preempt personal and social exchange; 2) mobility--rapid transit is more than a public service!; 3) velocity--everything is speeded up, minutes replace hours; 4) complexity--multi-tasking spills over from the computer to daily living. The pattern of family life no longer is carried over from one generation to another. In fact, within one generation a typical family can migrate from being strongly embedded in a social structure of community to becoming isolated.

Effects of modernity and family types

The family in our contemporary culture is subject to two forces; 1) the tendency toward isolation as contrasted with being well integrated in its social context; and 2) the tendency toward being tightly structured (morphostasis) as contrasted with being loosely structured as a unity (morphogenesis). When these two tendencies are placed in the form of a quadriplex, we can see four different family types as indicated in the figure below.

EFFECTS OF MODERNITY AND FAMILY TYPES

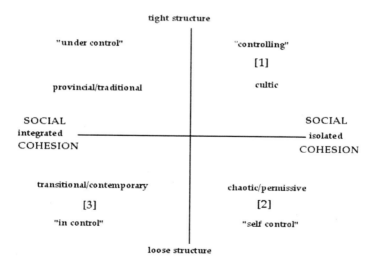

1. reactionary modernity
2. utopian modernity
3. redemptive modernity

Figure 1.1

When the social structure is rigid and social cohesion high (integrated) the family unit can be said to be 'under control.' The upper left hand corner of the quadrant represents this in the form of a provincial or traditional family unit. While my family of origin was well-structured and under control--parental discipline was firm but realistic--we were well integrated into the community through extended family as well as neighbors with whom we had regular exchange of social relationships. As a farm boy, even when roaming around the small town everyone knew that I was 'Albert Anderson's son' and on occasion reminded me of that!

The upper right quadrant of the diagram represents a tightly structured family unit, but one that is isolated within its own community. The result is a cultic unit, whether one or a number of family units. Often this takes the form of a religious or radical anti-social social structure. I call this 'reactionary modernity.' The lower right quadrant represents a very loose social structure but also one that is isolated from the context of its community. This tends to produce a chaotic and / or permissive social unit. We see evidence of this most everyday in news reports of children getting into trouble due to lack of parental supervision. Members of families that are chaotic tend to feature a 'self-control' type of behavior where each one does his or her 'own thing.' I call this 'utopian modernity.'

The quadrant in the lower left represents a family structure that has moved out of the more traditional or provincial form of being 'under control' to being 'in control' though also more loosely structured and with less continuity with the traditions and customs of previous generations. This is what I call 'redemptive modernity.' My family of origin held very closely to the traditions and customs of previous generations as to kind of food and language. Needless to say, our contemporary family has a quite different linguistic tone as well as taste! Intergenerational movement of family structure and life from the upper left to the lower left quadrant--from being under control to being in control--can be viewed as the optimum response to culture change due to modernity. In this case, well integrated social unity is preserved. One effect of modernity and also with postmodernity is the move directly from the upper left quadrant to the lower right quadrant where freedom from traditional structures tends to become more chaotic along with loss of stability.

Lack of stability undercuts the moral and spiritual fiber of the family structure which, in turn can lead to a moral crisis with serious social consequences. The next chapter explores the dynamics of family life under the stress of postmodernity that leads to a crisis of morality along with suggestions for the recovery of the moral and spiritual character of both individual and family life.

Chapter 2

The Crisis of Morality

Common to all of the complaints about modern society is the feeling that we have experienced a loss of moral values or, that values are no longer based upon absolute and universal moral truth. One way of viewing this problem is to suggest that the values by which people live today have become totally subjective and disconnected from belief in objective moral principles. There was a time when we could assume that personal moral values were closely aligned with objective moral truth. We could assume that what a person stated as a personal value was also connected to what the same person believed to be an objective moral value. We expected that a commitment to a set of moral values would determine how a person would act and the kind of choices that were made. That is to say, we assumed that the moral content of a person's character would be determinative of their decisions and actions. This no longer seems to be true.

In our contemporary culture, personal values have become separated from beliefs. Values have become related more to existential needs and desires than to the intrinsic worth or merit of a belief. Values now reflect more what individuals reveal by their behavior and choices than by what they say when asked to define the moral truth of what they believe. For example, in North America, up to 90% of the population will express some kind of belief in God or a Divine Being to whom they look for guidance and help. At the same time, these same people can be observed spending their time and money on things that bring immediate gratification rather than long-term fulfillment. The majority of people believe that marriage should be a life-long commitment and yet, more than half of all marriages fail due to a perceived loss of personal value in the relationship.

As a result, the basic moral structure of our social institutions of family and community appears to be falling apart. In response, we look to the church and educational institutions for moral and spiritual teaching as a way of reversing this trend. Unfortunately, this is not the answer. Those who seek to establish the moral values of society can no longer do that by merely re-stating the traditional belief system on which moral values were originally based. We cannot change values by speaking of what we ought to believe. We can only re-direct the personal values of persons in our modern culture in such a way that they are reconnected with what is believed to be true. What one asserts about family values is what one believes ought to be the case. Personal values are what one spends money, time and energy on with hopes of achieving or experiencing some personal gain or good. In our culture, behavior is more a reflection of values than beliefs. What should we conclude from this? Are the moral values which once were believed to be universal and objective now relative to each culture? And are personal and individual values no longer dependent upon objective moral truth? Social theorists are quick to offer their own commentary on these questions.

Stanley Hauerwas says that in our contemporary culture we face a challenge to traditional values that can result in a series breakdown in family values.

> It is alleged that we are living at a time when there is a breakdown of morality, or rather that a hedonistic self-fulfillment ethic has replaced past commitments to duty and responsibility, and the family is among the first and the most important casualties of this breakdown. This usually sets the stage for a call to return to traditional values in an effort to save the family from the acids of immorality. And by saving the family we can save our society.[6]

Hauerwas goes on to comment that some cannot distinguish between change and crisis, and quotes Dr. Tamara Hareven:

> The family has never been a utopian retreat from the world, except in the imagination of social reformers and social scientists. Some of the major problems besetting family life today emanate from the heavy demands placed upon it by individuals in society who require that it be a haven of nurture and a retreat from the outside world. The modern family's growing discomfort suggests the need for expansion and diversity in what we expect from it and its adaptation to a new social condition with diverse timing schedules and multiplicity of roles for its members, rather than seeking refuge in a non-existent past.[7]

Brigette and Peter Berger suggest that the question of moral values centers around the dynamics of authority and love, which are structures found in the bourgeois family:

We should recall again what has been one of the most salient characteristics of the bourgeois family: its balance between communal and individual requirements, and more specifically, its balance between authority and love. The bourgeois family, from the beginning, was 'child centered,' lavishing care and affection on its children. But at the same time, it provided stability, authority, and predictability. What exists today by way of suggested alternatives is not reassuring on these counts. This is as true of the various utopian experiments, which often emphasized love but have been singularly lacking in stability, as of the more professionally conducted child-care facilities, which very commonly supplied neither love nor stability.[8]

Failure to anchor moral values in the personal character of individuals results in moral ambivalence. Personal values become the basis for cultural moral standards. In this case, the moral culture of a society no longer reflects moral character, but personal values. An example of this can be found in the writing of the American psychologist, Marshall Lowe. He suggests that personal values, even though distinguished from cultural moral standards, are finally the basis on which public moral values are based.

> Values, which are created by individuals, must be differentiated from morals, which are produced by the culture. Culture can be seen as a system of consensually validated social expectations deriving from the personal values of diverse individuals. Morals provide the social standard for differentiating between the good and the bad.... There is a delicate balance between allowing the individual the freedom to choose values which have personal meaning and at the same time providing him with the stability of a morality shared with others.[9]

In this definition, morals are held to be relative to social and cultural expectations. Values are thought to be discerned by individuals, from which moral standards are derived as a social norm. This would appear to make public morality relative to the agreed-upon social determination of what is good, while leaving individuals free to follow privately held values as the basis for individual moral actions. We are not told what the source of the individually held values might be, except that they have "personal meaning." There appears to be no consideration here for the way in which one's character might also be determinative of both personal values and the social standards which provide moral guidance. How we view moral reality will usually determine moral values and actions.

Three Versions of Moral Reality.

The medieval world-view of reality was basically metaphysical. The physical world as well as the world of sense-experience and human behavior were regulated largely by appeal to abstract and well-defined concepts that transcended the ambiguous and uncertain temporal and historical order. This gave precision and universal status to what was considered to be both good and true. Moral character could be formed by acquiring the virtues of honesty, truthfulness, and goodness through discipline, contemplation, and devotion to these ideals. Moral values were grounded in this version of reality, and moral character cultivated as one of the goals of an educated person.

In the post-enlightenment period of European intellectual history, the scaffolding of this metaphysical view of reality has suffered from a series of earthquakes. The rise of existentialism, following the rejection of Hegel's philosophy by the Danish philosopher Søren Kierkegaard, turned the metaphysical quest for reality upside down. What formerly was sought as essential truth now was discovered through existential reality. Whereas character was formerly assumed to be the basis for moral decision, for the existentialist, character is the result of personal decision. Authentic existence becomes each person's quest and possibility, rather than conformity to some essential order.

With the rise of scientific empiricism following Francis Bacon, the behavior of nature, when studied with scientific objectivity, was considered to be a revelation of the reality of things. Reality was viewed as only accessible and verifiable through the rigor of scientific method. The social scientists applied this methodology to the behavior of persons through psychological and sociological experimental research, searching for clues as to which behavior was considered to be 'good' and which 'bad' (pathological). The moral criteria of both the metaphysical essentialist and the existentialist were set aside as an intrusion into scientific objectivity. Behavior itself became virtual reality. Those who could change behavior through techniques of modification claimed to be able to achieve more effective adjustment of humans to their inner conflicts and outer struggles to adapt and conform to life in the 'real world.'

When we now think of moral development and the formation of character, we must first of all inquire about which version of reality we have as our presupposition. A version of reality is what we might call an epistemological model. Epistemology has to do with a theory of knowledge. Each of the versions of reality which I have described represent an epistemological model. While there may be more than these three, and while there may be overlapping between them, I use these versions of reality in order to suggest that epistemological presuppositions are critical in our discussion of moral values.

I have tried to represent these three versions of reality which compete with one another in our postmodern world in the following diagram (Figure 2.1).

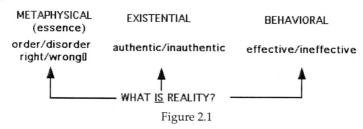

Figure 2.1

In the metaphysical version, reality is rooted in eternal and essential principles which are determined to be fixed and ordered. Deviation from these structures of reality are to some degree in disorder and thus considered to be morally wrong. In the existential version, reality is rooted in what one holds to be authentic as against inauthentic. In the behavioral version reality is pragmatic and functional.

Where relationships, such as marriage and family fail to provide openness and intimacy of one to the other, each version of reality responds differently. The essentialist views the moral status of the relationship as grounded in its conformity to what is 'right' because it is in accord with the true 'order' of things. The existentialist, however, might judge a dysfunctional relationship to be inauthentic and of no value, even though it conforms to an external order. For the existentialist, values, and thus, moral and ethic principles, are not rooted in the structure of relationships, but in the quality of the relation itself. For the behavioral perspective, what is of value, and therefore what is good, is what is effective as contrasted with what is ineffective. The use of a sexual surrogate, for example, to treat a problem of sexual dysfunction in a marriage, would be considered immoral by both the essentialist and the existentialist. For the behaviorist, a method of treatment that restores effectiveness to the relationship is not considered to be immoral if it succeeds in its purpose.

How should we respond to these competing versions of reality, each with their own moral criteria? Can we attempt to turn our society back to the pre-enlightenment version by rebuilding the scaffolding that secures morality to a metaphysical version of reality? Are we to reject all claims to personal values that collide with the objective reality of what is true and good? We might well heed the warning of Robert Bellah:

> Modern individualism seems to be producing a way of life that is neither individually nor socially viable, yet a return to traditional forms would be to return to intolerable discrimination and oppression. The

question, then, is whether the older civic and biblical traditions have the capacity to reformulate themselves while simultaneously remaining faithful to their own deepest insights.[10]

If we discover those 'deeper insights' that were contained in the older traditions, we will, I argue, be able to find our way forward without having to 'set the clock back' with regard to our contemporary age.

A Theological Version of Moral Reality

From the perspective of the Judeo-Christian version of reality as found in the Bible, we can find a place for each of the three versions I have discussed without making any one of the three the only version. If our fundamental presupposition is that all reality is created by God and upheld and redeemed by the power of God, we might gain the following insights.

First, God's character provides the moral basis for God's creation

As Creator, God is not viewed as impersonal power, but as a moral agent to whom all of creation is accountable for its meaning as well as its goodness. The biblical account of creation asserts the goodness of all that God has made: "God saw everything that he had made, and indeed, it was very good" (Genesis 1:31). The moral character of the created world is defined by the character of God. "For you are not a God who delights in wickedness; evil will not sojourn with you" (Psalm 5:4). The Psalmist attributes moral character to God as one who is faithful, just, merciful, and filled with compassion in his deeds as well as his words: "The Lord is faithful in all his words, and gracious in all his deeds. . . .The eyes of all look to you, and you give them their food in due season. You open your hand, satisfying the desire of every living thing" (Psalm 145: 13, 15-16).

What the metaphysical version of reality seeks to establish by appealing to impersonal concepts of the good, a theological view of reality finds moral stability and certainty in the character of God as Creator. Instead of abstracting away from the created world to find the moral absolute as a formal principle, the biblical tradition finds the moral absolute in God's Word of creation and redemption.

Second, the moral character of creation is revealed through human persons as the image bearers of God

While the Psalmist views creation as an expression of God's power and majesty, human persons are described as the bearers of God's moral character (Genesis 1:26-27; Psalm 8:1-4). To be made in God's image and likeness is to have a human moral character like that of the divine. Humans are thus moral agents not because of adherence to abstract moral law but because they bear the very moral character of God. This is why violence against another human is an offense against God. When the first murder is recorded in the Bible, God confronts Cain: "What have you done? Listen; your brother's blood is crying out to me from the ground!" (Genesis 4:10). Later, the Lord reiterates the moral connection between humans by saying, "I will require a reckoning for human life. . . for in his image God made humankind" (Genesis 9:8).

The intrinsic moral value of each person is an absolute moral reality as part of human nature as such, as each bears the human image of divine moral character. A theological version of reality is grounded in anthropology, not sociology nor psychology. Cultural moral standards are, at best, only relative moral indicators of the intrinsic moral character of humans created in the divine image.

Third, human character is expressed through the moral quality of social relations as well as the moral responsibility of scientific endeavor

The failure of an existentialist version of reality is not because it values the moral quality of human existence over the impersonal and ideal moral principle. The failure of existentialism is due to its value of the individual over the social relation. Søren Kierkegaard's attempt to escape the abstract and impersonal spirit of Hegelian philosophy led him to force reality into the narrow confinement of the self existing on the threshold of dread. By his own request, the only epitaph that he desired for his tombstone was 'The Individual.'

A theological version of reality overcomes this fatal plunge into personal despair by viewing humankind as intrinsically social being. The biblical account of creation has already corrected the existentialist error by saying, "It is not good that the man should be alone" (Genesis 2:18). The 'goodness' of human existence is not a solitary, existential reach for a transcendent reality, but the mutual recognition of the divine image in another's presence. When the woman is created alongside the man, they simultaneously and mutually awaken to their own human existence in the divine image: "This at last is bone of my bones and flesh of my flesh" (Genesis 2:23).

We now see that the moral character that underlies human moral decisions and actions is not the possession of individuals, but the moral quality of core human relationships. What the existentialist seeks in the name of 'authenticity' of individual existence, a theological version of reality finds in mutual respect and responsibility for the moral character of each person with whom one is related. For this reason, the biblical emphasis on moral character is defined in terms of social relationships. Husbands and wives, parents and children, slaves and masters, are all reminded by the Apostle Paul that the spiritual reality of their faith is expressed in the moral quality of their social relation. "Be subject to one another out of reverence for Christ," is Paul's admonition, followed by instructions to married couples, parents and children, as well as slaves and masters (Ephesians 5:21-6:9).

Fourth, the formation of human character takes place where personal values are created out of moral experience

We began this discussion with the suggestion that personal values have become detached from beliefs in our contemporary culture. As a result, attempts at moral development and formation of character through the teaching of moral principles will have little effect. I have suggested that one must begin with values and move toward beliefs. Or, another way to express it is to say that moral character must be perceived as having personal value.

When the Bible presents the moral challenge to have faith and live in obedience to the Word of God, the appeal is often made to the personal value that will be received as a benefit. When Moses attempted to bring the people of Israel out of Egypt, the discipline of obedience by which a former slave people could be formed into a community of character was presented as a journey to a land "flowing with milk and honey" (Exodus 3:8). The images of what would be achieved and experienced were vivid and compelling. This was an appeal to values rather than merely to moral duty. When Jesus warned against laying up treasures here on earth where thieves and corruption could attack, he urged his followers to "store up for yourselves treasures in heaven. . . for where your treasure is, there your heart will be also" (Matt. 6:19-21).

The formation of Christian character is not achieved by the teaching of Christian doctrine alone, nor by setting down rigid rules of moral discipline. Rules are necessary to set boundaries, but it is relationship, rather than rules, that forms character. When the Bible speaks of character, it does so in terms of core human moral and spiritual values, rather than religious rituals and regulations. The critical moral experiences which contribute to the formation of character do not take place in the church, but in the family and in the daily lives of people in their primary relationships.

The Relationship Between Moral Values and Moral Order

There is a moral order that anticipates and under-girds moral authority. The kinds of moral order, in turn, are based on constructs of reality, or fundamental orders. We can look at four distinct kinds of order as constructs of reality, and see how each lead to a perception of moral order and moral authority (Figure 2.2).

MORAL ORDER AND MORAL AUTHORITY

KINDS OF ORDER	MORAL ORDER	MORAL AUTHORITY
NATURAL ORDER	ideological	coercive
CONVENTIONAL ORDER	cultic	punitive
INTERPERSONAL ORDER	systemic and contractual	value intensive
REDEMPTIVE ORDER	personal and covenantal	empowering

violence
alienation

Figure 2.2

In the natural order, the moral order tends to be strongly ideological. Ideology becomes merged with nature--for example, the 'blood, soil and race' ideology of Hitler. In South Africa, the Afrikaaner claimed a moral right to the land by virtue of race, language and religion. This kind of moral authority is coercive--might makes right. In this order we find the highest potential for violence. Some will claim an absolute right to kill others to protect their space and rights.

In the conventional order, the moral order tends to be strongly cultic. Convention and tradition become codified so that deviation from this conventional order is thought to be 'unnatural.'

Paul says in 1 Cor. 11:13-14: "Judge for yourselves; is it proper for a woman to pray to God with her head uncovered? Does not nature itself teach you that for a man to wear long hair is degrading to him, but if a woman has long hair, it is her pride?" Nature in this case, is not a biological reality, but a conventional practice and custom that has become codified in such a way that it caries moral authority. The moral authority is punitive--the offender is ostracized from the community. In this order, we find the highest potential for alienation, which has its own destructive tendencies, and can also lead to violence.

In the interpersonal order the moral order tends to be systemic and contractual.

Personal relationships that follow commitment create a community of life that has a moral character that makes demands upon the individuals who have created it. Communities which are created out of this concept of order presuppose a kind of free and autonomous, or democratic social structure by which contracts are made and kept. The systemic nature of this moral order is based upon the interlocking network of social contracts by which individuals are bound. The moral authority is value intensive- -the moral character of the community, or family, is thus the place where values are shaped and where moral authority is lodged. A marriage for example, under this concept of moral order, is a social contract in which values are implied in the form of mutual good and the good of the society at large. On the other hand, when the value for one or the other or both, becomes marginal there is often insufficient moral incentive to continue the relationship. In this case there may be a conflict between the conventional order--it is wrong to divorce, and the interpersonal order--it is wrong to continue a relationship that has no value.

As an example of a conflict between two kinds of moral order and moral authority, the U. S. Supreme Court held in Planned Parenthood vs Danforth that husbands have no rights if their wives wish an abortion, since "abortion is a purely personal right of the woman, and the status of marriage can place no limitation on personal rights."[11] This clearly is an ideological kind of moral order that presupposes what we have called the natural order. The law then serves as a moral authority to coerce compliance.

When the personal order of human social relations is presupposed, there are contractual and systemic aspects to the community formed by these commitments and loyalties in a way that overrides both natural and conventional orders of existence. Where there are no values that contrac- tually emerge out of community, there will be no moral authority other than a reversion to natural or conventional forms of order.

Still, the interpersonal order, with is contractual basis for moral author- ity does not yet touch the structure of relationships that constitute family. Hauerwas argues that the kind of moral and contractual freedom that constitutes obligations does not satisfy the moral demands which family represents. "The family," he writes, "in spite of all the attempts to make it one, is not a contractual social unit."

> The family in our society thus appears morally irrational. It is simply part of the necessities of our life that the free person should learn to outgrow. For to be part of a family is to accept a limit that I have not chosen. Of course I can try to explain my commitment to the family, my obligations to parents, brothers and sisters, on grounds that even

if I did not choose them I have benefited from them. Therefore, it is not irrational to think that I may owe them something. However, this kind of argument cannot explain the assumption that there may be obligations to parents even if they are not the best of parents, or that we should continue to care and be concerned about relatives even when they are not our friends. Moreover, it fails to explain why I would for any reason decide to become a parent myself. Any reason I might give for having a child, in the terms of an ethic of autonomy, would appear immoral, on grounds of the use of another as a means for my own satisfaction, is irrational, since a child would only enter the world as a threat to my autonomy.[12]

Thus, I propose a fourth kind of order and moral authority: the *redemptive order,* where the moral order is personal and covenantal.

The biblical concept of covenant makes all other orders contingent upon the love and purpose of God as the source of moral authority. The natural, conventional and interpersonal orders each have their own moral order and forms of moral authority, but each are also contingent upon the moral authority of divine covenant love. Covenant order is not merely interpersonal, based upon the assumption that each person is a free moral agent, but it is personal and intimate, so that the character of the relation as an embodiment of love creates a form of moral empowerment to love in return. The moral authority is empowerment--the summoning forth of a moral power of personal being, as a power to create relationships which are covenantal in nature, and not merely contractual. Again, Hauerwas comments wisely on this point when he suggests that it is through intimacy that one person makes unique claims upon another. He quotes Ferdinand Mount:

> Intimacy always entails personal authority. The claims of a child for care and love, even if unspoken by child or mother, are just as much a moral authority over his father as the father's claims for filial affection and/or obedience and respect. For authority in this sense does not depend upon inequality nor does it wither away under the beneficent rays of equality. It depends solely upon one person acknowledging another person's right to make claims on him in particular.[13]

Yet, the fact that intimacy is implicitly a moral order is not enough for Hauerwas. He adds, "Intimacy and care are indeed important, but equally important is the initiation of children into the moral beliefs and institutions which we value. When such beliefs are absent the rightful authority of parents is correctly perceived as a masked authoritarianism."[14] Hauerwas does not explain to us what keeps a belief system from becoming merely a conventional order, when its moral authority becomes coercive. The biblical concept of covenant with its principle of contingency does allow for moral truth to be embodied in a structure of divine and human love rather than merely in beliefs as institutionalized dogmas and doctrines. Yet, it must also be said that Hauerwas, with his emphasis on the ethical nature of a community, with a character which embodies love, does implicitly bring this dimension to his treatment of moral authority. Coercive power is based on fear, both in the leader and in the follower. "Leaders tend to lean on coercive power when they are afraid they won't get compliance."[15]

Summary and Conclusion

The language of covenant communicates a sense of spontaneous and unconditional loyalty and commitment that emerge from a source transcendent to the natural, conventional, and interpersonal social order. And yet, covenant love emerges through and in the form of these other orders, each with their own loyalties and commitments. Here is the source of the creative tension, and yet positive value which can arise out of such a view of family. Theodore Roszak suggests that spontaneous and unconditional loyalty are the absolute bond of kinship. The forms and rituals of marriage and family, he argues, are the sacramental aspects of this unconditional loyalty, which is the "one precious need of the person which no Utopian substitute can provide."

> There will always be a failed loyalty behind us that can never be duplicated. The provisional and contractual arrangements we invent to take its place will rarely achieve the continuing intimacy of a good marriage; they can never supply the biographical continuity that the family alone keeps in trust for its members. . . . What we need in order to become what we are is not liberation from the family, but a family that lets its young weave their knots into an original fabric. The proper place to work our genealogical karma is not in a psychiatrist's office, but in an open childhood, among those whose lives must always be the prime facts of our identity.[16]

The mediation of love that empowers the being of another is the moral structure of family, and particularly, the moral authority that under-girds the function of parenting. When parenting is viewed as empowerment, the mask of authoritarianism can be removed--and parents and children can meet "face to face," and eye to eye, with real hearing, as Karl Barth says.[17] This is the praxis of family.

Chapter 3

Theological Aspects of Parenting
As God's Covenant Partners

When I began teaching a course on Theology of the Family with my colleague, Professor Dennis Guernsey, I suggested that we talk about the dynamics of parenting before we considered the factors that constitute healthy and effective marriage relationships. The reason for this I said, was that persons who enter into marriage represent the effect of their prior parenting as individuals. We cannot make an intervention into contemporary marriage and family relationships, I argued, without first dealing with the quality of parenting that leads to the kind of persons that enter into marriage as husband and wife.

Dennis agreed, and in his own contribution to the discussion reminded us that there is no such thing as a mere individual, but only 'members.' In saying this he was critiquing the rampant individualism that permeates our modern culture where even the term 'individual' is no longer useful when talking about family because the family is only one group of which one is a member. Each person exists in a collage of memberships that have competing demands and seemingly legitimate expectations of its members. He reminded us of two of his favorite quotations from an authority in the field of human social relationships, Carl Whitaker of the University of Wisconsin: 1) who ever human persons are they are only 'fragments of families,' and 2) his famous definition of a wedding: "A wedding is two families sending forth a scapegoat each hoping to reproduce itself."[18] Before we look at the role of parents in the development of mature and responsible adults prior to entering into marriage and family commitments, we need to look at what it means to say that humans are 'persons.'

The Formation of Human Persons

Human personhood certainly is a mystery--not only a question of why there should be persons at all, but a fundamental mystery in the experience of one's own personhood as well as in experiencing the other as person. True, we are less naive today about the multifaceted phenomenon of personhood, now that our scientific prowess has probed into the deepest recesses of the human experience and offered explanations for what used to be considered the influence of either angels or demons upon human personalities. But with less naiveté it does not follow that there is less mystery. For mystery is the threshold of the personal set within the concrete structures of physical existence. Without the mystery of human personhood, love and relationship would be little more than an organic 'chip' on which all the microscopic elements are 'wired' in such a way that predictability insures increasing efficiency in mating as well as meeting.

For example, recent brain research led James Ashbrook to conclude that as early as the sixth week of pregnancy the crucial crystallization of sex difference begins. Until that 'moment' the embryo is undifferentiated, neither female nor male; it is simply 'human potentiality.' As a result scientists now hold that "the basic plan of the mammalian organism is female and stays that way unless told to be otherwise by masculine hormones." Around the sixth week, fetal androgens begin 'organizing' the neuroanatomy of behavior for future reproductive activity. These androgens 'tune' certain cells to the hormones which will flood the body at puberty. Specifically, the androgen 'tuning' suppresses the capacity for monthly cycling in males. As birth approaches, the masculinizing hormones, primarily testosterone, have so affected the development of the brain that a 'trained observer, holding a microscope slide [of the hypothalamus] up to the light, can tell the sex of the brain with the naked eye. Male brains, says Ashbrook,

> in general and the left hemisphere in particular are more likely to malfunction. A higher percentage of 'autism, schizophrenia, and psychopathy' appear in the male population, along with a tendency toward aggression. If a man suffers right side paralysis and loss of speech, the effects are more likely to be permanent. Female brains present more right hemisphere malfunctions, especially mood disorders, along with a tendency toward affiliation. If a woman suffers right side paralysis and loss of speech, she is more likely to recover her ability to move and speak. Further, sex-related difficulties are overrepresented and underrepresented in such various areas as 'eating disorders; sexual/physical violence; incest, alcoholism; premenstrual syndrome; pregnancy and

childbirth; body image; issues of power, entitlement, self-esteem; and decisions regarding career, lifestyle, and family.' Sex-gender differences make a difference that is a difference *because the cultural contrasts are derived from biological substrata!*[19]

Well. Did we really need to know all that! The point is, that reducing personhood, even the sexual aspect, to physical brain activity does little to resolve the mystery of being human. In questioning this approach, one has passed over the threshold of the impersonal to the personal, from the nonhuman (or subhuman) to the human, and from that which is merely creaturely to a human form of creatureliness. Several assumptions flow out of the discussion at this point.

Creatureliness is a necessary but insufficient condition for human existence as persons

One cannot be human without also necessarily being a flesh-and-blood creature placed somewhere on the continuum that makes up the life of all creatures. Human persons may not develop out of sheer creatureliness, but they do develop as creatures as well as persons. Therefore, those creaturely aspects of existence that humans share with nonhuman creatures are essential to the development of the person. This assumption entails the fact that the uniqueness of the human creature results from a determination that has its source outside of the creaturely realm. That is, the form of the human is determined by that which is transcendent to creatureliness--there is no telos (or principle) hidden within sheer creatureliness that can reach beyond the limits of creatureliness itself to give rise to the human. The impersonal does not contain within itself the personal--though the reverse may well be true. Theologically, this transcendent source is understood to be the creative power of the Word and Spirit of God. There is then a contingent relation between creatureliness and humanity. The human person in its personal existence must be sustained by something--some personal reality--beyond its own creaturely existence. This is a mystery that requires a theological answer.

Second, human existence is intrinsically and originally social and only consequentially psychological

This assumption entails the conclusion that individuality, as a particular experience of self-awareness with its attendant psychological manifestations, derives from an experience of unity and relation with others. In the creation account in Genesis 2, the solitary human is under divine judgment--it is not good to be alone. Only when there is a complementary experience of humanity in terms of what we might call cohumnity does the form of the human appear actually (not merely potentially) complete. The 'we' exists before the 'I,' or one could say that the 'I' does not exist except as it encounters and is in relation with another human 'thou.'

Not only that, but in the creation account male and female emerge simultaneously not sequentially. Only after the story tells us that the man ('adam) was put to sleep and the woman was fashioned out of one of his ribs, is this 'earth creature' differentiated sexually as male, and not merely 'man.' In other words the 'man' that exists prior to the creation of woman is not yet 'male.' Old Testament Scholar Phyllis Trible says that, "Only after surgery does this creature, for the very first time, identify itself as male. Utilizing a pun on the Hebrew word for woman, 'issa, the earth creature refers to itself by the specific term for man as male, 'ish. . . . The unit 'ish and 'issa functionally parallels ha-'adam and ha-adama.'" Trible therefore concludes that the creation of human persons as 'male and female' ('ish and 'issa) occurs simultaneously, not sequentially. "His sexual identity depends upon her even as hers depends upon him. For both of them sexuality originates in the one flesh of humanity."[20]

Furthermore, in the biblical account the specific roles of husband and wife, father and mother, are not included in the original creative act. Roles are adjunctive to human personhood as male and female, not necessary. The description employs the explicitly sexual terms (male and female) that have just been introduced into the story. To this vocabulary the narrator adds the terms for parental roles, achieving a juxtaposition of relationships--man and woman to contrast with father and mother. Each couple is a unit of equality, one, equality of creation; the other, the equality of roles. Interestingly however, parents are not part of God's creative activity. They appear in the story as adjuncts to the creation of woman and man. In other words, sexuality makes father and mother possible; parental images are subordinate to and depended upon sexual images. Roles then, are secondary at best; they do not belong to creation.[21] The essential differentiation of man and woman can find fulfillment in roles, but is not characterized by these roles. Where disorder occurs in relationships, cultural and traditional role orders may be used to express the command of God (e.g. Paul, in 1 Tim. 2). But in this case the sexual differentiation itself at the biological level through which roles are identified is already being transformed (cf. Paul, Gal 3:28).

Third, existence as person derives from existence in relation

This, of course, logically follows the previous assumption. To attribute the quality of 'personal' to creaturely being is to denote being that is differentiated in its unity in such a way that 'relationship' takes place as a manifestation of personal being. Theologically this is what is meant by asserting that human persons are created in the 'image and likeness of God' (Gen. 1:26-27). It is this aspect of being in the image and likeness of God that differentiates between human and nonhuman creatures by determining that relation to God as Creator and Lord. That is, one can make the formal distinction between human and nonhuman creatures only by recognizing the distinction between created human persons and God the Creator. Without this formal distinction as a theological assertion, distinctions between human and nonhuman creatures would be relativized to the variations that occur on the continuum of creatureliness itself. Karl Barth argues that sexual differentiation as male or female is the only differentiation between human persons. This is not the case with animals who remain 'undifferentiated' in the solidarity of their species; sexuality does not become a history of personal identity for them as it does for humans. Because God is differentiated in the unity of his being so too humans created in his image are differentiated in the unity of being; the concrete form of this differentiation for humans is expressed through male and female sexual differentiation.[22]

Theologian Otto Weber reinforces this point when he says:

> All the other relationships can be interchanged: the father is also the son, the mother is also the child, and in the differentiated society the "master" can also be the "slave," and the "king" can easily become a component of the "nation." But the man will never become woman, nor the woman become man. It is an unmistakable trait of the mythological self-exaltation of man that this differentiation is denied as a fundamental and essential one (the androgynous myth). . . . But if God is the covenant God who grants us community and determines us for this community, then that polarity is established between us men, between I and Thou, which takes on its most concrete form in the predetermination of man for sexual duality. [23]

The polarity of personal being that is constituted by the image of God in humans, is expressed through the sexual duality and reciprocity of male and female. Human personhood is experienced as concrete creaturely existence, so that biological factors are the means of expressing personal attributes of being. Personal differentiation at the human level is necessarily constituted to be male or female being, not because the physical or creaturely aspect of sexual differentiation has the power to create personal being, but because the material content of personal being first of all takes place as creaturely being before it can be considered as an abstract or formal possibility. In this case, the sexual differentiation,

that humans share with other nonhuman creatures becomes the sign of
the personal differentiation that constitutes the human. As we shall see
later in this book, formation of personal identity as male or female, male
and female, is grounded in the image of God. Parenting is an important
aspect of this developmental process.

*Finally, human being as differentiated from nonhuman creatures, is be-
ing that is characterized by openness toward the power that constitutes
it*

This means that the openness of being that is characteristic of human
being is what constitutes the freedom of being that is unique to humans.
Theologically understood this is the spiritual dimension of human existence. The basic unity of the body / soul duality is endowed with spirit in
such a way that there is a spiritual openness toward other beings. This
is the *quintessence* of personal being that locates the spiritual dimension
of human life directly at the core of personal existence. This assumption
will have telling significance when we discuss the matter of spiritual
formation and the family.

In summary, we may say that the form of the human is social, personal,
sexual, psychical and spiritual. Developmentally, it may be that there is a
sequence by which each builds upon the other as shown in Figure 3.1.

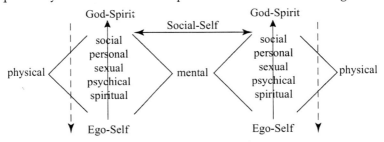

Figure 3.1

Reading from top to bottom, we see that the progression is from social
to personal, to sexual, then psychical and finally spiritual. As spiritual
beings, we then have an orientation to God as Spirit that runs right back
through each of the other sub-sets or sub-systems of the self. The dotted
line represents the growth of the self through each of the spheres, beginning with the social and moving toward the spiritual. The solid line moves
from the self through each sphere toward God. This depicts the integration of the self as the self and in relation to the other. The physical and
mental aspects of personal life impinge upon each of the spheres and so
the physical and mental health of each have an effect upon the spheres.

This serves to preserve a balance and positive tension between the physical and mental aspects of the personality for each of the components. If the spiritual dimension should be moved to the side and relate primarily through the mental side of the self, the religious self will become either rationalistic or mystical--both essentially movements away from the concreteness and embodiedness of the self.

In the same way, there are both physical and mental aspects to a healthy psychical and sexual life. And should these become primarily either physical or mental, this will represent a distortion and dysfunction for the self in its process of growth and development.

These system components are not 'stages' through which one passes developmentally in a strict linear fashion. Rather, the model should be viewed more like a spiral staircase, where one continues to make progress developmentally but with each 'rotation' through the process enters into and experiences each 'system' from a more mature (hopefully!) perspective.

Parenting Persons, Not Merely Children

Our discussion so far has been at the purely theoretical level. At the practical level, becoming human is a process that begins at birth and continues more or less until one's creaturely life is ended. It is to this process that we now turn our attention. While our perspective continues to be theological, we can look at the process itself quite straightforwardly as a process in which the social and behavioral sciences have an equally vested interest, as does theological science. It is my hope that this discussion of parenting will help us to form a developmental model for becoming mature human persons that integrates a theological perspective with the other behavioral disciplines. "The mother-child relation," says John Macmurray, "is the original unit of human existence."[24] I would prefer to substitute 'parent' for 'mother.' This is not to suggest that mothers can or ought to be replaced, but that parenting, not mothering alone, represents more the intended role in the development of personhood. The physical or biological process through which children are brought into the world cannot alone account for the care and responsibility of parenting children. At present (although one cannot say how much longer), children come into the world through the biological process of conception and birth involving both a mother and a father. Should it come to pass that the father is thought of more as the 'donor' and the mother the 'carrier,' it nonetheless remains merely a creaturely function. Physical paternity surely entails what parenting means by way of accountability for the development of human life, but it cannot of itself, as a creaturely act, totally account for the responsibility of parenting.

Parenthood is accountability to the command of God, not merely to the necessity of physical and creaturely existence

The commandment to honor one's parents does not mean the submission of one who is weak and helpless to one who is stronger and older. Rather, it is the recognition that these particular 'elders' who brought us into physical existence, bear on our behalf the commandment of life, which is also the promise of life, as determined by relation to the Word of God. This responsibility of course can be borne by other than biological parents in exceptional cases. And as we shall see, it can be borne by one of the biological parents in cases where it is impossible for both to do so.

In further qualifying what is meant by the concept of parenting, we must add that, although the parent may fulfill the role of educator, parenting is more than educating. If educating presupposes an originative or creative instinct in the child that can be developed and trained, in contrast, parenting assumes an instinct for communion that can be called forth and affirmed. This instinct for communion is stronger than 'libido'; it is the longing for the world to become present to us as a person. The educator summons into existence latent creative powers, that may or may not result in the development of persons into mature humanity. The parent however summons the latent mystery of the 'I' into relation, which is a summons into responsibility, into communion. Thus, parenting is necessarily humanizing when it takes place under the divine commandment, while educating may or may not be.

For example, a physical therapist can 'educate' the muscles and nervous system in such a way that coordination and movement is possible. This type of education also takes place with nonhuman creatures. In the same way, one might suggest that a psychotherapist can 'educate' through a stimulus-response mechanism in such a way that desired behavioral change is effected. But is this too not basically a creaturely and prehuman process? In this sense, education may fulfill certain limited goals without yet fulfilling the role of parenting. The concept of family derives from the concept of parenting and is dependent upon it for its significance in regard to the development of persons. The family as a collective unit is not the center of focus in the Bible. Rather, the relation of parents and children is central, and it is upon this relation that both the command and the promise rest. In focusing upon the parent / child relation, we are not disregarding the other significant relations that a child experiences, namely sibling relationships and relationships with other members of the extended family, such as grandparents, aunts and uncles. These other relationships are subsumed under the category of parent/child and are basically ancillary, although by necessity they also may become surrogate.

Theologically, parenting has its antecedent in the Old Testament concept of the Fatherhood of God. According to Ephesians 3:15, God is the Father of whom the whole family in heaven and on earth is named. In Isaiah 63:16, appeal is made to God as Father beyond all human fathers: "For you are our Father, . . . our Redeemer from of old is your name." Jesus accentuates this when be warns, "And call one your father on earth, for you have one Father--the one in heaven" (Matt. 23:9). And Israel is continually reminded that she exists solely by a fatherly action of God: "Do you thus repay the Lord, O foolish and senseless people? Is not he your father, who created you, who made you and established you?" (Deut. 32:6). "Know then in your heart that, as a parent disciplines a child, the Lord your God disciplines you" (Deut. 8:5; cf. Deut. 1:29-30; Hosea 11:1; Jer. 3:19-20).

Human parents stand in a relation to their children in a way analogous to the way in which God is related to his people, as Father

The seniority of parents over their children is relative, not absolute. Also, both parents, the mother and father, equally bear the responsibility of fulfilling, by analogy, that which is represented by the Fatherhood of God. That is, it is impossible from a theological perspective to equate the male role in parenting with the concept of God as Father. Whatever distinctive aspects belong to the male role of parenting, they must be established on other grounds. God's Fatherhood includes all of the nuances of parenting represented by analogy in human parents. For example, both nurture and discipline, both compassion and chastisement are exemplified by the Fatherhood of God, as generally portrayed in the Old Testament.

Everything said thus far implicitly assumes that personhood or selfhood, is as much a result of as it is an originally given determinant of human existence. The formal truth that supports this assumption is contained in the assertion that humanity as personal selfhood is experienced as cohumanity. In naming the animals, Adam could not 'parent' the beasts of the field in such a way that they became more and more human. There was apparently no 'givenness' with regard to human selfhood in their nature. Yet in 'naming' the woman as his copartner, the man discovered and experienced the openness of his own being to another. It is in this structure of cohumanity and as a consequence of this experience that he became a 'person.' It is in this developmental concept of personal human existence that the ontological determination of human selfhood in persons lies with the openness of being on the part of another person toward the self. The development of the self into full personhood can then never be posited as a project of self-development, aided and abetted by environmental technique. This of course radically qualifies all claims that parenting is a neutral process in the development of the self with respect to determining the actual content of the self. However, at this point, this is a highly abstract and theoretical statement of the case.

The material content of parenting is love given and experienced as openness of being in a structure of mutual interdependence. As Hans Urs von Balthasar, writes, "No man reaches the core and ground of his own being, becoming free to himself and to all beings, unless love shines on him." The creation of the original human person was an act of divine love, not merely of supernatural power. Supernatural power can create beasts, but not persons. Divine technology was shown to be insufficient in Genesis 2 when it came to 'making out of the dust' a counterpart to the solitary male. Adam can be a creature through the power of divine fiat, but he can become a human person only through a process of differentiation, recognition, and response to another human self. Von Balthasar likens this creative act on God's part to that of a mother's love:

> God, who inclined toward his new-born creature with infinite personal love, in order to inspire him with it and to awaken the response to it in him, does in the divine supernatural order something similar to a mother. Out of the strength of her own heart she awakens love in her child in true creative activity. . .The essential thing is, that the child, awakened thus to love, and already endowed by another's power of love, awakens also to himself and to his true freedom, which is in fact the freedom of loving transcendence of his narrow individuality.[25]

The failure of love at the level of cohumanity is consequently a deprivation of personhood, not merely an ethical fault

Likewise, a failure of love in response to God is a loss of personhood or, at the very least, a deformity of the self, not merely a religious fault. This is also why an unwillingness or a failure to love is already an act of violence against the person of another. This lies behind the teaching of Jesus in the Sermon on the Mount

(Matt. 5) where hatred is already murder, lust is already adultery, and nonresistance to evil is a positive approach to the humanity of others. Loving one's enemies is more than a tactic of nonresistance; it is the only creative act possible when the social structure has itself become inhuman. The liberation of a recalcitrant child from the destructive stance of rebellion and disobedience cannot be done by appealing to the child itself. No single person can attain true freedom of personal being unless he or she experiences the openness of being on the part of another in the context of a social structure of coexistence. Commenting on this same correlation of love between parent and child and subsequent capacity to love and trust others, Brigitte and Peter Berger say:

> Aristotle's famous view that if children did not love their parents and family members, they would love no one but themselves, is one of the most important statements ever made about the relation between family and society. The family permits an individual to develop love and security--and most important, the capacity to trust others. Such trust is the prerequisite for any larger social bonds. Only in the family are the individual's social tendencies aroused and developed and with these the capacity to take on responsibility for others. A person who has developed no family bonds will have a very hard time developing any larger loyalties in later life.[26]

The Bergers go on to say that an attack on the family structure in favor of democratic values that equalize the roles and relationships to a purely political or economic order is perverse and inherently destructive to personal life. The parenting role is not such that it can be delivered over to technicians or functionaries. We would say that this is because parenting is part of a developmental process by which 'humanization' occurs, not merely socialization.

From this we conclude that the development of persons into some degree of maturity will be directly related to the actual demonstration of love within the primary social structure of each person's life. This is what we mean by parenting. Ordinarily, biological parents or adoptive parents form the primary social structure for this parenting to take place. However, as has been argued, parenting is never a neutral pedagogical activity. It will be either constructive or destructive, depending upon the degree to which openness of being is experienced as a positive force of interaction between the persons involved. The openness of being is one way of describing the effects of love, where each person in the relation encounters the other in such a way that real contact and communication takes place. This mutuality of personal encounter is the inner core of love.

The role of parenting is to affirm the humanity of the child

John Macmurray reminds us that the notion that children are subhuman until they are humanized through education and rational development is not only unbiblical but false:

> If the notion that children are little animals who acquire the characteristics of rational humanity through education, whose personalities are "formed" by the pressures brought to bear upon them as they grow up--if this notion seems to us simple common sense, and matter of everyday observation--it is because we share the traditional outlook and attitude of a culture which has been moulded by Greek and in particular by Aristotelian ideas. So much of common sense is the relic of past philosophies! Whatever its origin, this view is radically false.[27]

This notion, adds Macmurray, is not derived from empirical study of human persons, but is a priori and analogical. If it begins by empirical study of organic life, it betrays itself by making a logical move from organic to personal being. The study of persons, in particular of the mother/child relation, counters Macmurray, reveals an intrinsic personal and human capacity that belongs to infants and is not found in nonhuman offsprings. The human infant is already completely human. It is not simply that the child has value because he or she has the potential of becoming human, but because he or she already is that which the human adult is. The human infant of course does not know this. That is, the child cannot affirm this for itself from the beginning. Therefore, in addition to its physical weakness and vulnerability as creature, the child is especially vulnerable precisely because it is a human child. This vulnerability emerges as a need deeper than mere physical dependence. And it is this vulnerability that makes the contingency of human existence at its very inception a matter of both intense (and even tragic) concern as well as exquisite joy.

Social scientist Clara Mayo corroborates this when she says, "In man, this dependence of offspring is much longer than in animals and is guided by more than the biological heritage. Only sustained social contact enables the child to develop a sense of self and a capacity to cope with the tasks that the environment presents."[28]

The role of parenting is to create and sustain the personal life of the child

The physical act of procreation is not itself, of course, an act of creating human life--even non human creatures bring forth their young in similar manner. Therefore, in saying that parenting entails the responsibility to 'create and sustain' personal life, we must immediately qualify that statement. Allowing for the fact that the exact point on the physical process by which human life emerges from conception cannot be determined with precision, parenting nonetheless actively undertakes the responsibility for protecting the physical existence of the child even before it leaves the mother's womb. Because the personal life of the child is dependent upon physical life, parenting actively prepares for the child's personal life by affirming and safeguarding its physical existence as far as it is humanly possible. We must not confuse human with physical or mere creaturely life. Therefore it avoids the stance of positing personal life in the form of rudimentary embryonic existence. It is not necessary to think of a fetus as a 'person' in order to regard it as human. And because it must be regarded as human, it must be protected in its most vulnerable stage from being treated inhumanly. But that responsibility can be placed only under the role of parenting.

The role of parenting is to contextualize and historicize the self as existing before and with God

I view the role of parenting as a responsibility that exists by virtue of the command of God--be fruitful and multiply (Gen. 1:29). This is obviously a theological assertion, and yet it is not an artificial or contrived position. The command of God is not itself an arbitrary intrusion into an otherwise self-sufficient world. Rather it is the positive determination by which human life comes into being, as well as the attendant providence by which it is sustained and oriented toward its true goal. Parenting is ordained by God as the means by which a child acquires a history and a story that provides a context for self-identity. Because the child is essentially a person, deviations and distortions must be dealt with as personal. Thus the role of parenting is to create an environment that brings the behavior and actions of a child into accountability to others as both liberating and reconciling. A child must be held accountable for its own destructive tendencies and for the other's good.

Responsible existence in cohumanity with openness to the presence of God at the boundaries of the self is the basis for the inner development of the image of God and moral character. The project of the self is not to maintain innocence as a desperate attempt to survive under the terrible and impersonal mandate of law, but to 'thrive on grace' as empowerment to live under the law of love. God's own covenant love is the paradigm for parenting. The narrative of God's parenting of Israel is really 'our story,' and when we find our place in God's story, our story finds meaning and hope.

Chapter 4

God's Covenant Love as a Paradigm of Parenting

When Dennis Guernsey and I first began to teach our course on Theology of the Family more than twenty-five years ago, we had a continuing disagreement as to the meaning of the word 'covenant.' I insisted that we could not speak of humans making covenant with each other in the same way that God made a covenant with humans. Dennis referred to the marriage vow as a 'covenant' between a man and woman. While I acknowledged that the term was often used in this sense, I argued that marriage was really a social contract entered into by two persons and that God attached his own 'covenant promise' to that relation. A covenant in a theological sense, I insisted, had to be unilateral--that is, made by one person on behalf of others rather than bilateral--that is, made by mutual action and consent. To say that a marriage vow was a 'covenant,' I argued, meant that one had to make it on behalf of the other, whereas we all know that in our culture marriage is a mutual commitment on the part of each.

"You have just been too much influenced by Karl Barth," Dennis would respond. "You have not yet grown out of your early training at Dallas Theological Seminary," I answered back. This exchange always took place in front of our students, much to their delight! It became sort of an annual ritual at the beginning of each course, and reappeared from time to time during our teaching together.

In October of 1996 I was invited to give the inaugural lecture in a series honoring Dennis at Seattle Pacific University in Seattle where he was on the faculty at the time and, as it happened, only two months before his untimely death due to a brain tumor. As we sat in his home prior to a quiet supper, Dennis talked about his attempt to convince his colleagues in the Marriage and Family Department of the importance of covenant as a paradigm of family. Struggling to express himself due to the aphasia he was experiencing as a result of the tumor, he groped for the right word. "You know what it is" he said, "You always used it when you spoke of the importance of covenant. The people in my department don't seem to get it!" His search for the elusive word continued, and my attempts to guess what it was were unsuccessful. Finally, he resorted to reciting the alphabet in hopes of bringing it to the surface of his mind. "A, B, C, D . . ." he slowly recited, and then coming to Q he stopped and said, triumphantly, "That's it, *quintessence*! You always said that covenant was the quintessence of family!' He sat back with a satisfied smile, as though he had opened a door through which sweet memories entered to flood his wounded spirit with healing grace. Then he slowly shook his head and said, "But they just don't seem to get it."

Covenant as the Quintessence of Family

So here it is again, Dennis. For you and for others in hopes that they finally do 'get it.' And once again, it is Barth who reminded us that "It is God's election and covenant that gives unconditional and compelling character to the requirement of monogamy . . . In His election and His covenant it is not merely the electing divine Partner who is utterly one . . . the creaturely and elected partner . . .is always singular as well." In other words, what might begin as ambiguous and uncertain due to human motives and misunderstanding, becomes singular and certain when God becomes the electing divine partner in the union. In the book that we co-authored I wrote, "Is marriage, then, a social contract that can be broken when one or both of the contracting parities violate the contract, or is it a covenant partnership that once entered into, can never be dissolved? Well, it is both. While a social contract based upon mutual conditions of good will and reciprocity does not contain within it the quintessential aspect of covenant love, covenant love can come to expression through a social contract . . . From the human perspective, the existence of a marriage is a social contract explicitly grounded in a relation of human sexuality, male and female, which finds its implicit source of covenant love in God's own commandment and gift of love."[29]

In a technical sense, 'covenant' as used in biblical theology means the unilateral relation established by God with his people Israel, through specific actions by which he summoned individuals and finally an entire nation into a history of response. There are several different types of covenants in the Old Testament; the primary use of the concept is grounded in the Abrahamic covenant by which God swore to make of Abraham a great nation. This covenant promise centered on the creation of a people of God through the generations of Abraham's descendants. Abraham's role was to believe in God's promise and to obey him through enacting the covenant sign of circumcision. The unconditional nature of the covenant as God established it entailed unconditional obedience, though the covenant itself was not conditioned upon obedience. In this divine covenant which is the presupposition of creaturely existence as human fellowship, God overcomes whatever negative or even indiscriminate tendencies there might be in humanity itself. Human relationships do not have to be arbitrary or accidental. This is why marriage as a social contract and family itself can be preserved from its own self-destructive tendencies through 'covenant partnership' with God. The implications for this are several.

First, because covenant is the basis of family, order precedes and overcomes disorder

When viewed apart from covenant, creation appears as sheer randomness and capriciousness. Surely this is what caused Hobbes to postulate the pragmatic imposition of rational forms of power in order to preserve human existence from chaos. In contrast, I suggest that covenant is not a 'rationalization' of disorder that God imposed as a consequence of sin and disorder. Rather, it is the original and divinely established intention by which creatureliness itself becomes an order of covenant partnership.

Covenant partnership, then, is a divinely determined order of existence for human beings. Genesis 2:24 places human existence within an order of cohumanity as the necessary and therefore logical result of the development of persons through the parent and child relation. The parenting relation is thus informed by the covenant partnership relationship, from which it derives its goals and ends. Considered pragmatically, parenting may well be a desirable end. From the perspective of covenant, however, it is not a means to an end but the end itself.

Practically speaking, we do not ordinarily enter into relationships that constitute family with a clear understanding of doing so because it is a 'sign' of divine covenant. Our initial impulses are to some degree always either pragmatic or idealistic. Even our first parents were deceived by both idealism ("You shall be as God," said the serpent) and pragmatism ("It is desired to make one wise," thought the woman). In this regard, every act of human commitment carries an implicit inevitability of betrayal--not the betrayal of one person by the other, but the betrayal of our own intentions and commitments, the breaking of our vows when we meet frustration and failure. And so disorder enters where originally there was order. This is especially true if we view marriage and family as contractual and not covenantal, for then betrayal, or at least disillusionment, becomes factual and the union merely theoretical and finally unreal. Covenant partnership, however, is itself the basis for a true 'disillusionment,' where illusions have become the basis for motivations and actions. But the divine covenant partner will permit no annulment of either his relation to them or their relation to one another. It is the reality of covenant that makes order the original reality and disorder only a deviation and distraction.

Yet covenant as the original order for marriage and family is not merely a fatalistic principle--you made your bed now lie in it--but rather is itself a creative principle of renewal and recovery. For covenant is not that which consigns us to our past, but that which orients us to our future.

To a certain extent, human covenant partner relations are provisional in the form of a social order. Even the customary words of the wedding vow echoes this fact--'till death do us part.' Yet marriage and family are a 'sign' of the covenant, and despite their provisional character as a social form, one cannot disregard this 'order' without also contradicting the original and divine covenant-partner relation.

The second significance of covenant as a paradigm of family is that selection is affirmed and sustained by election

Because life appears to confront us with a random series of possible choices any one of which can end up determining the course of our future, the possibilities can be quite paralyzing. Many of our selections, though at the time just what we thought we wanted, have turned out to be disastrous. Our selections can also be quite demoralizing. As youngsters, most of us have had to suffer through the pain of being selected for something that did not interest us, whether it was as a dance partner or as a member of the 'wrong' team in a pick-up game. One wonders how Eve felt on being presented to Adam as his 'selection,' when, as a matter of fact, there was no other alternative! In this case, certainly, selection is election--I choose you, and by my choice, you have no other choice!

Parenting is ordinarily nonselective. That is, we do not choose our parents and if our parents choose to have a child they are really electing to parent whatever child they receive through the apparently random process of genetic formation. In a sense, parenting is the affirming and sustaining of what appears to be the result of an indeterminate process. This is itself a 'sign' of the covenant that is initiated by God's election of what otherwise, would be an indiscriminate creature.

However, marriage and the creation of a family ordinarily do involve selection. Choices are made out of many possibilities for a mate. The temptation is great either to envision the ideal mate and project that ideal on a prospective partner, or to select a mate purely pragmatically (i.e., she has the values I want or need in a mate). Succumbing to either temptation, in my judgment, is the single greatest source of marital unhappiness. Stanley Hauerwas wisely comments that "we always marry the wrong person!"[30] I think that he means that our projection of an ideal mate upon the person that we marry always turns out to be quite different from what the persons actually is! My own observation is that when two people marry, the woman always expects the man to change but he never does, while the man expects the woman never to change but she always does!

It is helpful to remember that the basis for God's election of Israel was neither idealistic nor pragmatic. "It was not because you were more numerous than any other people that the Lord set his heart upon you and chose you--for you were the fewest of all peoples. It was because the Lord loved you, and kept the oath that he swore to your ancestors" (Deut. 7:7-8). God did not choose Abraham because he was the 'right person' but once chosen, he became the 'only person' through whom God would fulfill his covenant promise. For God, selection is invariable election. And the response then must either be to resist or to accept that election. That the elected may sometimes choose to resist is itself a mark of God's freedom and grace, not of one's natural rights or autonomy.

Our own creaturely humanity is more diffused than that. Covenant partnership is developmental in character. We discover our election in the process of our selections. Of course, there is more tolerance for error at some levels than at others; for example, to select some thing that appears beneficial to our life is less significant than to select some person for a lifelong mate. Good parenting is meant to assist us in accurately distinguishing between things and persons from the perspective of that which contributes essentially to the development of our own personal character as a covenant partner. Here too in the trial-and-error relationships involving companions and friends, there is a developmental process where, under proper guidance, we discern more accurately the different levels of relationship.

However, this experience not only gives us some skill in determining what is more appropriate and what contributes more genuinely to our own personal development but is also a process of discerning the reality of election as a confirmation and sustaining of our selecting and being selected. As we come to terms with the role of being parented, we are implicitly accepting election. One can oppose one's parents because of disagreements and even incompatibilities of style and temperament. However, within certain limits, one can develop into a mature covenant partner only by 'honoring' one's parents as a sign of God's covenantal care and provision. The exceptions to this, of course, do not constitute an alternative model of parenting but rather testify to the distortions that are woven into the fabric of human existence. To become cynical and refuse to honor that which is not agreeable to one's own wants or needs is to distrust election itself. It is not difficult to see why children who grow up under such circumstances lack the competence to make good covenant partners in marriage and family relationships.

There is only a hint of the grateful recognition of election in the Genesis 2 account. When presented with the woman, the man responds, "This at last is bone of my bones and flesh of my flesh; this one shall be called Woman" (Gen. 2:23). No other creature presented to Adam brought forth this response--each was only a possibility created to fill his need for companionship. God may have indeed summoned them forth out of the earth for Adam's consideration, but Adam reviewed them and named them, exercising his own power of choice.

But there is no such activity involved in the creation of the woman. The man is passive--rendered inactive by divine command. Upon awakening he recognizes the distinction between that which is for him because it is of him and that which can only serve him and can never be for him. Though clothed in mythical language, this story informs us of the original formation of humanity as covenant partnership. More than that, it expresses the joy at recognizing and accepting the election of God in that which is also selected.

Karl Barth points out that the joy of fulfillment at the erotic level found in being a covenant partner is presented only twice in the Old Testament: Genesis 2 and the Song of Solomon. All other references to marriage and family, he says, are related to the problem and possibility of posterity, of human fatherhood, motherhood, the family, the child and above all, the son. In the Song of Solomon we see that the picture given in Genesis 2 is not just incidental or alien to the rest of the Old Testament. In this Song, says Barth, we see, from the standpoint of a woman, the completion of what the man utters in Genesis 2. Here we have the question of an incomparable covenant, of an irresistibly purposed and effected union. "I am my beloved's, and my beloved is mine" (Song of Sol. 6:3).[31]

What we discover--almost, as it were, by accident--in selecting a mate and in being selected is that God also participates in this selection by virtue of election. This is why the marriage vow is not itself capable of sustaining the relationship as the expression of human wisdom (in making the right choice) or of human endurance (I made the wrong choice, but I will see it through to the end). The marriage vow can only be a sign of the covenant, and those who make the vow can find lasting joy and love only in being covenant partners--receiving each other as God's elect.

*A third mark of the covenant upon the family is the fact that faithful-
ness outlasts and overcomes faithlessness*

Throughout its description of Israel's tragic unfaithfulness and betrayal of covenant love, the Old Testament portrays God as a faithful spouse who will not abandon his beloved. In parable and in pronouncement the prophets summon Israel to consider the faithfulness of Yahweh who is espoused to Israel his bride. Unconditional love is the very core of the covenant relation between God and his people. Covenant partnership is God's determination that such unconditional love be experienced. As a sign of this covenant partnership, marriage and the family participate in the same unconditional character of love.

As part of this unconditional love one relinquishes the right to exist alone. Even as God relinquished this right in order to create and sustain a covenant partnership with his creature, so also must humans uncondition-ally relinquish this right in their original meeting and encounter.

Another aspect of this unconditional love is a commitment to the life of the other. Not only does one no longer have a right to exist alone, one now finds his or her own existence in the other. Moses was not averse to reminding even God of his unconditional commitment to share the life and destiny of his chosen people, those who bear his name (Exod. 32:11-14).

Also in this unconditional love is an acceptance of the gift of the other. All ethical obligation has its source in the love of neighbor (Rom. 13:10). This is an unconditional 'debt' that we owe one another. It is this debt that God assumes in entering into covenant partnership with his own creatures.

The covenant is exclusive as well as inclusive. It excludes all that stands against the determination of covenant love itself. But it also in-cludes, unconditionally, all that belongs to covenant love. Undoubtedly a shadow always lies over the human dimension of covenant partnership. Inconstancy and unfaithfulness shadow every human relationship. We cannot purge this alien possibility by either religious or humanistic ideal-ism. But all this, says Barth,

far from altering, proves finally even in its negativity that the covenant, as God willed, concluded and now maintains it, is a covenant
of love and marriage. Love is always love even if it is not deserved
or reciprocated by the beloved, even if she rejects and disgraces it by
unfaithfulness. Similarly, marriage is always marriage even though
broken by Yahweh's partner. Yahweh is always the Lover, Bridegroom
and Husband. And His lost people is always His beloved, His bride
and His wife.[32]

As the fundamental basis for marriage and family, covenant partnership is tough and unrelenting when confronted with disappointments
and even unfaithfulness. The first sign of a contradiction in committed
relationships is not the end but the beginning of experiencing covenant
love. Covenant partnership is also resourceful and hopeful. Where dead-
ends and repeated failures occur, a new pilgrimage can take place. Because
the covenant exists only provisionally in terms of social and temporal
institutions and traditions, it can leave its own ruins without leaving
anything of significance behind.

Many a marriage has experienced the demolition of its walls, which
were carefully built both idealistically and pragmatically. Those who
are prepared to be covenant partners and have indeed entered into the
creation of marriage and family will not long be detained by such ruins,
but will continue to build a new style and a new place.

No social institution has the resources for such endurance and renewal.
For this reason the family as constituted by the covenant love of God is the
source of renewal and stability for society. Yet the family must 'grow its
own members' through the development of persons capable of covenant
partnership. Thus it turns out that the parenting process is original to the
building of strong families. God is the parent who loves before he is the
covenant partner, and so it is with parenting that the paradigm continues
to unfold.

The Relation of Covenant to Creation with Implications for a Theology of the Family

From a theological perspective, the form of the family, either as an
ideal form (transcendental), or as a descriptive form (phenomenological)
does not define family. Family is defined by its goal, expressed in terms of
purpose, and working through design. Therefore, creation cannot serve
as a design for family in terms of its ultimate purpose or goal. Creation
does determine to some extent, however, the form and even the design of
family through the biological and natural order of human creatureliness.[33]
Several implications flow out of this concept.

The principle of contingency

There is a contingent relation between creation and covenant. That is, there is no necessary relation by which we can abstract the goals of covenant love from creation. The Divine covenant has its antecedent in God's loving purpose, and therefore precedes creation logically, though not chronologically. The covenant in enacted in the midst of creation where humans have already discovered the necessity of family as a sociological and even physical form of survival and growth. There are clans, tribes, and extended family structures, as well as the biological nucleus of mother and infant.

The impetus for these various forms, however, are indiscriminate and bound to nature and natural survival, and also reflect particular forms that belong to cultural factors. There is a certain solipsism in all such creaturely and natural forms of the family. These forms tend to modify themselves as self-existing entities, and therefore do not point beyond themselves to a purpose and goal that lies beyond their own existence.

When covenant emerges through the existing form or forms of the family, there is a modification of form in terms of purpose and goal, not necessarily in terms of function. Thus, the uniqueness of covenant as that which represents the telos, or teleological goal of family is not in some creaturely or natural form. These forms are relatively good, and relatively bad; because they can be relatively good as creaturely and natural forms, they can serve the purpose of covenant love and be modified to carry out the design of covenant love. This helps to explain why the covenant promise can be carried forward by the existing polygamous form of the family in the days of the patriarchs, and even through the later period of the monarchy (David, for example).

We also see this principle in the case of Abraham (Gen. 12:ff). There is already an existing family structure whose origin is rooted in antiquity, and this is no different in kind from any other family structure, except for cultural peculiarities, which do not account for the origin of family, but only for how families might function as a sociological and cultural fact. Family, for Abraham, however, becomes modified through the promise of a son, whose origins are, as it turns out, both natural and supernatural. Isaac represents an interception of the natural determinism of family, and opens up this biological, sociological, and cultural existence to a future which cannot be extrapolated out of what already has been, or even out of any possibilities which are in the present. Isaac is born 'from above,' as it were, and therefore related more to the future than the past.

The principle of entitlement

Covenant love, as the teleological goal of family, gives more than natural rights, it grants entitlement. For example, in the case of Isaac and Ishmael, and also in the case of Jacob and Esau, the natural rights of the first-born are set aside, and the entitlement to be the bearer of the covenant promise comes to the one who has no natural rights. The family, as bearer of covenant promise, thus rests upon more than kinship or blood lines. This is the basis for the New Testament and Pauline teaching concerning those who are made inheritors of the promise to Abraham through a spiritual kinship to Christ, whose own family of origin does not constitute his relation to Abraham, but the fact that he is 'born from above.' (Galatians 3). Here too we see a modification of family in that the deterministic principle of rights is nullified in favor of the principle of entitlement. While biological factors and blood lines continue to bear forward the destiny of family in a particular and even necessary sense, these factors are modified by the factors of election and choice, which brings entitlement to those who would have no natural right.

The principle of entitlement is enacted when the twelve tribes enter into the promised land and each tribe is allotted a share in the land. But this entitlement to a share in the promised land does not give an intrinsic right to the physical descendants of the original tribal heads to the land. The promised land is never owned outright by those who live in it and those who have entitlement to it. God remains the 'owner' of the land, and those who have entitlement are stewards of the land. They reap the benefits of the land, but do not have it in their disposition to buy or to sell as an absolute right. This is made clear in the celebration of the year of the Jubilee, which is the 50th year, or when seven, seven-year sabbatical periods have been completed. In the year of Jubilee the land which has been sold, or even which has been lost through some means, even bad management, returns to those who have entitlement through dependency from the original tribal heads (cf. Lev. 25:8-24; Nu. 36:4). There is continuity of the entitlement, but this continuity rests upon the divine mandate and promise, not upon outright ownership.

Two things are implied in this entitlement: 1) one cannot be disenfranchised from one's entitlement, even through failure or foolishness; 2) the entitlement is itself not an intrinsic right to have the property at one's absolute disposal. For family life this means:
- parents have 'entitlement' not natural rights or power over children.
- husbands and wife have 'entitlement' not absolute power of disposal

over their own lives, and the lives of their spouses (cf. Eph. 5).
- children have 'entitlement' in the form of parity, a full share in the good--telos--of family.

The principle of commandment

Commandments are expectations based on entitlement. Without entitlement as their presupposition, commands become defeating and tyrannical. Covenant love grants entitlement, but also gives commands in the form of expectations and rules based on this entitlement. Without such expectations, and without the commands, covenant love would dissipate into either pragmatic permissiveness, or 'law and order' repression of the human spirit. For those who have entitlement, covenant is to be 'performed', and the principle of commandment is the performance of covenant love (Deut 4:13). The family, as God's design for humans, does not merely uphold law and order, but has the positive power to exercise the principle of commandment and to bring forth the 'performance' of covenant love. Commands that do not communicate the power of 'performance' are destructive and demeaning to the human spirit.

The implications here should be quite obvious. The commandment of God is not merely a moral principle attached to parental authority. Rather, the commandment is rooted in the promise of covenant love which is more of a moral paradigm than a moral principle. For example, Hauerwas says:

> The scripture's authority for that life consists in its being used so that it helps to nurture and reform the community's self-identity as well as the personal character of its members. . . . scripture creates more than a world; it shapes a community which is the bearer of that world. Without that community, claims about the moral authority of scripture--or rather the very idea of scripture itself--makes no sense. . . .The refusal to ask our children to believe as we believe, to live as we live, to act as we act is a betrayal that derives from moral cowardice. For to ask this of our children requires that we have the courage to ask ourselves to live truthfully. . . The task for parents is to direct their children's attention to those paradigms which provide the most compelling sense of what we can and should be.[34]

The principle of shalom

Shalom means more than peace as the cessation of hostilities; shalom means wholeness and harmony; shalom represents rest and renewal, for example, "peace in the land" (Lev. 26:6). The principle of Sabbath rest is the principle of shalom. Shalom is used more than 250 times in the Old Testament and is translated generally by *eirene* (peace) in the New Testament. Unlike *eirene*, shalom is the opposite not so much of war as of any disturbance in the communal well-being of the nation. Throughout the Old Testament shalom denotes well-being in the widest sense of the word: prosperity (Ps. 73:3); bodily health (Isa. 57:18; Ps. 38:3); contentedness, on departure (Gen. 26:29); on going to sleep (Ps. 4:8); at death (Gen. 15:15); good relations between nations and men (1 Kings 5:26; Judg. 4:17), and salvation (Isa. 43:7; Jer. 29:11).

Shalom has a social dimension, not being bound up with the political aspirations of Israel, and has a public significance far beyond the purely personal. Shalom is closely bound to righteousness (Isa. 48:18; Ps. 85:10); with the concrete ideas of law and judgment (Zech. 8:16), and even with public officials (Isa. 60:17). Shalom is found in the climax of the blessing in Num. 6:24ff, where it sums up all the other blessings and where it is closely associated with the presence of Jahweh. The one who has received this gift of shalom is fulfilled, or complete, and thus has realized the *teleios*, or 'perfection' of which Jesus spoke: "Be perfect, therefore, as your heavenly father is perfect" (Matt. 5:48). Thus, *teleios* renders one aspect of shalom not immediately apparent in *eirene*. The telos of family is the realization of covenant love. Family is a sign of this perfection in the form of the fulfillment and completeness that is indicated by the filial relations that are established *for* the individual person, and not *by* the individual person. Belonging is a gift, not an achievement. The *quintessence* of family, thus, is this shalom of covenant love, which is experienced in a positive contingent relation to God who is its source and guarantee.

The Contours of Covenant in the Parable of Love in the Book of Hosea

The Old Testament prophet Hosea wrote during the last days of the life of the northern Kingdom (780-721 BC). He used the paradigm of covenant and marriage between Jahweh and Israel as a mirror of the faithlessness of Israel and the faithfulness of Jahweh. In Hosea chapters 1-3, we see the contours of a paradigm of covenant, based on the metaphor of marriage and family. For example, "On that day, says the Lord, you will call me, 'My Husband, and no longer will you call me 'My Baal'" (2:1). "I will make for you a covenant, on that day . . . " (2:18). In Chapter 11, Hosea presents the paradigm of parenting using Israel as a child, "When Israel was a child I loved him, and out of Egypt I called my son" (11:1).

Divine covenant love is **realistic**

"When the Lord first spoke through Hosea, the Lord said to Hosea, 'Go, take for yourself a wife of whoredom and have children of whoredom, for the land commits great whoredom by forsaking the Lord.' So he went and took Gomer, daughter of Diblaim, and she conceived and bore him a son." (Hosea 1:2-3). What are we to make of this? Remember, that this is a parable that Hosea was asked to perform, not merely teach. As a parable of God's relation with Israel it is meant to portray the faithless life of Israel as betrothed to the Lord. Rather than abandoning Israel due to her unfaithfulness, God shows his intention to maintain his covenant love. From this we conclude that divine covenant love is realistic. Unfaithfulness is anticipated and included. There is no ideal that determines the object of divine covenant love--it begins with what is, not with what ought to be.

From this we not only can learn what it means to experience God's covenant love, we learn what it means to bring marriage and family life into partnership with divine covenant love. In a purely contractual kind of relationship, failure of one to live up to the terms of the contract frees the other from covenant obligation. Our love is always imperfect and subject to failure. When we make a commitment to love each other and bring that relationship under the blessing and power of God's love, we must be as realistic as God and be prepared to face and deal with unfaithfulness under the discipline of divine love.

Divine covenant love is **responsible**

Moving from chapter one to chapter three in the book of Hosea, we assume that Gomer, the one chosen to represent Israel has relapsed back into a former way of life, even after being the accepted out of grace and chosen by love. "The Lord said to me again, 'Go love a woman who has a lover and is an adulteress, just as the Lord loves the people of Israel, though they turn to other gods and love raison cakes'" (3:1). The reference to raison cakes is not just to eating a pastry, but to offering 'cakes' to an idol! Divine covenant love is unconditional on both sides. God's love is not conditional upon human faithfulness; human responsibility to remain bound to the covenant relation is unconditional. Promise-making cannot be contractually avoided in a relation upheld by divine covenant love. "So I bought her for fifteen shekels of silver and a homer of barley and a measure of wine. And I said to her, 'You must remain as mine for many days; you shall not play the whore. . . '" (3:2). From this we gather that in addition to being realistic, divine covenant love does not abdicate its responsibility upon the failure of another. Both parties are held responsible by the covenant; God is responsible to seek out and restore the object of love, and the one who is loved is responsible to return and live under the constraints of covenant love.

Divine covenant love is resourceful

Here we move ahead in the book of Hosea to the last chapter, where Israel has finally come to the end of its spiritual delinquency, not by its own choice, but due to the consequences brought about by her disobedience and unfaithfulness to the Lord. "Return, O Israel to the Lord your God, for you have stumbled because of your iniquity. Take words with you and return to the Lord. . . " (14:1-2). What follows then is an incredible series of promises, offering rich resources for renewal and restoration (14:4-9).

- I will heal their disloyaliity;
- I will love them freely;
- I will be like the dew (I will prosper you).

"O Ephraim, what have I to do with idols? It is I who answer and look after you. I am like an evergreen cypress; your faithfulness comes from me" (Hosea 14:8). Covenant love is a source of renewal.

Summary of Divine Covenant Love From the Book of Hosea

There is a promise: you are wanted. "When Israel was a child, I loved him, and out of Egypt I called my son" (11:1). All children born into the world need to know they are 'wanted' regardless of the circumstances that led to their birth. Self-identity begins with the internal security and sense of 'being wanted.'

There are constraints: there are limits. "I led them with cords of human kindness" (11:4a). The Hebrew literally reads: "the cords of a man," i.e. human restraints; Moffat's translation reads: "the harness of love." God is portrayed as a human parent who sets limits based on the family structure and unity where each not only belongs, but is held by the relation itself as an animal might be 'harnessed' to a task; but in this case, the 'harness' is the cords of love that will not let another slip out of the family bond.

There are commandments: this is how to love. "I led them with . . . bands of love" (11:4b; cf. Deut 6:1f). Commandments are not rules imposed arbitrarily, but teachings that make the commandment of love specific. Parents need to show 'how to love,' not only demand that children love. To 'lead' children with 'bands of love' points to the curriculum of love. Covenant love can only be taught through 'home schooling.'

There is freedom: you are free. "I was to them like those who lift infants to their cheeks. I bent down to them and fed them" (11:4c.) The Hebrew text here is difficult to translate. The New Living Translation reads, "I led Israel along with my ropes of human kindness and love. I lifted the yoke from his neck, and I myself stooped to feed him" (11: 4 NLT). I like this translation because it captures the image of removing the yoke of slavery into which Israel had fallen and setting them free. Having farmed with horses who were forced to work all day with a steel bit in their mouth, and having the experience of seeing the horse shake its head in relief and freedom when that 'bridle' with its painful bit was removed, I think that I then catch the power of the metaphor.

Divine covenant love is a harness without a yoke; it is a bridle without a 'bit.' Would that we were born with this instinct, but then we would not need parents!

Chapter 5

The Praxis of Parenting

Someone once told me that good parenting takes practice. That may be true, but very often practice is only a repetition of incompetence. It was said of a pastor on one occasion that he was quite a capable leader as he had twenty years of experience in ministry. Another pastor that knew him replied, "Actually, he had only one year of experience repeated nineteen times!" The point being that he really never learned anything beyond his first year. I fear that many parents end up 'practicing' parenting and only discover that practice does not make perfect!

Parenting in the Praxis Mode

Students always complain when I introduce such a technical term as praxis, but it is important to define parenting as more than doing what comes naturally. Praxis is quite different from the mere application of truth or theory. It surely is an activity that does include some theory, but as a responsibility for the development of human personhood, along with character and spiritual formation, even though it does not require a license, like driving a car (perhaps it should!), effective parenting is measured by the product.

Aristotle once described two quite different ways of viewing an action. The first kind of action he called *poiesis*. This word simply means an action that produces a result, like a carpenter constructing a cabinet, or a contractor building a house. The end product completes the action regardless of what the future use may be of the product. This future use or purpose, what Aristotle called a *telos*, does not enter into the process of making something (*poiesis*).[35]

For example, a builder might be asked to build a house in accordance with a specific design and blueprint. When the house is finished, the contractor is paid in full if the building has been constructed according to the design. If, after several years, persons living in the house commit illegal or immoral acts, the builder of the house cannot be held liable for these actions. In other words, the ultimate use of the house, or its telos, was not part of the builder's responsibility. This is what Aristotle meant by *poiesis*. The product completes the action.

There is another kind of action, which Aristotle called praxis. While this includes some elements of poiesis, it goes beyond merely producing a product according to a design. With praxis, the telos, or ultimate purpose and value of an action becomes part of the action. While the design serves to orient the action toward its goal, the ultimate purpose, or telos, informs the action so as to correct the design if necessary in order to realize the ultimate purpose. One involved in praxis, therefore, is not only accountable to implement the design with skill, but to discover the telos through discernment.

In the drawing below (Figure 5.1) the action stands between the design and the telos, with the telos reaching back into the action from the future. The one who performs praxis must have discernment of the ultimate purpose or goal that is becoming evident through the action. It is also the case that only in the process of the action are certain truths concerning the final purpose and goal discovered. The action itself can reveal these truths. This is what makes praxis quite different from practice as the application of truth through a skill or technique.

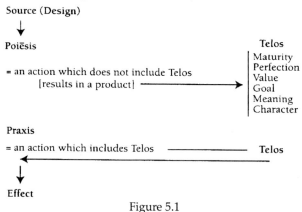

Figure 5.1

The praxis of family is to look at what families are actually producing or becoming through the actions of being family, particularly with regard to the function of parenting. In a biblical mode of praxis truth is disclosed through the action as well as revealed in a design. "My word," says the Lord, "shall not return to me empty, but it shall accomplish that which I purpose and succeed in the thing for which I sent it" (Isaiah 55:11). As with our postmodern culture, what has meaning is not so much abstract truth but that which is real and has authenticity. This is why a biblical theology of marriage and family already anticipates what postmoderns look for, not a 'modern' view of truth as abstract universal principles, but concrete and embedded truths that constitute the narrative of authentic community. This why in the drawing above the effect of action is part of the truth of the act itself, not merely that it is a replica of a theoretical design.

Because praxis has its telos, or goal, in producing maturity, the trajectory of parenting extends far beyond the limited time (usually about 18 years) that children remain at home and are subject to direct parental authority. It is not difficult to delineate the particular set of competencies that we use in describing what we expect of--say--a thirty-year old young woman or man with regard to being able to make and sustain commitments and promises, to demonstrate moral character, and to embody a rich and healthy spirit-life with God. We all know what we mean when we say that someone is a person of faith, good character, and maintains effective social relationships. We say that such a person has maturity.

Obviously, the trajectory of parenting extended to a thirty-something young person must go beyond establishing 'house rules' and curfew deadlines! It is something like using a rifle with a thirty-inch barrel to hit a target one hundred yards in the distance. Allowance must be made for a variety of factors that will affect the track of the bullet once it leaves the end of the barrel. Because of these factors, if one aims directly at the target it will miss every time! A few practice shots will reveal adjustments due to the pull of gravity and the wind before the proper effect is reached. While this analogy has its limitations, it does point to the problem facing parents. One does not have opportunity for 'practice.' And what one does with the first child may not work with the second. Every child is born into a different family, we are reminded.

For this reason, a praxis approach to parenting must go beyond simply 'doing it by the book.' In the best of all worlds, an inter-generational family unit has a wealth of advantages, where the younger parents have guidance, support and encouragement from the elders. Although even here, we often discover that the 'sins of the fathers are visited upon the children!' In other words, bad parenting can be passed down from generation to generation! One of the reasons for this book is to recognize and preserve the praxis of parenting that 'hits the target' and correct the aim of that which does not. One of the crucial areas on which we need to reflect is the role of power and authority in parenting.

Dynamics of Power and Authority in the Formation and Nurture of Identity

The balance of stability and love rest at the core of the development of children into mature and responsible persons. These two factors are the irreducible minimum of a viable socialization context. By stability I mean both authority and predictability. The key to the development of children within family is a covenant love that has both unconditional loyalty as its base, and authority as its structure.

Distinguishing power from authority

In Chapter Two I described the four kinds of order and the moral authority that provide a basis for determining the kind of moral values that impinge upon our relationships. The model can be presented here again for the sake of defining the relation of power and authority with respect to the role of parents in the development of self-identity for children.

MORAL ORDER AND MORAL AUTHORITY

KINDS OF ORDER	MORAL ORDER	MORAL AUTHORITY
NATURAL ORDER	ideological	coercive
CONVENTIONAL ORDER	cultic	punitive
INTERPERSONAL ORDER	systemic and contractual	value intensive
REDEMPTIVE ORDER	personal and covenantal	empowering

Figure 5.2

Each kind of 'order' determines the kind of power that will be used

- In the natural order, power needs to be 'harnessed' in order to control it.
- In the conventional order, power tends to be merged with the authority which resides in the conventional moral order. Submission to authority is required under the category of duty, honor, and obedience to the moral law. One only has power if one has a position of authority.
- In the interpersonal order power resides not with those who use

nature to control, nor does power become lodged with those who become authority figures as conservators of the conventional moral order; rather, authority mediates power to those who are expected to use it to uphold the contractual commitments which form the structure of society. With the mediation of power there is also a kind of conferral of authority, with authority lodged in autonomous, free moral agency.

- In the redemptive order, power is not tied directly to authority, but linked with personal being; consequently empowerment is the telos of authority as a praxis of community. In both the interpersonal and redemptive order, there is a shift of power from the strong to the weak. Lewis Smedes puts it this way: "Parents gradually get weaker and children gradually get stronger; parents gradually relinquish authority and children gradually move into freedom. . . healthy parental authority aims precisely at the child's ultimate liberation from it."[36] Smedes appears to define power and authority as virtually the same thing, as the interpersonal order tends to do. The shift of power does not need to result in the 'weakening' or disempowering of the parent if power is connected with personal being rather than with authority as a structure of moral agency. The biblical concept of power as *exousia* is helpful in making clear this distinction between power and authority. Jesus spoke as one who had authority (*exousia*), that is, they sensed the power of his person as compared to those who wielded power due to their official status.

Releasing Power From the Need to Control

Moral authority, argue the Bergers, cannot be exercised through coercion, but must take place in the family where this authority is mediated through structures and rituals of love.[37] It is love that mediates power to others through its use of authority. The commandment to love is the moral basis for the commandment to obey; in commenting on the commandment for children to "honor their fathers and mothers," Smedes says: "If there is a single reason why parents have a right to their children's respect, I suggest it is authority. . . .Parental authority, rightly understood, is the one quality all parents have which corresponds to the honor that children are asked to give them. Authority, moreover, is the backbone of family life."[38]

However, as we have already made clear, authority must be distinguished from power, and authority must be understood with respect to the particular kind of order within which it operates. If parents operate out of a natural order primarily, authority will be used to control, for the harnessing of power is the authority of the natural order. This leaves children without power or can force children to harness their own natural power and to retaliate in order to control parents.

One might look upon the typical 'temper tantrums' of a small child as one form of using natural instincts to gain power and so control the situation. The same thing can be said with regard to the conventional order and the use of authority to command respect as a way of conserving the traditional or conventional order. This is exemplified by the conflict the Jewish father and his daughter experienced in Fiddler on the Roof. "Tradition," he cries out. This is the backbone of his argument against his daughter marrying outside of the Jewish religion.

Smedes is right if we consider authority as the mediation of power through the interpersonal order. However, if we operate with the distinction between power and authority made above, the empowerment of the weak does not involve a transfer of power (i.e. authority), but the empowering of the weak so as to live under authority, that is, under the command of God as rooted in his own covenant love.

Rollo May suggests that there are five kinds of power.[39]
- exploitative power-----power over
- manipulative power----power over
- competitive power-----power against
- nutritive power--------power for
- integrative power------power with

Clearly, both nutritive and integrative power are more expressive of covenant love.

In the end, of course, the command, honor your father and mother, never really is annulled. There is a weakening of the authority of parents in terms of the natural and conventional order to be sure. This authority is attenuated so greatly with the development of the power of love in the children that in their own adulthood they form structures of authority in new forms of the interpersonal order, and begin again the generational cycle of marriage and family. Yet, in the redemptive order the children are also empowered to keep the commandment, and to remember to honor their parents. The mark of having been parented is the continued remembrance and honoring of someone with whom your own destiny is shared. Smedes has a perceptive comment: "The key to the parent's power lies inside the memory of the child."[40]

For example, Jacob, before dying, said to his son Joseph: "Promise to deal loyally and truly with me. Do not bury me in Egypt, but let me

lie with my fathers; carry me out of Egypt and bury me in their bury-
ing place." (Gen. 47:29-3; Gen. 50:4-14) Joseph, then, made his brothers
promise that they and their descendants would carry his bones out of
Egypt to the promised land when God should deliver them (Gen. 50:24).
Moses took the bones of Joseph with him during the exodus from Egypt
400 years later and Joshua buried them in the family plot (Exodus 13:19;
Joshua 24:32)!

Covenant love as the Mediation of Power: The Foundation for Strong and Secure Self-Identity

The development of personhood in the sense of being empowered to
participate in covenant community is related to the degree to which individuals within family are encouraged and supported in their own 'power
of being.' Power of being is strongest when it is manifest as unconditional
loyalty as the expression of love.

- Love is not a dependence upon someone stronger than oneself, but
it is the strength and power of being to sustain what Roszak called
the 'unconditional loyalty' which is at the heart of family.
- Love is not being drawn irresistibly like a magnet to the power of
others, but it is the power to remain loyal and faithful to the other
even when there is adversity and conflict.
- Love is not a helpless need for someone else to fill a vacuum in our
lives, but it is the overflowing of our own fullness of being expressed
as openness of being to the other in many contractual ways.

Here we see that social contracts which range from everyday arrangements, to marriage itself, are under-girded by the power of personal being
that sustains love in and through the contract. Maurice Friedman makes
this point forcefully when he writes:

> In the relations between parent and child and teacher and student,
> it is again the recognition of otherness, of the uniqueness that has its
> own right and must grow in its own way, which informs the mutual
> contact and the mutual trust. . . For this trust to exist, the teacher or
> parent must be really there, really facing the child, not merely there
> in spirit. To be here she need possess none of the perfections which
> the child imagines, but she "must have gathered the child's presence"
> into her own story "as one of the bearers" of her "communion with
> the world, one of the focuses of" her "responsibilities for the world."
> She does not have to be concerned with the child at every moment, but
> she must have gathered the child into her life in such a way that steady
> potential presence of the one to the other is established and endures.
> The catastrophe for the child comes not if the parent or teacher turns out
> to be less than perfect, but if she is trying to seem to be a certain type

of person in order to win the approval or dependence of the child. The essential problem of the sphere of the interhuman, as we have seen, is this duality of being and seeming. . . In the interhuman realm, "truth" does not mean saying whatever comes to mind, but letting no seeming creep between oneself and the other. It does not mean letting go before another but granting that person a share in one's being.[41]

Dynamics of Parenting and Development of Personhood

The image of God as co-humanity is the theological basis for the uniqueness of human personhood experienced in primary social relationships. The image of God is itself understood in a developmental sense, i.e., the capacity to experience one's personhood is a developmental capacity. Children are not born with the full capacity to relate as persons, though they are fully persons and fully human at birth. Thus, the image of God is qualitatively present from he beginning (at least birth), but is developed in a quantitative sense through the development of the capacity to love. Covenant love is the telos of the praxis of parenting; this telos is the moral basis for the authority given to parents and the moral content of the praxis of family.

Experience of family is indispensable to the development of personhood; it is the 'world' of the child, as the Berger's put it:

> Children need a world to grow into. [This world is not merely a physical environment, but a social environment in which socialization occurs.] Socialization is impossible without a strong sense of belonging existing between the child and one or more 'significant' adults. Minimally, therefore, every human society must provide community in the social locale where children are raised.[42]

In this sense, family can be said to be that 'locale,' or 'world' where this socialization takes place. "Identity is not something an individual is born with; rather it emerges from specific social processes."[43] Identity is itself a development process which occurs as the child experiences a world mediated through the socialization of primary relationships. Not all experiences of family are positive ones, however. Theodore Roszak points this out dramatically:

> The violation of personhood begins in the cradle, if not in the womb. . . . We are born into other people's intentions. We learn our names and our natures at their hands, and they cannot teach us more truth than they know or will freely tell. Can there be families whose love is not treason against our natural vocation?[44]

One could respond by saying that there are ideals that stand above such filial parochialism and that love is rooted in ideals, not in traditions or even in human dispositions and temperaments. But even here Roszak will not yield his point: "We know that every ideal that supports the family has been used to tell a lie." This reminds us of a statement by Stanley Hauerwas, "No one rules more tyrannously than those who claim not to rule at all because they only want to love us."[45] Roszak goes on to comment: There must be a family beyond the family so many are struggling to escape. From this he argues, there must be personalities who become the sacramental carriers of the unconditional loyalty and commitment which children need in order to become fully personal and human. He puts it this way:

> We meet as strangers, each carrying a mystery within us. I cannot say who you are; I may never know you completely. But I trust that you are a person in your own right, possessed of a beauty and value that are the world's richest resources. So I make this promise to you; I will impose no identities upon you, but will invite you to become yourself, without shame or fear. I will defend your right to find authentic vocation. For as long as your search takes, you have my loyalty.[46]

Several points can be made that relate to the role of parents in the development of personal identity in the child. First of all, there is the importance of the parent/child relationship in the formation of a theology of the family. Second, much of the insistence upon the marriage relationship as primary stems not so much from a theological necessity as from the influence of contemporary culture. Because erosion of the family as an institution and the subsequent emphasis upon marriage as a depository of nonbinding commitments, the affectional function is held to be all-important. Third, Jesus Christ in his mediatorial function made God fully 'knowable' but that it yet remains necessary for the child through the parent/child interaction to learn 'how to know.' Though the divine Word has 'spoken,' the human person must still be taught 'to hear.' And fourth, the teaching of the child 'to know and to hear' God is accomplished through the process of socialization--of inculcating the values, beliefs, attitudes, roles, and norms associated with the stream of holy history. This is a process within each generation in which the reconciliation process is repeated and made complete. A significant dimension of that witness involves the 'older' transmitting the knowledge of God, his mercy and his grace in Jesus Christ to the 'younger' so that when they ask "What do these things mean?" they receive their answer.

It is the function of parents through the process of socialization to transform the human raw material of society into good working members. Through the process of socialization the past becomes the future, the parent becomes a person to the child in such a way that the child becomes a person to the parent. The products of socialization (i.e., values, beliefs, attitudes, roles, and norms) are developed through the natural dependencies of the child, that is, its need for care and information. The child either does or does not 'learn' to know God, to become fully human, to be differentiated as male or female. For every person someone or something stands in the parenting role and begins the re-creation of the image of God. Unfortunately, that process does not work well for many. For others it works relatively well. Probably more than we would like to admit, the grace of God is conditioned by that process. By conditioned we simply mean that his grace is either facilitated or frustrated by the parenting process as it is mediated to the person. Part of the human condition is freedom--and part of that freedom as parent is to participate in or hinder the grace of God from generation to generation.

Parenting and the Development of Persons

It was from Dennis Guernsey that I learned what is involved in the socialization process of parenting though his teaching and writing.[47] The parenting role can now be set out in more detail. This involves a five-fold developmental process. This is not to imply that socialization is an all-inclusive term nor that the following is all-inclusive.

The first task of the parent is the task of attachment

Because the human infant is absolutely dependent, the role of care-giver is primary. Studies have shown that there are specific kinds of anxiety an infant experiences in the first few months of life which relate to the infant's critical physically and psychologically needs. It is through the attachment process that the natural anxiety of affect dependence is mediated, trust is engendered, and the basic self begins to emerge. The initial position of the infant, however, is one in which the self is in the dependent position. It is wholly at the mercy of the primary care-giver. At no other time is the human more vulnerable. There are no defenses. There is no ability to care for one's self. The totality of the emerging person's self is defined by the responses of their 'first love,' that is, their primary care-giver, usually the mother. If the relationship is warm, nurturing, and infused with joy, the infant develops the basic and necessary ability to trust, founded upon the certain and predictable responses of the care-giver. If, on the other hand, that care is thwarted by circumstances, ambivalence, or by the dysfunction of the care-giver's ability to relate unconditionally to the infant, a state of mistrust is generated and the consequences are life-long. Failure to achieve attachment at the very beginning, can leave the self unable to attain intimacy later in life.

The second task of parenting is the task of differentiation

Very early in the first year the infant begins to realize that he or she is not joined to the mother. When she leaves the room the infant is left behind. When the infant cries because of pain or discomfort the mother doesn't always respond immediately. Other objects in the infant's world begin to take on significance, whether they are stuffed animals, hanging mobiles, or parenting alternatives such as the father. The task of the primary care-giver at this stage is to encourage the infant to expand his or her world to include other sources of meaningful stimuli and to avoid the extremes of limiting the infant to the world of the mother or of abandoning the infant to the multiplicity of outside care-givers who may or may not create a reliable nurturing world for the infant.

This stage of differentiation is later played out in bold relief in the adolescent years, when the infant--now grown to be a young person--must be released from the bonds of the parental family. If the earlier process of differentiation operated at either of the extremes, the parental experience with the emerging adolescent takes on an overly centrifugal or expelling character or an overly centripetal or binding character. The seeds for the parent/adolescent experience are sown in the quality of relationship between the infant and the primary care-giver.

The third task is the task of separation and individuation

Healthy parents raise their children not to need them. They work themselves out of a job. Unfortunately, many parents begin this task far later than is necessary. Although it begins as early as ten months with the infant's growing skills (such as learning to walk by itself), the task itself is stretched out over the very early years. "Me do it" is the bane of every parent during these months of the child's early life. What is at stake is the child's sense of mastery of its world apart from the mother, and the freedom to fail if necessary and to know that its failures will not end in catastrophic loss or disaster. At this stage the parent(s) are faced with the delicate balance between the child's independence and autonomy and its dependence upon the parent.

Latent within this stage and the task of separation and individuation is the issue referred to in the literature as 'rapprochement.' This term is defined as the natural ambivalence experienced by the child when it begins to realize the implications of its growing independence and autonomy. If the child gets too good at it, it will not need its mother. Often during these months or years there is an upsurge in separation anxiety, in which the child backs away from its emerging independence and experiences a normal time of anxiety or clinging to the mother. What the child needs is the reassurance of the care-giver that her presence and support can be depended upon and that as the child ventures out into the world the care-giver will be a steady source of support and encouragement. The message must be "You can't go wrong if you grow up. It's OK not to need me. I'm with you even if I don't do things for you."

The fourth task of parenting is the task of establishing constancy

This task is predicated upon the successful completion of the first three. It has to do with the final outfitting of the self in the child so that it is able to tolerate the natural ambivalences of relationships and the ambiguities of life. If the primary care-giver has been basically dependable, nurturing and loving, and has been able to release the child to become a self of its own, the next stage for the child is to realize that the mother, or anyone else in fact, cannot be there always and in every way. The child learns to depend upon itself at all times, and to forgive either itself or others when appropriate. No one can be perfect, and to demand perfection of oneself or of others is unrealistic. Constancy implies the attribution of permanence and trust even when the immediate results suggest otherwise.

The fifth task of parenting is the task of generalization.

During this time the child recognizes its interdependence upon others. This is when the position of the self becomes 'I/thou.' It is the position of the prodigal son returning to his father. It is the dialogue between the self and the other in which the person declares "I am responsible to and for you as well as for myself." It is the position of emerging community; of mutual interdependence--the position in which the 'one another' imperatives of the New Testament become relevant. It is the position in which the law of Christ is being fulfilled.

Summary

In terms of parenting these five tasks are developmental, each necessary for those that follow. Thus, the absolute dependency of the person as infant is secured through the process of attachment to the dependable care-giver. The self begins to emerge in an environment of acceptance and joy. Next, the infant begins to differentiate itself from its care-giver and to develop a sense of its own self as distinct from others. Having become aware of its growing sense of differentiation, the infant/toddler enters into the journey toward separation and individuation even in the midst of rapprochement or self-doubt. From the resolution of this doubt comes the quality of constancy or the ability to trust and to forgive both self and others. And last of all comes the stage of generalization or healthy interdependence in which the child begins to recognize its responsibility not only for itself but also for the welfare of others.

These necessary tasks are foundational to the biblical injunction to leave one's father and mother and to cleave to one's spouse. Whether that leaving involves the commitment to marriage or the commitment to others in community, the process is not complete until mutual interdependence is effected. Parenting, therefore, is the arena in which the human person learns the necessary skills to function as an adult-whether married or single.

Chapter 6

Marriage as Covenant Partnership

"One ought to marry at all costs," Plato reportedly advised, "for if it proves to be a happy relationship, one will experience bliss and heavenly delight. If it proves to be an unhappy relationship, one may then become a philosopher, and experience the joys of the mind."

The fact that this quotation betrays a certain cynicism concerning the estate of marriage only shows that there is nothing new under the sun. And yet, if sociologists and psychologists are accurate in their assessment, marriage and human sexuality together constitute the greatest crisis for contemporary society. We may generally anticipate that roughly one-third of all marriages contracted in any given year in the United States will end in divorce--and in certain sections of the country, the ratio is one out of two. For several years, Los Angeles County has granted more divorce decrees than the number of marriage licenses issued. There can be little doubt that the critical problem underlying the general malaise of family life in North America is the instability and unhealthiness of marriage as a social unit. It is further postulated that this dis-ease in the state of marriage is a symptom of a more fundamental confusion of human sexuality, linked with a basic incompetence in developing and sustaining mature covenant relationships.

I do not intend in this discussion to set forth a basic theology of sexuality, nor will I review and critically analyze the literature on sexuality and marriage. My concern is more limited: it focuses upon the specific nature of marriage with respect to the basic encounter of male and female in covenant partnership as set forth in the preceding chapters. I have attempted to present a developmental model by which persons experience their own human selfhood as cohumanity, and by which they develop competence in creating and sustaining covenant-partner relations. While I have established the concept of covenant as the basic paradigm of family, I have not as yet delineated the basic structure of family itself. In now taking up this task, our first step will be to look at marriage as it stands independent of family as a sociological entity, and yet as the theological and practical sources of family. We ought not to consider marriage a component of a general concept of family. Rather, understood theologically, marriage stands as the concrete foundation of family. Karl Barth says that marriage is not subordinate to family, but family is subordinate to marriage.[48] Consequently, our task is to set forth a theological and critical basis for understanding the nature of marriage as an expression of human love and sexuality. Coupled with this theological endeavor will be certain pastoral perspectives, for our aim is not merely to view marriage theoretically, but to provide a basis for preventing marital breakdown as well as for healing and renewal where the breakdown has occurred.

Marriage as a Covenant Partnership

The language of covenant as applied to the marriage vow does not mean that humans can make covenant in the same way that God does. The divine covenant with humanity is unilateral, not bilateral. Marriage as a mutual exchange of vows is a bilateral social contract which God "joins together" (Mark 10:9). The promise exchanged by those who enter into marriage makes them 'covenant partners' with God. Marriage is a unique event of co-humanity which has its own purpose and value, and which is an eschatological sign of the goal of humanity (cf. Genesis 2:23-24; Eph. 5:22-23). Thus sexuality as a component of co-humanity makes marriage a possibility but not a necessity, for personal fulfillment as male or female is based in cohumanity. Sexuality is not made sacred by marriage, but is sanctified by true humanity, that is, by co-humanity. The New Testament Christian community already anticipated this eschatological reality in viewing the brother / sister relation as the primary one; but even here we should note the sexual differentiation and gender identification involved.

God quite clearly prefers that marriage be monogamous, yet also expressed a purposeful presence through the sometimes confusing and problematic social structure of polygamous marriage. The blessings of the covenant intended through Abraham for all the families of the earth unfolded through God's gracious presence to bless the offspring of Jacob and the four women who produced the twelve patriarchs. God prefers that marriage be a life-long commitment and 'hates divorce' as Malachi expressly stated. Yet God's presence in the lives of persons who have experienced the tragedy of a marriage that has failed leads many to conclude that remarriage for divorced persons is a witness to God's gracious presence. The ministry of affirming God's presence as a source of reconciliation and healing does not annul God's preference as intended for the human good.

Promise-making as the creative hope of marriage

The greatest threat to the family for the future is not poor marriages, or conflicted family structures, but loss of belief in the making of promise. Craig Dykstra, says:

> Families are people who make promises to each other. When we see what these promises are, we see what a family is . . .It is not the failure to keep promises, in and of itself, that destroys family. Such failure happens in every family and can be expected. Family can remain family in he midst of unfulfilled promises. What destroys family is the collapse of promise-making. It is when the very making of promises is no longer believed and believed in that families die.[49]

Thus, love, as the expression of promise-making and keeping is the core of marriage. When we view humans as bound to each other in the form of cohumanity we realize that individuality is derived out of relationship, and that relationship itself is the core of being human. A promise is thus not merely an ethical matter, but a moral structure of the encounter between persons, of which the marriage vow is but one example. Jürgen Moltmann says:

> The human being is the being who can make promises. He can and will be, for himself and other people. . . He does this in promising and in keeping the promise, in faithfulness. In his promise, a person commits himself, acquires a particular Gestalt, and makes himself someone who can be appealed to. Through faithfulness the person acquires his identity in time, because he remembers, and permits himself to be reminded, and recollects the promise he has given. It is in the historical link between promise and fulfillment of the promise that a person acquires his continuity. And it is only through this continuity that he finds his lived identity.[50]

An unresolved issue is the status of non-married adults who have freedom and autonomy, but no shared promise. The early church legitimated the single life style as a vocation alongside of marriage. But, as Stanley Hauerwas says:

> Singleness was legitimate, not because sex was thought to be a particularly questionable activity, but because the mission of the church was such that "between the times" the church required those who were capable of complete service to the Kingdom. And we must remember that the "sacrifice" made by the single is not that of "giving up sex," but the much more significant sacrifice of giving up heirs.[51]

The church must provide a language and liturgy of promise by which both the married and the unmarried can be bound to the Kingdom of God and to each other.

Toward a Theology of Marriage

At the outset, we must also make clear a subtle but important distinction between a theological and an ethical view of marriage. Emil Brunner asserts that marriage, in the full sense of the word, represents an ethical solution to the problem of the relation between the sexes.[52] In his view, the erotic sexual impulse, originally created as good, has become through sin, the greatest danger for the individual as well as for society. Thus, he posits marriage as the only optimum containment for this otherwise unbridled impulse.[53]

Sexuality, argues Brunner, is sanctified only through marriage, unless one chooses total abstinence. But abstinence is essentially a negative means of ethical life. And Brunner believes that the sexual drive under the power of sin is not likely to be controlled successfully because it is basically an 'unnatural' form of human existence. Brunner rejects Barth's claim that human sexuality is a determination of human existence as the image and likeness of God and thus exists prior to and independent of marriage as a true order.

We can contrast Brunner's ethical view of marriage with Barth's more theological view. The question of the sexual implications of cohumanity as male and female does not coincide with the question of marriage, argues Barth. In other words, "the ethical question in relation to the sphere of male and female cannot be exhaustively discussed in the problem of marriage."[54] Brunner says that sexuality is sanctified as an ethical existence under the command of God only in the marriage relation. Barth disagrees, arguing that the command of God "sanctifies man by including his sexuality within his humanity, and challenging him even in his bodily nature and therefore in his sexual life, in his answering of the problem of sex relationship, to be true man."[55] What Barth means is that the sexual relation of man and woman has already been constituted a true order of humanity as an integral part of total humanity as male and female. Marriage, as an exemplification of the total encounter of male and female in covenant partnership, thus integrates sexuality into total humanity.

I do not want to caricature the positions of Barth and Brunner to make it appear that they are further apart than they actually are. The difference is subtle because both advocate monogamy as the sole form of physical sexual expression under the command of God. And yet the difference between a theological view of marriage and sexuality and an ethical view is important. Brunner does posit a basic I-Thou relation as intrinsic to the image of God. But because he rejects the notion that this also includes sexuality as male and female, he must of necessity introduce marriage into the discussion of sexuality as the ethical presupposition of a sexual self-understanding as man and woman.

This has serious consequences for understanding the role of sexuality in the case of the unmarried person as well as for a discussion of the matter of homosexuality. If, following Brunner, we say that the marital pair is the basic model of man and woman as a community of love and all other relations are peripheral to it, then marriage will be offered as the highest, if not the only possibility for authentic humanity.

On the other hand, following Barth, humanity as determined by God is cohumanity, existing concretely as either male or female. Marriage then, is not the only ethical justification of sexuality understood as authentic male and female humanity, even though it alone offers the only partnership in which sexual relation has its intended consummation and completion, This decentralizes the view that marriage is the only context in which male and female sexuality can be discussed ethically. Thus, sexuality is liberated from the need to be denied or repressed. The command of God, says Barth, requires no 'liberation from sex' as a negative ethical act.[56] Marriage is not seen as a 'containment' of that which has no other ethical point of reference, but as the 'contextualizing' of that which comes to expression in the total encounter of man and woman. "Coitus without co-existence is demonic," says Barth--"within as well as outside marriage."[57] Because sexuality is set within the command of God in terms of authentic humanity, marriage does not constitute the basis for a sexual ethic, but itself comes under the true order of sexuality as cohumanity. Marriage, as encounter between man and woman, rather than constituting a sanctification of 'unbridled sexuality,' is sanctified in the command of God that relates sexuality to coexistence as personal humanity,

We shall have more to say about what it means that marriage takes place under the 'command of God,' but for now it must also be said that this divine command does not take place independent of the human act of response and recognition. While marriage is more than love, it involves the mutual recognition, choice, and commitment of two people in covenant partnership. God joins together actually as well as theoretically. He joins together in and by the encounter and decision of the two who form the union; not only on the basis of this human act of love but coincidental with it and as its objective validation. What begins as affection and feelings of love, says Brunner, is absorbed into personal will expressed as commitment in marriage. According to Barth, love, in contradistinction to mere affection,

> may be recognized by the fact that it is determined, and indeed determined upon the life-partnership of marriage. Love does not question; it gives an answer. Love does not think; it knows. Love does not hesitate; it acts. Love does not fall into raptures; it is ready to undertake responsibilities. Love puts behind it all the Ifs and Buts, all the conditions, reservations, obscurities and uncertainties that may arise between a man and a woman. Love is not only affinity and attraction; it is union. Love makes these two persons indispensable to each other.[58]

Even if the entrance into marriage is superficial, even if it is virtually a blunder, continues Barth, what was not marriage can later become marriage.[59] This is so because fidelity awakens love as the result of a relationship that honors coexistence as a concrete manifestation of the divine command. Fidelity, then, is the human source of stability and permanence in marriage. As the positive expression of will to partnership, fidelity can reawaken a love that barely exists or has even died.

But fidelity is more than a commitment to the other person based upon feelings of love. If it is only that, love's failure to sustain its own cause when it is not reciprocated will undermine it. Fidelity is the surrender of one's own cause to the cause of the other. Coexistence then becomes a partnership in which the particularity of the other becomes an irrevocable source of one's own destiny.

Hidden in this particularity is the origin of the concept of monogamy. Despite the fact that one can love more than one person at a time --for love itself is not the only source of fidelity--one can experience the exclusivity of the divine command with only one other. Inevitably we become confused when we base the principle of monogamous marriage on the notion of the exclusivity of love. This is where Brunner failed in his argument for monogamy. He asserts that natural love is in its essence monogamous, despite the tendencies toward polygamy expressed in various cultures.[60] Barth rightly argues that Brunner's notions are based on human experience rather than on divine command. "It is God's election and covenant, says Barth, "which gives unconditional and compelling character to the requirement of monogamy. . . In His election and His covenant it is not merely the electing divine Partner who is utterly one. . .the creaturely and elected partner. . . is always singular as well."[61] Despite the tendentious theological argument that Barth uses to make his case, it remains compelling precisely because the divine determination of cohumanity is concretely and particularly male and female. Even at the level of physical sexuality, complementarity is essentially a polarity between two. Thus, though one can love more than one person simultaneously in terms of general human encounter, one cannot be bound in a relationship of fidelity to more than one at the same time. And the singularity of sexual union expresses this quite particularly.

Having said all this, are we tempted to respond with the disciples, "If such is the case of a man with his wife, it is better not to marry" (Matt, 19: 10)? We hope not. While we have set marriage within the absolute determination of a divine command, we have not set it above the reality and practice of human existence. Those who seek to enter into marriage ought to be counseled to consider it seriously, but also to view it realistically, not ideally. Marriage can never be the solution to problems of personal unhappiness or loneliness. It can never be the relational horizon within which one expects to meet all his or her personal needs. Marriage offers an expression of love and sexuality not realizable in any other human relationship, but it is no more human than any other human task or relationship. And in particular, because marriage takes place under the divine command, says Barth.

> The sphere of the relationships of man and woman as they are embodied and lived out among us human beings is not simply a labyrinth of errors and failings, a morass of impurity, or a vale of tears at disorder and distress. For by the grace of God...there are always in this sphere individual means of conservation and rescue, of deliverance and restoration, assured points and lines even where everything seems to vacillate and dissolve, elements of order in the midst of disorder. .. And if there is no perfect marriage, there are marriages which for all their imperfection can be and are maintained and carried through, and in the last resort not without promise and joyfulness, arising with a certain necessity, and fragmentarily, at least, undertaken in all sincerity as a work of free life-fellowship. There is also loyalty even in the midst of disloyalty and constancy amid open inconstancy ....thus even where man does not keep the command, the command keeps man....He who here commands does not only judge and forgive; He also helps and heals.[62]

Is marriage, then, a social contract that can be broken when one or both of the contracting parties violate the contract, or is it a covenant partnership that, once entered into, can never be dissolved? Well, it is both. While a social contract based upon mutual conditions of good will and reciprocity does not contain within it the quintessential aspect of covenant love, covenant love can come to expression through a social contract. It is my opinion that all humans can express a dimension of covenant love because they are created in the divine image and likeness. But God is the source of covenant love, which he expressed through his actions of bonding with Israel and then with all humanity through Jesus Christ. From the human perspective, the essence of a marriage is the social contract explicitly grounded in a relation of human sexuality, male and female, which finds its implicit source of covenant love in God's own commandment and gift of love. In this sense, marriage is not a product of each individual's effort, but rather a mutual task. A shared task or purpose is what orients a marriage relationship to the future, and causes it to endure. Stanley Hauerwas says this in a forceful and helpful way:

> Unless marriage has a purpose beyond being together it will certainly be a hell. For it to be saved from being a hell we must have the conviction that the family represents a vocation necessary for a people who have a mission and yet have learned to be patient. Marriage and family require time and energy that could be used to make the world better. To take the time to love one person rather than many, to have these children rather than helping the many in need, requires patience and a sense of the tragic. Indeed such activities remind us of how limited we are, but at least we in the Christian tradition claim that it is only through such limits that we learn what it means to be free.[63]

Diana and Richard Garland define the primary task and purpose that offers creative partnership as a calling of the marriage partners to seek and find God's will for the marriage. They tend to define this as something above the task and purpose which marriage itself has in contributing to the community of which it is a part. "The marriage relationship," they suggest, following the model of Christ and the church in Ephesians Chapter Five, "has a transcendent purpose in God's scheme of things." To the extent that they mean that the marriage itself has a purpose or task beyond that of each individual, and beyond the role of each person in the relationship, I would agree. They give five suggestions as a basis for thinking of the task concept of marriage.[64]

1) Marriage is a unity, with a task and purpose of its own beyond those of the individual partners:
2) the task or purpose of each marriage is unique and cannot be imposed by a standard definition of the function of marriage;
3) the task or purpose of a marriage is often not explicitly defined but can be found in the structure of the relation rules and values that define the couple's life together;
4) the task or purpose of a marriage varies over time;
5) a significant source of meaning in marriage comes from the partner's roles as co-creators; marriage requires creative use of space, structures of relationships, and their own history; or, we might say,

their own story.

Marriage as Sexual Partnership

The relationship of human sexuality to marriage is a matter of particular concern and often of confusion. Marriage counselors tell us that most marital problems include some dimension of incompatibility or dysfunction at the level of sexual relationship. We are reminded here of Barth's warning: "coitus without co-existence is demonic."

But there is even more confusion in the so-called 'premarital' experience of sexual relation, Does sexual relation itself constitute marriage in God's eyes? If so, then what does 'premarital' mean in terms of the sexual relation? Sexual intercourse between man and woman is presupposed by the command of God by which human existence is set within a divine order. To be human is not only to be male or female, but to be male and female. Not only does God determine us to be either male or female, but also that we are to be male with respect to the female, and female with respect to the male. This reminds us of Paul's teaching that "in the Lord woman is not independent of man nor man independent of woman. For just as woman came from man, so man came through woman" (1 Cor. 11: 11- 12). Coexistence is the mutual recognition of the determination of one for the other and one with the other. To relate in such a way that this determination does not result in coexistence is a fundamental disorder, what Barth calls 'demonic.' That which stands in defiance of the command of God has its source in the evil one, not in some neutral human determination of its own.

It is instructive to note that the Mosaic Law stipulated the penalty of death for those who violated the integrity of the vow of betrothal as well as the marriage vow itself. Adultery occurs when a person who is married has sexual relation with someone other than the spouse. But it also occurs when one who is betrothed and has not yet consummated the marriage has sexual relation with someone other than the betrothed. The implication here is that an explicit contract has been made, one which is binding upon the persons involved, and one in which the community itself has a stake (Deut. 22:22-27).

Yet the Law did not invoke the death penalty upon those who had sexual relation and who were neither married nor betrothed. Instead, the man was bound to seek out the father of the woman and negotiate the required marriage contract with the woman (Deut. 22:28 -29). In this situation the act of sexual intercourse brought no specific penalty upon the lives of those involved. However, the sexual act consummates an implicit contract that requires ratification as an explicit and public contract of marriage. One might say in this case that coitus precedes coexistence, but that coexistence contextualizes the coitus in such a way that the offense against the true order is taken up into the marriage as a responsible act of covenant partnership. This, of course, is a precarious position to be in. The distance from the 'field' where the act occurred to the 'father's house' where the act is contextualized constitutes a quite specific risk and danger. The couple is without support and affirmation of either family or community. Passion, and even affection, has not yet been resolved into will and intention. While a 'union' has been consummated, it is without the integrity of community affirmation; the coexistence that constitutes the necessary human context has not yet been made visible in marriage.

It is quite clear that the couple have come under the 'command of God' through the act of sexual intercourse, questionable though it may be under the circumstances. What is required is obedience to this command through the negotiation of the appropriate wedding contract, Failure to follow through in this way then places the man and woman in jeopardy due to disobedience. The 'sin' involved then is not specifically the act of sexual intercourse, though this can become the occasion for the sin, but the sin would be the failure to obey the command of God. One must not press this situation too far, but it is helpful for us to sense the distinction between responsible sexual relation and irresponsible relation. Not every act of sexual intercourse constitutes marriage--but if it does not, then it constitutes disobedience and becomes sinful. What we are arguing for here is responsibility before the command of God, not sexual permissiveness.

Theologically, then, we might say that the marriage--not the wedding ceremony--constitutes the contextualization of sexuality as both an implicit and explicit will to coexistence. "The equation of marriage with the wedding ceremony is a dreadful and deep-rooted error," says Barth. "Two people may be formally married and fail to live a life which can seriously be regarded as married life. And it may happen that two people are not married and yet in their precarious way live under the law of marriage. A wedding is only the regulative confirmation and legitimation of a marriage before and by society. It does not constitute marriage."[65]

The transition from affection to love and then to marriage and consequently to the founding of a sociological unit recognized by others constitutes the intersection of several concerns. The theological concern is for the recognition of and commitment to the form of coexistence that contextualizes the sexual life in a partnership that exists under the command of God. To this central concern there may be added the domestic aspect of marriage, which involves the severing of one domestic relation and the setting up of another. This can never take place only as a presumption of individual or even mutual interests on the part of the couple. The recognition of the new relation by parents (or by those who fulfill this responsibility) is the affirmation of the marriage by the 'closest neighbors,' says Barth.[66] In this sense, existing social relations (parents, children, friends) expand to create a new social unit without confusing their own relation to the marriage.

We should also consider two other aspects of marriage--legal and ecclesiastical. While the state cannot constitute marriage by declaration from a theological standpoint, coexistence in true humanity coincides with the structures of society by which order is upheld over disorder, As the manifestation of the existence of the new covenant through the life of Jesus Christ, the church affirms creation in its fundamental order. Marriage does not belong to the church as a religious institution any more than it does to the state. While Christians are motivated correctly in recognizing and desiring the affirmation of the Christian community upon their marriage, "the so-called marriage altar," warns Barth, "is a free invention of the flowery speech of modern religion."[67]

The domestic, legal, and ecclesiastical forms of recognizing marriage all enter into the 'making visible' of the marriage relation as the coexistence of two people as covenant partners, We have mentioned them briefly in order to take note of their significance, but they are not our central concern. Our focus, rather, is upon marriage as that which necessarily belongs to coexistence consummated through sexual union lived out under the terms of lifelong partnership.

However, as we indicated earlier, the transition of two people into this relation is somewhat ambiguous and often precarious. What emerges here is what typically is discussed as the problem of premarital sexuality. From a pastoral perspective, it makes considerable difference whether or not one views the marital relation ethically or theologically. The person who sees marriage as the ethical validation of suspicious sexual inclinations might presume that the ideal is a totally nonsexual relationship prior to the wedding night. Those who hold this view tend to equate marriage with the wedding ceremony. However, for the one who sees marriage as the result of an encounter that involves mutual commitment to a life of covenant partnership, 'premarital' will mean something other than 'pre-wedding night.'

At the practical level, for two persons who encounter each other in such a way that mutual love develops into a significant relationship of sharing and communion, physical sexuality may become a tyrannical and somewhat autonomous component of the relation. If the wedding ceremony itself is the only justification for having or expressing these sexual desires, there can only be a negative relation between sex and personal love. There cannot be a truly integrative motivation because, ethically, a 'thou shalt not' intrudes. A dichotomy can then occur between physical expression and personal love, with unmediated guilt casting a dark shadow over the relationship. As often happens, sexual desire, disengaged from a positive integration into coexistence at the personal level, assumes an almost demonic power of its own. This, of course, proves to the one who holds an ethical view of marriage that sexual desire outside of the marriage vow is basically a negative force--not realizing that, in this case, the presupposition itself has created the fact.

From a theological and pastoral perspective, however, the goal of counseling is to enable couples prior to their wedding to sustain a basically integrative relation between physical sexuality and personal love, This includes a mutual commitment to abstinence from sexual intercourse until the time that the marriage can be consummated as a covenant partnership, upheld by God and the Christian community. In this case, abstinence is supported by the very motivations of love itself, not by setting up an ethical dichotomy.

But what is appropriate pastoral response when couples have become involved in sexual relations prior to a wedding, or have even lived together as a domestic unit prior to a formal ceremony? In this case, the integration of sexual feelings into personal expressions of love precipitates consummation of the marriage prior to its public declaration in the form of a wedding ceremony. A wise counselor will increase the contextualization of the sexual relation through enhancing the covenant partnership of the couple rather than depriving the relation of this support through ethical disapproval. How can the covenant partnership be 'enhanced' in such a situation? One way is for the intentionality of the couple to become more than a mutually expressed desire to live together or to have sexual relations; in other words, the marriage has now begun in a progressive way toward its consummation in a legal and public wedding ceremony. Of course there will be tensions, and each individual situation will require unique and sensitive counsel and support. We are not suggesting here the toleration of a permissive or indiscriminate approach toward sexual relation. But neither are we suggesting that sexual intercourse itself is intrinsically immoral or evil. And it is vitally important to the health of that relation that once sexual relation has been integrated with personal love and shared life that every resource available be used to bring the relation to the optimum level of covenant partnership expressed in the conventional form of marriage. The relation is brought under the command of God at the time that it is consummated sexually, personally, and socially. This is what it means to say that 'God joins them together.'

Chapter 7

The Ecology of Family Relationships

My parents, with their roots firmly established in the Scandinavian ethos and culture of the Old World, were traditional in their concepts of marriage and family and provincial in their practice. What they considered to be normal with regard to marriage roles we today would call hierarchical, male-dominated, and task-oriented. No sociologist bothered to do research on marital satisfaction in our town.[68]

Where it once was considered standard practice to conscript children into the community labor force from adolescence onward to work alongside of adult men and women, we now view that as abusive child labor and invoke laws against it. It now seems to be the parent's responsibility to keep children happy with disposable toys and ego-building cheers at every little league and soccer game within a day's drive. I often wonder what these same children will do when they become adults and realize that no one will be standing on the sidelines cheering for them!

In that small rural community in middle-America where I grew up, a married woman who worked outside the home was viewed with suspicion, if not disdain. Divorce was unthinkable, not because marriages were successful, but because divorce was unacceptable. With every young boy and girl socialized into prescribed role expectations and families firmly woven into the patchwork quilt of intergenerational community life, self-identity, stability and continuity of life were taken for granted.

No more. It is not only that the social structures of these communities have been unhinged from their foundation, the moral values once invested in these social structures have now been withdrawn and invested in quick-return 'junk bonds' promising individual freedom, self gratification, and a guaranteed minimal allotment of high tech appliances. We can't go back to the 'good old days,' nor should we. Nostalgia is not a nostrum to

alleviate anxiety nor a remedy to soothe the psyche of a lost generation.
Home Alone II was not as entertaining as was the first film. Cleverness is
cute, but its shelf life is short. Stand By Me strikes a different chord, even
as the tragic often speaks to us out of the depths of the soul. Robert Bellah
describes the contemporary situation as one of deep ambivalence.

> [Secular] therapists see a need for the social ties that they cannot really
> comprehend--they cry out for the very community that their moral
> logic undercuts. Parents advocate "values" for their children even
> when they do not know what those "values" are. What this suggests is
> that there is a profound ambivalence about individualism in America
> among its most articulate defenders. . . . Modern individualism seems
> to be producing a way of life that is neither individually nor socially
> viable, yet a return to traditional forms would be to return to intoler-
> able discrimination and oppression. The question, then, is whether
> the older civic and biblical traditions have the capacity to reformulate
> themselves while simultaneously remaining faithful to their own
> deepest insights.[69]

That last sentence brings into focus exactly what I want to pursue in
this chapter: "The question, then, is whether the older civic and biblical
traditions have the capacity to reformulate themselves while simultaneously remaining faithful to their own deepest insights."

As Bellah reminds us, there were often deep insights contained in
some of those antiquated social customs and structures. Reformulation
of social structures, roles and responsibilities in light of biblical teaching
is not an option, it is a mandate. Insights connect us with abiding truth
through times of transition. And it is the discovery and preservation of
these insights that will enable us to maintain continuity with biblical truth
while tacking through the cross currents of modernity.

What is normative in biblical teaching is not a certain structure or form
of family, but acting and living in ways that create, nurture and support
persons within their social structures, including marriage and family.
This is why the verb 'familying' gives meaning to the noun 'family.' For
the Apostle Paul, being family is a process of spiritual formation, even as
living in the power of the Spirit redeems and restores family.

The thesis of this chapter is that: Spiritual formation as family ministry
is the fundamental theological insight that integrates the psychological
and social aspect of human personhood with the life-long task of growing
toward maturity in Jesus Christ. I will develop this thesis in two ways:
by examining first, the social structure of human spirituality, and second,
the ecological structure of social spirituality. This examination develops
further the two primary themes, that family is something you do, and

that the social structure of 'being family' provides the ecological context
for the spiritual formation of its family members.

The Social Structure of Human Spirituality

In a work that is extraordinary in light of his youth and precocious
insight, Dietrich Bonhoeffer, at the age of 21, wrote his doctoral dissertation at the University of Berlin This dissertation accomplishes what no
other work since has achieved in the integration of spirituality, sociality,
and human personhood. While his dissertation was ostensibly an attempt
to define the nature of the church, he began with a creative and profound
examination of the social nature of human personhood as the basis for
stating his thesis that Jesus Christ exists in the spiritual structure of human sociality as community (*gemeinde*) rather than in the institutional
form of the church.

Spirit, he wrote, is necessarily created in community, and the general
spirituality of persons is woven into the net of sociality.

> It will appear that all Christian and moral content, as well as the entire
> spirituality of [persons], is possible and real only in sociality. Not only
> do the concepts of sin and of the church become more profound, but
> a way opens up to a Christian evaluation of community life. . . . Here
> we have to show that [a person's] entire so-called spirituality, which is
> presupposed by the Christian concept of person and has its unifying
> point in self-consciousness. . . is so constituted that it can only be seen
> as possible in sociality.[70]

Because the reality of spirit is first of all a social reality rooted in the
nature of human personhood, Bonhoeffer can argue that the social structure of human personhood is intrinsically spiritual. The Spirit of God does
not constitute something alongside of, or merely inside of a person as an
individual. Rather, the Spirit of God joins the human spirit at the core of
its social reality. Human spirituality is the core of the self as it becomes
a self through social relation with others. Jürgen Moltmann argues in a
similar way when he says, "The Holy Spirit does not supersede the Spirit
of creation but transforms it. The Holy Spirit therefore lays hold of the
whole human being, embracing his feelings and his body as well as his
soul and reason. He forms the whole Gestalt of the person anew by making believers 'con-form' to Christ, the first born among many brethren
(Ro. 8:29)."[71]

Personal being is both structurally open and structurally closed,
Bonhoeffer suggested. Self-consciousness arises out of consciousness of
the other in the concrete social situation. What he called the 'structural
openness' of persons is what we might call transparency, but Bonhoeffer

also includes in his definition an interchange of affect, shared identity, and common experience. He is referring to more than a psychological state; he is describing an actual social structure of being through which the self is differentiated and determined as unique and individual.

Being open to the spirit of other persons awakens and intensifies one's own spirit. Personal being is structurally open and closed. There is no self-consciousness without consciousness of the other, that is, of community.

> God created man and woman directed to one another. God does not desire a history of individual human beings, but the history of the human community. However, God does not want a community that absorbs the individual into itself, but a community of human beings. In God's eyes, community and individual exists in the same moment and rest in one another. The collective unit and the individual unit have the same structure in God's eyes.[72]

What Bonhoeffer calls structural closedness is not a withdrawal of the self from the other, but the uniqueness of the self that results from an actual interchange in core social relations. The meeting of two persons constitutes a 'third' reality which he calls 'objective person,' or 'objective spirit.' The basic social category is the I-Thou relation. The Thou of the other person becomes the concrete form of the divine Thou.[73]

> Two wills encountering one another form a 'structure.' A third man joining them does not see just the two men joined together, but rather a third thing, the structure itself, opposes his will with a resistance which is not identical with the will of the two individuals, but can be greater than the resistance of the two individuals, or--if such an idea were possible--of the sum of all individuals. It is this 'structure' which is objective spirit.[74]

In a passage remarkable for its insight into the paradox of personal relations and personal intimacy he wrote: "Whereas in experience these acts isolate the I from the You completely, the intimate act is not primarily what constitutes the person as structurally closed. Rather, social intention is inconceivable without corresponding openness. On the other hand, social intention is directed toward the openness of the person, the intimate act toward the person's closedness." Grounding spirituality in the basic social structure of human being, he added, "Individual personal spirit lives solely by virtue of sociality, and 'social spirit' becomes real only in individual formation; thus genuine sociality itself presses toward personal unity. One cannot speak of the priority of either personal or social being."[75]

In our culture we tend to view intimacy as the degree of contact we have with others, primarily achieved through physical proximity and/or verbal communication. Bonhoeffer, however, observed that intimacy is a quality of personal being which is derived out of relation with others. In other words, intimacy is not a means to a relationship but the result, or gift of the relationship. As a result, seeking intimacy with another through a physical or even social relationship of touching and proximity is self-defeating. In being genuinely open and in relation with anther we experience personal intimacy as a gift from the other, not in using the other to fulfill the need for intimacy.

Because spirit is first of all a social reality rooted in the nature of human personhood, Bonhoeffer can argue that the social structure of human personhood is intrinsically spiritual. The Spirit of God does not constitute something alongside of or merely inside of a person as an individual. Rather, the Spirit of God joins the human spirit at the core of its social reality. Human spirituality is the core of the self as it becomes a self through social relations with others. The bi-directional nature of human spirituality is represented by the two great commandments first stated in the Old Testament and then reiterated by Jesus: "'You shall love the Lord your God with all your heart, and with all your soul, and with all your mind.' This is the greatest and first commandment. And a second is like it: 'You shall love your neighbor as yourself'" (Matthew 22:38-39; Deut 6:5; Lev. 19:18).

As originally created by God, social spirituality reflects the divine image and likeness constitutive of human personhood. The second creation account (Genesis 2) recasts the creation of the human as though only a solitary individual is present. Despite an obvious relation between Adam and God, the divine verdict is that it is not good for the man to be alone. With the creation of the woman humans are differentiated and yet bound together as social beings. The implication is that the divine image spoken of in Genesis 1 can only be complete as a social construct of personal relation.

Even as the individual self exists as structurally open to the spirit of another person, it is structurally open to the Spirit of God. When we speak of spirituality as a relation with God we are speaking of the social spirituality that is constitutive of the human person, not a religious instinct, feeling or practice. Social spirituality is what makes religion possible. Social spirituality is not only the source of authentic relation with God, it is the first casualty of sin and in need of redemption.

The 'works of the flesh,' as contrasted with the 'fruit of the Spirit,' are symptomatic of negative and pathological social spirituality--enmities, strife, jealousy, anger, quarrels, dissensions, factions (Galatians 5:20). These are some of the diagnostic categories by which the Bible identifies sin. They are not first of all violations of an abstract moral law; they are the breakdown of the social spirituality which is necessary for healthy family life, as well as for other healthy social relations. The therapeutic effects of spiritual formation through the indwelling of the Holy Spirit are likewise described in terms of healthy social spirituality--love, joy, peace, patience, kindness, generosity, faithfulness, gentleness, self-control (Galatians 5:22-23).

Bonhoeffer's concept of the social nature of human spirituality leads him to define sin as, "the will to affirm in principle oneself and not the other as a value, and to acknowledge the other only in relation to oneself."[76] While sin has its origin in the individual will to claim moral and spiritual autonomy by elevating self-interests over those of others, the effect of sin, Bonhoeffer wrote, is social and not merely individual. Consequently, while individuals must take the initiative in repentance, only the social structure itself can repent. "The community," he wrote, "has fallen into guilt; it must seek repentance, it must believe in and experience grace at the limits of time. It is clear that this can happen only 'in the individual.' Only thus can the hearing of the call be concretely comprehended, and yet it is not the individuals, but the collective person (*Gesamtheit*) who, in the individuals, hears, repents and believes. The centre of action lies in the collective person."[77]

The Ecological Structure of Social Relationships

The concept of ecological relationships was first developed in Biology (1869), and then brought into the sphere of social science by Kurt Lewin and Roger Barker (*Psychological Ecology*, 1944). The concept of ecological psychology was then developed with emphasis on how the environment restricts and affects the range of human personality and behavior. The introduction of ecology into psychology and theories of human development is well known through the work of Allen Wicker and Urie Bronfenbrenner.[78] Ecology describes the relation of an organism to its environment; in psychology, the ecological matrix includes the self in its social and physical field of experience and interaction. Those who work with ecological systems as a function of social structures identity four types (Figure 7.1):

- micro: immediate; for example, the nuclear family;
- meso: relation between two or more micro systems; for example, the school;

- exo: outside system which impacts meso and micro systems; for example, the school board;
- macro: incorporates all lower systems.

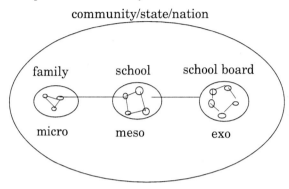

Figure 7.1

For example, a child who is acting out behavior problems in school (meso system) may be projecting difficulties experienced at home (micro system) due to marital discord or lack of one parent. In dealing with the child from the perspective of ecological family systems, the teacher needs to take into account any possible family dynamics from which the problem originates. Or, a husband who exhibits anger and even abuse in his family (micro system) may be experiencing difficulties in his work-place (exo system) that cause problems that only surface in his actions at home. Every person, to some extent, participates in more than one ecological system so that there is often a 'spill-over' from one system to another.

The ecological dynamics involve 1) reciprocity: there is a reciprocal impact of the developing person on the environment (every child is born into a different family!); and of the environment on the developing person; and 2) perception and reality: self-identity is a hermeneutical process where the ecological systems require continual interpretation and assimilation. Implications for family relationships include:

- we are not merely individuals, but members;
- there is private ownership of space, things, etc, but public use;
- any one's burden is every one's responsibility;
- every person has responsibility to move toward maturity; self-autonomy;
- self-reliance with accountability rather than independence.

The implications for a family systems model are significant. The social structure of human spirituality has been shown to be grounded in an ecological matrix. Persons are not only intrinsically social beings, but

human spirituality is located at the core of social being. Spiritual formation is thus an essential component in the development of self-identity
and competence in human social relationships. An approach to marriage
and family ministry that fails to take into account spiritual formation as
the core of each person's growth toward personal maturity is reductive,
partializing, and lacking in both spiritual growth and development of
social skills.

The biblical story of creation can be read as a pre-theoretical ecological
matrix in which humans are: 1) related to the physical world--created from
the dust of the ground; 2) related to each other--bone of my bone, flesh
of my flesh; and 3) related to a transcendent spiritual reality--created in
the image and likeness of God (Genesis 1-2). These three spheres of human existence interact with each other in such a way that the entire self
is represented in any one of the spheres. At the same time, dysfunction
in one sphere impacts the viability and quality of life in the other two.
W. W. Meissner suggests that "Development of spiritual identity, then, is
achieved through the same ego-functions that are involved in the natural
psychological identity."[79]

A schematic diagram (Figure 7.2) shows that the ego-self, with all of
its mental, emotional, and personal attributes, is equally invested in each
of the three spheres. The historical self (behavior), is what we experience
and what others obseve of our behavior in real time. Symptoms of dysfunction may occur as the historical self experiences some form of failure,
causing the person to seek assistance, or requiring others to intervene. In
this ecological matrix of social spirituality, each of the three spheres must
be considered as possible sources of the problem.

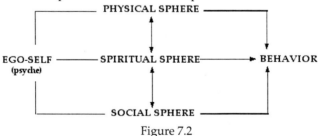

Figure 7.2

Spiritual formation must necessarily include the development of
human personhood as social being. The core social paradigm of human
existence includes spiritual formation as much as it does physical and
personal existence. One cannot isolate the spiritual dimension from either
the physical or social. This is the ecological basis for spiritual formation
as marriage and family ministry.

Spiritual Formation and Family Ministry: Implications and Suggestions

Let me propose some practical implications for marriage and family ministry as an outcome of the model I have presented.

We must move from models of curing to models of caring

Thomas Moore suggested that our preoccupation with curing patients as though they were diseased might better give way to a therapy of caring.[80] A therapeutic approach that is primarily interested in objectifying symptoms by reference to a diagnostic manual will have little notion of care and less competence to offer it. On the other hand, providing a context for spiritual formation in the practice of family ministry is not a matter of religious indoctrination or what is often called 'spiritual exercises.' Spirituality is a process of rebuilding self-identity through a renewal and redemption of the primary social systems in which the person exists. The primary social network need not be and often will not be made up of those in closest proximity. The story of Samuel illustrates this point simply but profoundly (1 Samuel 1-1).

Hannah is one of the two wives of Elkanah, her husband. She is barren and bereft of comfort, an object of ridicule by her counterpart, and unmoved by the solicitous but simplistic advice of her husband to 'cheer up'; his love ought to be worth more than ten sons! Little did he know how much her soul suffers under the introjected theology of her day--if she is barren, the Lord has closed her womb, she might as well be cursed.

As it turns out, Hannah's fervent prayer, accompanied by the promise to give her child back to the Lord if he will only open her womb, is answered. She names him Samuel, which means 'asked of the Lord.' When the child is weaned she brings him to Eli the Priest and says: "For this child I prayed; and the Lord has granted me the petition that I made to him. Therefore I have lent him to the Lord; as long as he lives, he is given to the Lord" (1 Samuel 1:27-28). And so she leaves him under the care of Eli.

Eli's two sons were notorious moral and spiritual scoundrels, hardly a model family in which to place a foster child (1 Samuel 2:12f)! What then accounts for the fact that Samuel early on has a soul that is open to the Word of the Lord? Hannah enters the picture again. Each year she makes for him a little robe and takes it to him when she goes up with her husband to offer the yearly sacrifice (1 Samuel 2:18-19).

We know this incident from Samuel himself. Each year, his mother must have recounted her story of barrenness and spiritual pain. Each year she must have told him of her prayer to God and of her vow. Each year Samuel must have heard that he was not only God's gift to her, but her gift to God. He discovered his identity as he was taken into the narrative of his mother's barrenness, her prayer, the promise of Eli, the subsequent birth and his placement in priestly service.

The story does not conceal the weaknesses and failures of the principle figures in Samuel's life. They are 'good enough' to use Donald Winnecott's phrase--not perfect, but they are adequate as a social network in which the boy's spiritual formation can take place.[81] Hannah's story is tragic as well as inspirational. It is surely not intended to suggest that mothers should give up their children to be placed in dysfunctional foster homes! However, even in this extraordinary act, we can discern the power of a primary bond between a mother and a child. Tenuous as it was, the social bond between Hannah and her son was reinforced regularly and ritually through the robe and story. Samuel's development into a person of spiritual perception and unimpeachable character as a prophet of God may well be accounted for by the family narrative offered by Hannah rather than religious instruction by Eli the priest. In developing models of family ministry we could well be guided by Hannah, who had no cure for the dysfunctional family of Eli, but nonetheless, offered a model of care which was intentional, spiritual, and, we might say, epigenetic and ecological!

We should go beyond the technique of fixing to strategies of freeing

The metaphor of brokenness has become the *leitmotif* in the contemporary culture of pop-psychology. In his play "The Great God Brown" Eugene O'Neil has one of his characters say: "We are born broken. We live by mending. The grace of God is the glue."[82] True as that may be, when we begin with the assumption that something is broken, then our first approach is to fix it. The economics of fixing what is broken has done more to determine the future of mental health services in one decade than a half century of theories about psychotherapy. 'Managed care' is itself an oxymoron.

There is a sense in which we should be grateful for a renewed focus on more cost-effective therapy where therapeutic outcomes are related more realistically to the practical needs and financial resources of those who are seeking help. We can also applaud the wider distribution of mental health services to those who can least afford it but who perhaps are in the greatest need. At the same time, some are asking, has mental health care lost its soul in becoming merely mental health service? In other words, is the problem causing the breakdown of life for many people today simply a dysfunction that can be fixed, or is it a disempowered spirit?

What is most remarkable about the ministry of Jesus was not only that he fixes what was broken, gives sight to the blind and working limbs to the paralyzed, but that he liberates the spirit of people from bondage. Not only does Jesus provide liberation from demonic oppression, but from psychic shame, cultic disqualification, and social alienation.

Jesus could fix what was broken. But he also taught that one is not free by simply having a problem removed. It is one thing to have a demon cast out and the symptoms disappear. It is quite another to regain spiritual health and wholeness. This point was made quite clearly by Jesus: "When the unclean spirit has gone out of a person, it wanders through waterless regions looking for a resting place, but not finding any, it says, 'I will return to my house from which I came.' When it comes, it finds it swept and put in order. Then it goes and brings seven other spirits more evil than itself, and they enter and live there; and the last state of that person is worse than the first" (Luke 11:24-26). Spiritual formation in family ministry restores and rebuilds the life of persons from the inside out.

We ought to move from moral imperatives to spiritual empowering

The temptation to impose moral imperatives in the hope of engendering spiritual conformity to biblical principles is hard to resist on the part of Christian therapists. Some speak of moral values and imperatives as a way of avoiding the appearance of offering only secular psychology. Others, who are often anxious about their own spiritual life, may feel morally compromised by clients who exhibit immoral behavior or attitudes. As a result, they impose moral imperatives on others as a way of reducing their own moral anxiety. The effect is the same. To offer moral imperatives to one in need of empowering grace is to give a stone when one is asking for bread.

Spiritual formation is a process of spiritual empowering more than it is a program of moral development. The contemporaries of Jesus were scandalized by his apparent tolerance of the lack of conformity to the moral law on the part of those to whom he brought the good news of the Kingdom of God. For example, they demanded that he apply the strict law of Moses and condemn to death the woman caught in the act of adultery. When none could claim that they were without sin and therefore not qualified to cast the first stone, Jesus said to her: "Neither do I condemn you. Go your way, and from now on do not sin again" (John 8:11).

Not only did Jesus liberate her from the punishment of the law, but he was in effect, saying: "You are really free, and do not have to live that way again!" Perhaps he sensed that her self-condemnation exceeded that placed upon her by any other. In freeing her from the condemnation of the law, he also affirmed in her an inner freedom from the needs and drives that brought about her immoral behavior.

In another incident, a woman of the city, "who was a sinner," Luke tells us, knelt before Jesus and anointed his feet with oil, bathing them with her tears, drying them with her hair. The Pharisee who had invited Jesus into his home, protested, "If this man were a prophet, he would have known who and what kind of woman this is who is touching him--that she is a sinner" (Luke 7:39). After lecturing his host about hospitality and love, Jesus said to the woman: "Your sins are forgiven. . . Your faith has saved you. Go in peace" (Luke 7:48, 50).

Spiritual formation as family ministry cannot afford to use moral judgments as a qualifying standard attached to healing presence. God's moral freedom is the basis for God's moral law. Unconditional grace mediated through the spiritual power of forgiveness is itself a moral quality of love. Moral imperatives without spiritual empowerment only cripple and condemn. To moralize under the guise of Christian ministry is itself a form of spiritual abuse and a violation of the law of love. The rules for loving are explicit, unambiguous and placed at the forefront of biblical teaching. The apostle Paul spells it out clearly:

> Owe no one anything, except to love one another; for the one who loves another has fulfilled the law. The commandments, "You shall not commit adultery; You shall not murder; You shall not steal; You shall not covet"; and any other commandment, are summed up in this word, "Love your neighbor as yourself." Love does no wrong to a neighbor; therefore, love is the fulfilling of the law (Romans 13:8-10).

In his inaugural lecture upon assuming the presidency of Fuller Theological Seminary titled, The Glory of a Theological Seminary (1955), Edward John Carnell offered the radical thesis that love is the epistemological core for the truth of orthodoxy. In daring to challenge the loveless rationalism of evangelical orthodoxy, and by suggesting that love is the imperative essence of biblical faith, Carnell earned the outrage of many on his faculty and cast a cloud of suspicion over his leadership among the still fundamentalistic constituency of the school. Rejection of his emphasis on the need for love in orthodoxy led him to resign as president in 1959 followed by a serious mental breakdown and his pre-mature death in 1967.

If it now seems incredible to some of us that the biblical emphasis on love should be so threatening to those who pin faith to propositions and link truth with logic, we only have to remember that Jesus was crucified on exegetical grounds. "This man is not from God because he does not observe the sabbath," cried out those who sought to destroy him" (John 9:16). Tearing the biblical text out of the womb of covenantal love and mercy, they used it to nail truth to the cross. In the name of biblical authority, some define morality in terms of traditional forms of marriage and family; they have forgotten God's moral judgment against the formal principle of the law when used to sanction loveless and lifeless formality. In the name of biblical authority, many pastors send women back to suffer at the hands of abusive husbands, citing the biblical text that women should submit to their husbands. They have ignored God's advocacy for those who are victims and his severe judgment against those who oppress and abuse.

In the name of biblical authority, modern-day 'Job's counselors' tell those who suffer from emotional distress and mental pain that confession of sin and spiritual obedience will cure them instantly and save them from secular psychology's sinister seduction. They have severed the spirit from the soul, leaving the soul to dangle on the bungee cord of psychology as unessential to spiritual health, while binding the spirit to the law with inelastic and unyielding steel strands of moral obligation.

Love integrates soul and spirit, psychology and spirituality. Love is the core of rationality and the goal of spirituality. Love is the systemic and ecological social structure that promotes personal and individual growth toward spiritual maturity in Jesus Christ. Paul has written for us the theoretical basis for spiritual formation as family ministry:

> But speaking the truth in love, we must grow up in every way into him who is the head, into Christ, from whom the whole body, joined and knit together by every ligament with which it is equipped, as each part is working properly, promotes the body's growth in building itself up in love (Ephesians 4:15-16).

If alienation, addiction, violence, abuse, obsession, and meaninglessness point to loss of soul, then family ministry can find in spiritual formation a theoretical and practical model of integration. Spiritual formation as family ministry moves beyond treating symptoms to the rebuilding of primary relationships in the psycho-social network where persons find a sense of belonging, a new sense of self-identity, affective wholeness, and self-worth.

Chapter 8

Families Are Not What They Used to Be!

A candidate who is running for President of the United States was recently interviewed on television regarding the comment made by his 21 year-old son who said that he was somewhat estranged from his father because he did not have a good relation with his step-mother, his father's third wife. In the interview, the candidate acknowledged this and replied, "Well, you know, we have a blended family and there are often many problems, but it is a personal matter and we are working on it."

Having a blended family member means that this man is in good company. Blending families by including children from a previous marriage is a process of awkwardness and artfulness, confusion and commitment. A 'blended' family is composed of a married or common-law couple with at least one stepchild (that is, a child who is the biological offspring of only one of the spouses in the family).

Statistics on the Changing Family Structure

There are few role models for blended families, and often little societal support as stepfamilies navigate through their day-to-day routines that may be as bewildering as walking a maze in the dark. The statistics on blended families are eye-opening. For example, 1,300 stepfamilies are formed daily. Each year 500,000 adults become new stepparents. Some 6.4 million children, representing a tenth of the nation's children, live with one stepparent and one birth parent (Census Bureau figures). Blended families now outnumber traditional nuclear families. And the number is likely to grow, based on current divorce statistics and trends. While these statistics may help blended families to feel less alone, they do little to address the complications of stepfamily living. The primary cause leading to blended families is divorce and remarriage.

Divorce has become common in America. In fact, an estimated 50 percent of first marriages end in divorce after an average of 11 years. Researchers consistently rank divorce as one of the most stressful life experiences. Each year 1 million American children experience divorce firsthand. However, a substantial number of these children will not be in single parent homes for long. When divorcing under the age of 45, 80 percent of divorced men and 75 percent of divorced women remarry within three to four years. And divorced adults with children tend to remarry quicker than divorced adults without children. Statistically, half of all children born since 1970 will live in a blended family arrangement.

Blended families face unique social, psychological and economic challenges. Sixty percent of second marriages fail. According to the U. S. Census Bureau 66 percent of marriages and those cohabiting end in break-up when children are actively involved, according to Stepfamily Foundation statistics. It is predicted that 50 percent of children in the United States will go through a divorce before they are 18. Approximately half of all Americans are currently involved in some form of step relationship. Very soon, according to the Census Bureau, more Americans will be living in stepfamilies than in nuclear families.

The American Family Association reports that the number of families that fit the traditional mold will probably be in the minority in the 21st century. The percentage of children who live with both biological parents, who remain married, dropped from 73 percent in 1972 to 51.7 percent by 1998. In 1960, 45 percent of households consisted of married couples with children. In 1998, that percentage had fallen to 26 percent. As a result, Families are smaller and less stable. Marriage is less central and cohabitation is more common. Within marriage gender roles have become less traditional and more open.[83]

Blended families face unique problems. Both parent and stepparent often do not treat children in the blended family equally. Many stepparents find it difficult to love their stepchild or stepchildren. The children may not accept the new 'parental authority' in the home. Discipline from a stepparent can often result in frustration, opposition, and disrespect. The new home has two sets of rules, and two types of discipline. Children have two homes, with two sets of rules and different methods of discipline. Extended families do not always accept the new spouse or the stepchildren.[84]

Households now defined by the U. S. Census Bureau as 'non-families' will eventually receive legal recognition as 'families' in virtually every state. Such arrangements will include unmarried heterosexual couples, homosexual couples, and friends who 'intentionally' live together. The current standard definition of what constitutes a family is a group of two or more persons related by birth, marriage, or adoption residing together. There will be increasing pressure to redefine 'family' as "a group of people who love and care for each other."[85]

> Most Western and many non-Western societies are becoming what some call 'high-divorce societies.' Co-habitation and out-of-wedlock births have increased dramatically. The 'feminization' of poverty has negative effects in wealthy countries, but it has had devastating consequences for poor ones. Since the 1960s the divorce rate has more than doubled. During this same period, non-marital births. Increased from 5 percent to 33 percent. In the United States there has been a 30 percent decline in the marriage rate since 1960. The number of couples cohabiting has increased eightfold since 1970. Some have predicted that 'marriage is doomed' and will be replaced by a constellation of relationships where couples have a series of long-term relationships with children from each. These facts lead some to conclude that the cure needed for such family disruption is a massive cultural conversion--the birth of new 'familism.'[86]

Don Browning argues that the Judeo-Christian tradition provides excellent resources for a new critical familism

Implications for the Church's Ministry to Families

The members of most churches today represent to some degree the demographics of their contemporary society. This means that when the church thinks of itself as a 'family centered' church, its perception may be far from reality. The traditional nuclear family represented by a father and mother for whom this is their first marriage, and one or more children who are biologically descended from both parents and only one parent is employed outside the home, constitute less than 20% of modern families. With an increasing number of single parent and blended families comprising the church membership, not only does this affect the program design of family ministry but challenges the leadership of the church to re-think its approach to its members with respect to its teaching and practice of welcoming and assimilating persons into membership.

Is it the family that is undergoing attack in our culture or only one form of the family? Is it only the encapsulated perceptions of a Western traditional mind-set that insists that the family be defined as nuclear? Perhaps it is that narrow definition of family that is under attack. In an attempt to react against the erosion of traditional family structure for the sake of traditional values, some have sought to link what we have come to think of as a traditional family with biblical and moral values. The very concept of a 'broken family' when applied to a divorce that leaves one parent with the children already suggests some loss of moral value. How much more of a loss is implied for some when confronted with couples who cohabit in committed living arrangements without a civil marriage. The demand on the part of gay couples for a 'right to marry' is both ironic and confusing. It is ironic on the one hand because the traditional concept of marriage itself is viewed as a 'human right' and confusing on the other hand because marriage of a same sex couple is contrary to a traditional definition of marriage as involving a man and a woman. Not only is the concept of what constitutes a family now in question, but also what constitutes a marriage.

When modernity alters the traditional roles of society, particularly those of the family, it usually causes a reaction in the name of conservatism. Those who speak out against change in the role of the family, as well as against changing roles within the family structure, claim an authority based on the conventional order of tradition and time-tested values. These 'values' are the abstract qualities of the good life, usually moral, which inhere in conventional life-styles. Thus, to alter the conventional roles is to challenge the intrinsic values of a society. In the final judgment, those who do so are considered to be immoral.

A moral authority then attaches itself to those who seek to uphold the conventional order of the family. It was, after all, the charge that his teaching corrupted the youth of Athens that brought Socrates to judgment by his peers, and led to his death. Because he questioned the traditional beliefs of his elders and encouraged young minds to question traditional authority as well, Socrates was charged with atheism and condemned to death. It is but a short step from the charge that those who attempt to change the traditional, conventional order are violating a moral law to the charge that they are violating the law of God. Those who become the guardians of the moral order will also become the prophets of God. Thus, conservatism has always had a religious aspect to its passion.

When the family is held to be the cornerstone of a society, it becomes a quasi moral order of the society. That which is considered unconventional family life when measured by the traditional role of the family will then be subject to judgment. Traditionalists will attack the 'new immorality' and issue a call for a return to the conventional to restore the 'righteousness' of the nation. For example, the breakdown of moral authority in a society is often traced to a loss of parental authority in the home--specifically, the undermining of the male authority of the husband and father by the woman. Although she merely wishes to exercise her right to equality and full partnership in the marriage, she may be seen as abandoning her 'place' as wife and mother if she pursues activities and interests outside of the home. A woman who feels led to seek personal fulfillment beyond her role as wife and mother will find it difficult to account for the moral passion directed against her unless she understands the connection in the popular mind between conventional order and conventional morality.

All of this takes a more serious turn when Christians link conventional moral authority with scriptural authority. When the Bible itself is read as teaching an absolute order of role relationships within the family unit--"'Wives, be subject to your husbands"--failure to comply is tantamount to disobedience to God. For the evangelical Christian, who takes the Bible seriously as the inspired Word of God, the issue becomes critical. Biblical authority becomes a higher order of authority than conventional authority when authority becomes an issue of biblical teaching.

What the Bible Teaches About Family Roles

Given the assumption that the Bible speaks with the authority of God, the question then becomes, What does the Bible teach concerning the family and roles within the family? Whatever assumptions one brings to the Bible will determine one's interpretations of the text. For example, one who holds that there is a fundamental natural order that is determinative of human existence in families will not permit the Bible to teach that which is contrary to the natural order. And when I say 'not permit the Bible to teach.' I mean only to suggest that we all read the Bible in an attempt to understand what it teaches, unless we adopt a sheer literalist approach to the language of Scripture, which is warned against within Scripture itself (see John 6:63). On the other hand, one who holds that order is indeterminate with regard to culture and nature will understand the teaching of the Bible to be relative and not absolute whenever it speaks in a cultural context. As a result, the interpreter is permitted to apply the teaching in a way that is consistent with the individual's own perceived good.

However, there may be a third way of perceiving the structure of order when it comes to the family, and that is a created, contingent order. Here we can find some positive implications for understanding how the authority of Scripture upholds the original and true order of the family while, at the same time, it does not fail to speak relevantly to each age. Just as the absolute, quintessential order is ascribed to God alone, even though it is embodied in a culturally relative social order, so the authority of God is embodied in Scripture, but not such that Scripture literally becomes God. That would be idolatry.

We can view love as the material content of the inner structure of relations that constitute family. This is a love that first of all resides absolutely in God, and then by his endowment, in humans who exist in his image and likeness. Relation, then, is the 'logic of laws' that regulate family life and roles. The authority of the rules or laws that regulate life is a contingent authority. It is never found absolutely in the natural order, nor absolutely in the individual and personal order. It is a valid authority in its own right because it is divinely determined to uphold and support the true order of relation.

However, there is a hermeneutical principle, a principle of interpretation, that we must recognize at all times when we seek to understand the authority of natural order as contingent upon the divine order. We must always seek the 'spirit within the words,' to use the language of Jesus (John 6:63), or to seek the 'logic within the rules,' to use another metaphor. Significantly, in the same general context where Jesus earlier spoke of the distinction between spirit and word, he says, "Why do you not understand what I say [*lalia*]? It is because you cannot bear to hear my word [*logos*]" (John 8:43). The logos is the incarnate Logos, which is God and which has also become flesh (John 1:1, 14). Thus, the contingent and created order does have a point of interpretation common to both God as absolute and the created order as contingent upon the Creator. The authority of Scripture, therefore, is a contingent authority. Or rather, we should say, the authority of Scripture is based directly on the authority of God himself as he has given himself to be known and apprehended in the created order, which includes the language and written testimony of witnesses under the inspiration of the Holy Spirit.

For example, when we deal with marriage, as my former colleague, Geoffrey Bromiley once wrote, "A law of marriage differs decisively from a theology of marriage. We should not conclude that all that is meant by a theology of marriage exists in biblical expositions of the topic. . . God reveals himself in and through the Bible. He speaks in and through it. Yet the Bible does not replace God. He has not just given us the Bible and left us to it. He himself is still the one with whom we have to deal."[87] Bromiley did not intend to weaken biblical authority, but to tie biblical truth and authority to God as the original and living source.

In the context of the church, which is the community of Christian believers filled with the Spirit of Christ, the authority of Scripture anchors the life of the believer in the historical person and work of Jesus Christ. But because the church, as the new community of God and thus the new family of God, is formed through the presence and power of the resurrected Christ by his Spirit, the scriptures are anchored in the contemporary presence and work of Christ through this community.

The Original Order of the Family

In this way we see that the original order of the family is grounded in the new family of God, and that the moral authority that upholds the order of the family as a social institution is grounded in the spiritual authority of love as expressed through Jesus Christ and as experienced in Christian community. The church, then, as the new family of God, demonstrates the authority of Scripture by renewing marriage and family where it has fallen into disorder, and by recreating marriage and family where it has been destroyed.

In the view of the Apostle Paul, the foundational social structures of family, marriage, parents and children, are basically affirmed as good and necessary, despite their imperfection (Ephesians 4). At the same time, through the gospel of Christ, all of these structures are radically qualified and brought under the grace of redemption through being connected to Jesus Christ. The role of the church is to make this connection.

The center of true humanity is thus bound up with this shifting of the criterion from seeking one's own good to that of the other person. This shows that the single commandment of love--to love God and to love the neighbor as oneself--is grounded in social humanity, not merely in individual humanity. But we cannot know this love fully apart from the gracious love of God addressed to us in Jesus Christ. Thus when we encounter the true humanity of Jesus Christ, a revelation of that humanity is also communicated through the gospel of Christ. For any attempt to define humanity on our own terms incorporates the fallacy of self-preservation into our social and ethical structures. As a result, change produced by social revolution alone cannot lead to the discovery and form of authentic human existence. The constant factor through social and cultural changes in human self-perception is the structure of humanity as a social reality of love. This love is experienced as a reciprocity of relations in which Jesus Christ is present as the objective reality of grace, freedom and responsibility. The law of God in Jesus Christ, while liberating us from the letter of the moral law, binds us to the moral responsibility of living by the law of love.

Ethical norms remain constant when grounded in the true humanity of the other person rather than in culturally conditioned self-perceptions of individuals, or the collective cultural mass. This is the answer to the question of relativism. The moral good of the other person constitutes an ethical criterion from which no one is exempt by virtue of doctrinal, ideological, ecclesiological or political commitments. When understood in this way, the meaning of that which is good is not first of all an abstract principle mediated through one's own perception of the good (modernity), but it is first of all a 'moral event' that takes place between persons created in the image of God.

Here we see how the centered family does not fall away from the absolute moral principles of modernity into the relativism of postmodernity. Rather, the foundation for human morality is grounded in the social being of humanity as God intended it. Immoral acts are not primarily violations of an abstract moral law but are violations of the moral structure of human life itself.

The Church's Responsibility to Cohabiting Couples

Wayne Oates argues that by-and-large, the church has turned a blind eye to these developments in marriage and family life. The nearly eight million people in the United States living together outside of marriage merit the careful attention and shepherding of all Christian pastors. "Pastors perform wedding ceremonies for about 80 percent of those who get married, and many of these have been living together," says Oates. He argues that church study groups need to address expectations of marriage and its disciplines. These can easily be forums for 'breaking the silence' about couples living together. "One of the tests of human character is the capacity to form and maintain lifelong relationships. Marriage is one of the most exacting of such relationships. It is also the relationship best fitted for the perpetuation of humanity in the birth and rearing of children."[88]

Don Browning concludes, "Whether the church places a new emphasis on betrothal, attempts to renew marriage itself, or tries to go in both directions at once, it must see its work as part of a larger multidimensional work of culture that it can inform but not in itself either control or fully implement."[89]

One example of the church's attempt to implement ministry to a growing segment of the population, where living together without benefit of civil marriage, is an attempt to create dialogue about the possibility of offering ecclesiastical marriage to elderly couples living together where civil marriage involves some tax penalty. In order to facilitate discussion without forming an official policy, in 1984 the American Lutheran Church produced a document titled, "Pastoral Care with Couples Living Together Outside of Marriage." This paper noted that the number of such couples increased from 640,00 in 1970 to 4.1 million in 1983. By some estimates, the paper stated, an average of 40 percent of all Lutheran couples now cohabit before seeking a church marriage.[90] In Sweden, a predominately Lutheran country, the paper reported an estimated 99 percent of couples, cohabit before marriage. In the United States, the study found that some elderly couples who marry may lose retirement or social security benefits if they marry, yet use up most of their resources on paying rent or utilities if they live separately.

The paper concluded by stating that coupling is most nurturing when it is not solely a private decision made by just two people. Members of families, congregation members, pastors of the couple, all should be taken into the couple's counsel and celebration. Further, it was suggested that some public recognition of a relationship is needed. If a couple believes that legal marriage is not the answer, can the church recognize and bless a committed, covenant relationship apart from governmental regulation? In other words, can an ecclesiastical marriage be performed in the absence of a civil one? While this raises ethical questions with regard to the deliberate attempt to circumvent governmental laws that penalize the couple who are married, it also raises theological questions as to what constitutes a marriage in the eyes of God? I have dealt with this question more fully in Chapter Six, above.

Our concern at this point is to trace out the deeper contours of marriage and family in hope of finding a 'point of contact' between the church and contemporary forms of marriage and family in order to serve as a redemptive and empowering resource, rather than merely withdrawing and retreating from engagement for the sake of conformity to its own principles. In order to do this, I want to think of a way of perceiving 'family' in the context of our postmodern culture that draws upon both biblical and sociological insights.

The Family Story: The 'Center' of the Family

I am indebted to my former colleague, Paul Hiebert, for the concept of centered as compared with bounded sets.[91] A 'bounded set,' says Hiebert is developed from sociological study of groups that are defined by certain structural or common characteristics. To exist with a 'bounded set' something must be defined by the boundary that sets it off from other objects or groups. Bounded sets are static and ordinarily require conformity to ideas, behaviors and appearances and a tendency to exclude or reject those who do not conform. As a result, Hiebert says, outward conformity of appearance and behavior along with ideological conformity to a set of doctrines or ideas can conceal the actual disposition of a person with regard to the truth or reality held by the group to be normative.

The disciples and followers of Jesus 'appeared' to conform to his own teaching as central to their existence, but in the end not all were revealed to be 'close to him' in heart and soul, Judas, for example. The 'bounded set' is defined by the frame, or the boundary terms and concepts. All those who fit within the framework are part of the 'set,' while those who fall outside the boundaries are foreign or alien.

In contrast, the 'centered set' is defined by the orientation or direction of one toward the center, regardless of distance from the center. In the centered set there is no clearly defined boundary that defines who is 'in' as against who is 'out.' In Hiebert's model of the centered set, some things (persons) may appear to be far from the center but actually have a deep inner orientation and actual movement toward the center. Hiebert used the model to explain why in mission work (he was in India) individuals who received the gospel in remote villages far from well established Christian 'centers' ought to be candidates for baptism even though they had not yet acquired all of the characteristics (belief system, behavior, dress) that belonged to those more 'centered.' While the centered set does not place the emphasis on a boundary line, there is a clear division between those orientated or moving toward the center as compared with those who appear to be 'near the center' but are actually moving away from it. Here we are reminded of the indictment by Jesus, quoting an Old Testament prophet, "These people honor me with their lips, but their hearts are far from me" (Matt 15:8; Isa 29:13).

The 'centered family,' then, is the network of primary relationships which orient each person toward a 'center,' or core reality, from which the character of each is determined. Figure 8.1 represents each of these configurations. Note that the one on the left (bounded) excludes everything not within the solid boundary, while the one on the right (centered) has no clearly defined boundary but a solid center.

BOUNDED   CENTERED

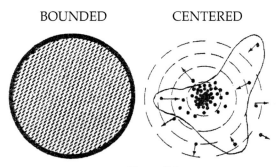

Figure 8.1

What is the "center" of the family?

In our class I liked to use the example of a 'family portrait' to make my point between a centered and bounded set as a helpful tool in family ministry. Most homes have a 'family portrait' hanging on wall or available for quick display! These pictures are 'framed' so as to include everyone in the picture and usually presented as 'our family' picture. In our contemporary society, few such family portraits capture the real story that lies behind and displays family relationships. Some portraits include blended families, where one or more child is 'in the picture' but whose mother is not. Or, a child is left out of the picture even though the father is present because he or she is in another family picture with the mother. Only a 'story' can explain how these people are related to each other. One student told me of her family pictures in which there was a woman who was not recognized as one of her relatives. Her mother informed her, "Oh that is 'Aunt Bess,' not really your aunt, just a woman who came to live with our family and was considered to be one of us." It takes a 'story' to connect real relationships when a framed portrait does not. The family story may include some painful memories, but is necessary to capture the reality that comprises the 'family portrait.'

The 'story' of Jesus includes some of that pain. It apparently became well-known that Joseph, the husband of Mary, was not the biological father of Jesus. While this has become a fundamental theological truth for orthodox theology, the gospel narrative of the 'virgin birth' is also one that does not 'fit into the frame' of a traditional marriage unit! In a similar way, one cannot connect the twelve tribes of Israel without telling the story of twelve sons born to one man (Jacob) through four women! In this case, a polygamous family unit was used by God as an existing cultural practice to produce the twelve tribes of Israel as a means of 'redeeming' marriage from below, so to speak. That story connects God's grace to humanity, though it was far from ideal. Perhaps we need to be reminded that, though many of the stories of marriage and family in our contemporary culture are not quite 'ideal' from a certain perspective, we can still see Gods grace present, if we are willing to listen to the story!

Each person's story has a 'center' where grace lives

It is the 'story,' or the narrative that serves as the living drama and context within which each person discovers her or his own 'story.' The role of parenting is to create and sustain the personal life of the child. Parenting introduces the child to the world in such a way that its personal identity 'moves along with it,' rather than being hidden in a dependency relationship with the parent; this is the 'history' of the self. The deepest need in a child is the urge to experience belonging as a history of its participation in a family story. This is the basic theme developed by Stanley Hauerwas in his book, *A Community of Character*. In developing our own character, or identity, Hauerwas says, it is important

> to be introduced to stories that provide a way to locate ourselves in relation to others, or society, and the universe. Stories capable of doing that may be thought of as adventures, for there can be no self devoid of adventure. What we crave is not dignity as an end in itself, but the participation in a struggle that is dignifying. Without self-respect, integrity is impossible. And self-respect comes from a sense of the possession of a self correlative to our participation in a worthy adventure. . . .Moreover, through initiation into such a story I learn to regard others and their differences from me as a gift. Only through their existence do I learn what I am, can, or should be.[92]

When is a story true? From a modern perspective, truth is an arbitrary and universal fact by which a story may be judged as 'true or false.' In a postmodern view of truth, each person's narrative contains the elements of what is true 'for that person.' At first glance, this appears to be sheer relativism as against the concept of 'absolute truth.' Hauerwas seems close to this view when he says, "And at least one indication of the truthfulness of a community's story is how it forces me to live in it in a manner that gives me the skill to take responsibility for my character."[93] However, in saying that each person must take responsibility for his or her own character, there is something more intended than the location of character in mere subjective or private inclinations or actions. In fact, as Hauerwas himself admits, at the very center of what we call character is a 'call to conversion' out of self-centered and self-serving living into a community of repentance and growth toward a 'way of life' in conformity to God's story--the gospel.

> The convictions that form the background for Christian growth take the form of a narrative which requires conversion, since the narrative never treats the formation of the self as completed. Thus the story that forms Christian identity trains the self to regard itself under the category of 'sin', which means we must do more than just develop. Christians are called to a new way of life that requires nothing less than a transvaluation of their past reality--repentance. . . Thus growth in the Christian life is not required only because we are morally deficient, but also because the God who has called us is infinitely rich. Therefore conversion denotes the necessity of a turning of the self that is so fundamental that the self is placed on a path of growth for which there is no end.[94]

The fundamental 'story' which provides the center of the family becomes the means by which the being of the other is disclosed to each, and
by which the being of each is taken up and incorporated into the being
of others as a shared origin, destiny and purpose. The centered family
is one that has an essential story, or narrative, by which each individual
creates his or her own story. Without such a story by which an individual
participates in a core community, or family, the self becomes dissociated
and disconnected from the unity of life, and has no participation in a
culture by which the self is related to ultimate reality through metaphors
and symbols. Yet, it is not enough to live vicariously in the story of community or family--one must have one's own story which becomes more
than a sub-plot within the larger story. The individuals in a culture become
the bearers of the story of the culture, even as the individuals in a family
become the bearers of the story of the family.

Implications

- Those who involve us in the story of their life pilgrimage are more
  significant than those who merely provide role functions;
- those who share in the discovery of our own story and who allow
  themselves to enter into its truth become family forever;
- the unity and wholeness of family issue from a shared story that
  unfolds in the making, despite changing roles and broken relationships;
- the assimilation of the Christian story into the family story provides
  the ecology of conversion and faith development;
- the centered family, with the Christian story as its symbolic life in
  the world, constitutes the church as the family of God.

Chapter 9

When Those Who Love You Hurt You

The pastor received a call from the Chaplain at the hospital. Linda, a member of his church had just been admitted with serious injuries due to a physical beating by her husband.[95] The husband was in shock and making a scene in the waiting room. Would he come right over? When the pastor arrived, he found that Linda had no broken bones, but would be in the hospital for several days recovering from lacerations and bruises. Al, her husband was crying and protesting that he did not mean to harm her but that he had just lost control.

The next day, Al came to the pastor's office for an appointment as he had promised. "I admit that I hit her but had no intention of hurting her. As God is my witness, I love her. I have asked God to forgive me and I want to pray with you that I will receive his forgiveness and yours." The pastor did not immediately respond. After a few moments he asked, "What really was your intention then?" Al replied, "She was mouthing off to me in front of the kids. She does not really respect my authority in the home. I had to do something to stop her. Pastor, don't I have a right to have my wife respect me and to expect that she will honor my role as the Bible says?"

When Linda returned from the hospital, the Pastor met with both Linda and her husband over the next several weeks for counseling. At the same time, Al had agreed to enter group therapy and was faithfully attending his sessions. Linda assured her husband that she had forgiven him and expressed hope that Al's contrition was genuine and that the incident would not happen again. Al, it appeared, had accepted her forgiveness but admitted that he felt deeply ashamed over what he had done. "It was not only that I did wrong to her," Al said, "but now the whole church knows about it. I don't think I can ever face these people again. Nothing that I can do will ever restore my reputation as a good husband and father."

In reflecting on this case, several questions emerge. Al claims to love his wife, Linda. How is it possible for love and violence to exist in the same relationship? Are we not led to believe that if one loves another person one could not (should not?) hurt that person? Can love and violence exist in the same relationship? In reflecting on this situation, several questions come to mind: 1) What response can be given to Al when he argues that the Bible says that the wife should submit to her husband's authority in the home? 2) How should the pastor respond with regard to Al's request for forgiveness? 3) If Al has experienced genuine forgiveness for the wrong that he did, both from God and from his wife, why does he still feel shame? 4) What strategy should the pastor now take to help Al overcome his sense of shame and find restoration and acceptance with the other members of the church? Before we address these questions, we need to look more closely at the dynamics of domestic violence.

Dynamics of Family Violence

A published report by the American Medical Association, revealed that one out of every four women in the United States experiences some form of abuse from a man she lives with or to whom she is related. One-third of all women who arrive at doctors' offices or hospitals seeking emergency treatment, and up to one-quarter of all those seeking prenatal care, are victims of domestic violence. Each year, 4 million women are severely assaulted by their current or former partner. More than half of female murder victims are slain by their husband or boyfriend.[96]

Those who research the cause of domestic violence say that family violence is different from all other forms of violence in that it has its highest potential for injury where there is the greatest potential for intimacy and love.

> You are more likely to be physically assaulted, beaten, and killed in your own home at the hands of a loved one than any place else, or by any one else in our society. . . . In our society, a person's earliest experiences with violence comes in the home--spankings and physical punishment from parents. We learn that there is always going to be a certain amount of violence that accompanies intimacy.[97]

I have found that this fact is one of the most difficult for persons to accept, other than those who have experienced it first-hand. We do not want to believe this. We cling to the illusion that abuse between married couples or between parents and children is due to the absence of love or, even worse, some emotional or mental disorder. Yet, we must face the fact that violence and love can co-exist as systemic components of primary relationships. And, may in fact, have more devastating consequences precisely because the recipients of family violence are dependent upon the abuser for some degree of care and even affection.

> That violence and love can actually coexist in families is perhaps the most insidious aspect of intimate violence because it means that, unlike violence in the streets, we are tied to abusers by the bonds of love, attachment, and affection. . . . Perhaps the greatest challenge to understanding intimate violence and devising adequate social polity is to see violence and love as coexisting in the same relationship.[98]

We are also told, contrary to conventional thinking, that persons who commit family violence are ordinarily 'normal' persons measured by accepted societal standards. In fact, say Gelles and Straus, "only about 10 percent of abusive incidents are caused by mental illness. The remaining 90 percent are not amenable to psychological explanation."[99]

> Initially, the response to family violence was to assume that abusive family members were mentally ill. But over the past two decades the tendency to diagnose the causes of violence as a psychological abnormality or mental illness has declined. We realize now that individual psychiatric care for violent family members is but one limited treatment for the problem. Since the roots of family violence lie in the structure of the family and society, we know that individual psychiatric treatment can be effective with only a small number of cases of violence and abuse.[100]

As it turns out, the dynamics of family violence are often fueled by an 'undeveloped moral sense' of personal rights related to relative degrees of powerlessness. Does this suggest, then, that there is a range of normal physical force that should be expected and tolerated in these domestic settings? Is it normal for parents to use physical force in disciplining a child, such as spanking or other forms of forcible punishment? Do not people who love each other often express their anger and frustration through harsh words and even pushing and shoving? Should we make allowance for force that is normal but which is not abusive?

The distinction between normal and abusive force, once used to distinguish between the force used in attempts to discipline as against violence which causes injury no longer has credibility among many sociologists.[101] For this reason, I prefer to speak of abusive relationships whether physical force is used or not. The use of physical means to exercise control over another can become a more overt form of abuse that is already taking place through the violation of a another person's dignity and personal space. We should also be aware of the fact that, while incidents of physical abuse may appear to be isolated and unconnected, a deeper pattern of abuse often underlies isolated incidents. One case of domestic violence may be closely connected to other acts of violence or abuse in the home. Studies have shown that incidents of child abuse are higher in homes where there is spouse abuse.[102]

In the above case, Linda's husband admitted that he was wrong to hurt his wife and put her in the hospital. At the same time he claimed that he had a right to discipline her. "She was mouthing off to me in front of the kids. She does not really respect my authority in the home. I had to do something to stop her. Pastor, don't I have a right to have my wife respect me and to expect that she will honor my role as the Bible says?" Not only does he express a feeling of humiliation and powerlessness that led up to his violence against his wife, he now finds justification for his action in a biblical principle (though he admits to going beyond what he felt allowed to do, for that, he is sorry). Here we are dealing with a deep feeling of moral righteousness that lies at the very heart of violence and may be part of the precipitating cause. When we understand this, we begin to see how difficult it is to use guilt as an appeal to change in behavior.

Violence as related to a primitive moral instinct

Psychotherapist, W. W. Meissner states it clearly. "There is a violence inherent in the moral sense. We violate children and arouse them to an inner rage when we keep them from the guidance and support they need to develop fully."[103] I must admit to being shocked at first reading this statement. The idea that our sense of moral right has within it the seeds of violence is somehow hard to accept. However, upon further reflection, it seems to be true when so often those who are offenders in cases of domestic abuse claim to themselves having been 'abused' and their moral self threatened by the objects of their abuse. What Meissner means by a 'moral sense,' however is not yet the same as a more highly developed 'ethical' sense. "Moral rules," he says, "are based on a primitive level of development. They are derived from fear, a response to threats of abandonment, punishment, exposure, or the inner threat of guilt, shame, or isolation. Ethical rules, however, are based on ideals to be striven for."[104] In other words, the 'primitive moral sense' is what causes children to throw a temper tantrum when they feel humiliated or deprived of some pleasure. We can punish them for their bad behavior, but may actually be causing a 'moral injury' to the undeveloped moral instinct of the child. In making an intervention into early stages of violence, there may also be the need to offer some protection of the offender's essence as a developing person and personality, says Meissner.

In abusive relationships, there may be a sense of personal inadequacy on the part of both the offender and the victim. In this case, the victim lacks the self-worth and ego strength to set boundaries or, as may well be necessary in some cases, to terminate the relationship as the first step in self-recovery from the abusive situation. This may explain the fact that victims of abuse often find it difficult to report abuse or, even when reported, fail to terminate the relationship.

In the following drawing (Figure 9.1), I trace out the effects of abuse as 'resistance' to the core of the self's own sense of entitlement behind which lies the primitive moral instinct. When this is violated it produces moral outrage, self-hatred and in many cases acts of violence. Because the violence has its source in the primitive moral instinct, the offender often turns to self-justification, as with Al in the case above. Punishment alone will not lead to change in behavior. Rather, there must be some form of empowerment that leads to moral self-worth, the ethic of love and finally a sense of self-fulfillment.

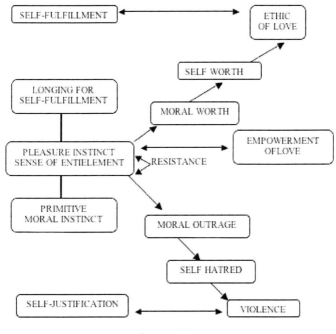

Figure 9.1

It is inevitable that each infant will experience frustration of the pleasure instinct to some degree, for the self is incapable in its earliest stages of development to accept delayed gratification of pleasure as a moral value. The fusion of pleasure and a sense of omnipotence takes place before there is a chance for the self to differentiate between the feelings of pleasure and power. Having the pleasure instinct gratified gives one an immediate sense of power. The infant experiences a feeling of omnipotence in receiving gratification from those who have the power to give it.

This sense of being 'all powerful' is an acquired feeling, it is not innate such as is the pleasure instinct. We are not born with a sense of power, but each of us possesses from birth a need for self-fulfillment. At the core of the pleasure instinct is a deep longing for the fulfillment of self through relation to another. This 'God-created' longing seeks fulfillment in its source; that is the love of God. Human love and relation is a reflection of that divine image which is experienced as a longing and desire for self-fulfillment. There is, in a sense, a 'moral right' to this fulfillment, so that if it is denied there is a sense of violation and even injury to the self. The earliest experience of this longing for self-fulfillment is the pleasure instinct in the child. The feeling of omnipotence for the child becomes attached to a sense of ownership of space, toys and even persons.

When the self acquires the feeling of being in control and having ownership of what is needed for self-gratification, the moral instinct shifts from pleasure to power of ownership. When the desire for pleasure is frustrated it is perceived as a threat to the moral right to possess that which is needed for one's gratification. The instinct to recover one's control over the situation can lead to abuse of the rights and person of others. The culmination of this process in acts of violence brings moral condemnation on the abuser.

The moral paradox of abusive behavior lies in the contradiction between the sense of moral outrage felt when denied what is perceived as necessary to self-identity (self-esteem) and the abusive (immoral) behavior that results. When Al came to me for counseling, he could not express this moral paradox conceptually, but he was surely caught in the moral self-contradiction of his intentions and actions. What he failed to understand was that abusive behavior does not suddenly spring up out of nowhere. There is a continuum of abusive that begins long before there is an overt expression of it.

Family violence is often 'disorganized violence'

Family violence tends to erupt; it is often chaotic and irrational. One aspect of this form of violence is that it cannot be predicted by the victims, though it may always be expected. This form of violence is systemic in nature, not merely episodic. One case of family violence may be closely connected to other acts of violence or abuse in the home. Studies have shown that child abuse incidents are higher in homes where there is spouse abuse.[105] Family violence operates on an 'exchange theory' principle of rewards and punishments. The principle of 'distributive justice' whereby each party in a transaction receives a fair reward or payment in kind, tends to break down in family relationships. Where one party perceives the other as not fulfilling an obligation or duty, the relationship cannot easily be broken off. As a result, anger, resentment, and some form of punishment or retaliation occurs. Gelles and Straus suggest that acts of violence occur when the costs of being violent do not outweigh the rewards.

> Clearly, the immediate rewards of using violence to work off anger or frustration are quite valuable to some individuals who would rather not wait to see the longer-term benefits of more reasoned and rational discipline and conversation with their children or partners. . . . Power, control, and self-esteem are other rewards of family violence. . . . Being in control, being master (or apparent master) of a situation, increases one's sense of self-worth. For men or parents whose sense of self-esteem may have been damaged or devalued by experiences outside of the home. . . control at home is even more important.[106]

Diagnostic Factors in Family Violence

Both 'normal' and 'abusive' violence can be placed on a continuum in order to show that abusive relationships begin long before there is physical injury. We seem to have an instinctive sense of when we are moving out of primary relationships into secondary ones when we leave the company of a good friend to stand in line at the Department of Motor Vehicles! While there is a sense of abuse when confronted by the impersonal nature of a bureaucracy, it is quite different from the same treatment by one who professes to love and care for us.

Primary relationships carry an implicit promise of mutual care, respect and trust. It is only on the basis of such qualities in the relationship that we risk ourselves to the intimacy of sharing our thoughts, personal space, and physical touch. When we form such relationships we expect to feel safe, free to respond, and nurtured in our own need for self-care. The moment that we no longer feel safe or free to respond, a violation has occurred, and abuse has begun.

In pastoral counseling I have discovered that teen-age dating patterns reveal tendencies toward abusive behavior under the sanction of accepted cultural roles in the relationship. Because men are often assumed to have the responsibility for initiating a relationship, women can feel disempowered and helpless when confronted with demands for intimacy which feel like a violation of personal integrity. Fearing rejection and possibly the loss of the relationship, the woman may feel pressured to respond. At this moment, the relation has become oppressive, coercive and demanding. Men are invariably shocked and defensive when this is pointed out to them. Nor are women always ready to call this abusive behavior. Only after marriage, in many cases, did the more overt abuse become apparent in the form of economic, emotional and physical forms of oppression and coercion.

Incidents of abuse may appear to be isolated and unconnected. The deeper pattern of abuse, however, is more systemic. The underlying problem of negative self-esteem and a self perception of powerlessness, can pervade all of the relationships an offender has.

When Don and Sally came to me for premarital counseling, we began the usual series of tests and discussions which focused on compatibility and role relationships in marriage. After a few weeks, Sally asked for an appointment to discuss a personal and private matter.

"Maybe I shouldn't be concerned," she began, "but I have felt increasingly uncomfortable with certain aspects of our courtship. Don seems to expect me to respond at times with signs of physical affection that I feel are inappropriate. If I do not respond, he sulks and will not call me for several days. Sometimes, this goes on for a week or more, until I call him and make up to him. If I do respond to him when he wants me to, then everything is really fine between us. Maybe it is just me."

As we talked, it became clear that there were other patterns in their relationship that exhibited the same need for Don to control her. He wanted her to dress in certain ways when they went out. If she did not comply, he would get angry and punish her by not taking her out.

"I really love him," she told me, "and I feel that he loves me. Maybe after we are married he will feel more secure and I will have more freedom to respond and please him."

What Sally revealed was a pattern of abusive behavior under the cloak of rather typical dating patterns in our culture. My counseling with them immediately moved into this area. Don and Sally were headed for a potentially abusive marriage. The seeds of abusive and violence were already being sown and were far from harmless personality quirks and lack of social skills.

The beginning of abuse in a relationship may be so imperceptible that it is like the proverbial story of the frog in the kettle. When the water at first is the same temperature as the frog, there is no discomfort. As the water is gradually increased in temperature, the frog makes adjustments to the change until finally, when the water reaches the boiling point, it is too late to jump out! Sally was ready to make adjustments to the behavior of Don for the sake of keeping a loving relationship. What she did not realize is that the water already was beginning to boil.

Abuse begins in a relationship when an almost imperceptible line is crossed where what was once safe, nurturing and empowering, becomes oppressive, coercive and demanding. Sally feels uncomfortable in her relationship with Don, but is powerless to express these feelings for fear of breaking the relationship, which she values on many other counts. Sally feels inadequate to set boundaries based on what she perceives to be appropriate responses. Don is unaware of her boundaries because they are unexpressed and because of his own need to find reassurance by controlling her response to him.

When I placed the positive and negative qualities of a relationship on a continuum and asked Sally to indicate where she would place herself in her relationship with Don, she immediately saw the pattern of abuse that was beginning. This is what the diagram looked like.

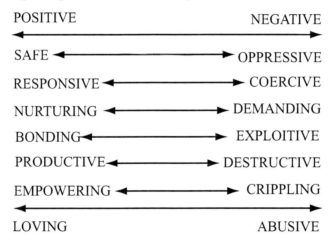

Figure 9.2

While Sally continued to feel deeply bonded with Don and did not feel that the relationship with him was destructive and crippling, she did not feel responsive and nurtured. She felt coerced to respond in many situations and that his demands upon her left her feeling uncared for. To some degree she also felt oppressed, and realized that she also felt vulnerable at the physical level and not always completely safe.

When Sally could place herself on each of these continuums as to how she felt about her relationship with Don, she became aware that the relationship was already moving from positive to negative and from loving to abusive. The next step was to discuss this with both Don and

Sally, using the diagram to help Don see precisely what her feelings were in regard to his demands upon her.

It was a painful and difficult experience for Don. In the end, however, it proved to be an effective intervention into the abusive tendencies in their relationship. When Don was asked to indicate on each continuum where his feelings were in regard to Sally's relationship with him, it became apparent that he too felt some level of coercion from Sally and, most important, felt disempowered and somewhat crippled by her assertive role in making decisions concerning her career without consulting him. It was somewhat of a shock for Sally to discover that Don also feel abused in the relationship!

As they began to communicate honestly about their feelings using this means of making more objective the effect of their relationship on each other, the boundaries of each became more clear. They discovered a means to conduct a personal audit with regard to these feelings and boundaries with a commitment to be open to each other's feelings in these areas and to maintain the integrity of each other's boundaries.

Recovering From Family Violence

The nature of abuse that occurs in personal relationships is a form of violence against the self's spirit which leaves an invisible wound which time alone will not heal. To suffer abuse is not only to experience psychological trauma, but spiritual desecration. The term 'desecration' implies the violation of something sacred, an intrusion upon that which is holy. In suffering sustained abuse, the self is not only injured so as to require healing, it suffers a violation for which only a restoration of the self's innate sense of spiritual integrity will suffice. This is what makes abuse in the context of intimacy so destructive and devastating. The psychological effects of trauma and abuse may sometimes be removed or alleviated through therapy. Recovery from abuse always involves a restoration of emotional and mental health. But the desecration of the self's spirit requires also a spiritual therapy that renews and restores health and wholeness to the spirit.

Trusting another person to care for us as we would care for ourselves is an openness of the spirit to the spirit of another. Trust is the sacred key given to another by which access to one's own secret self may be unlocked. Violation of this trust is unlawful entry into the sacred chamber of the self, a desecration of that which is most holy, for it is a gift of God. Abuse is unlawful entry into the sacred chamber of the spirit, a violation of the self's own sense of holiness. The spirit of the self is holy as it has virtue-

-it is essentially good; as it has value--it is of inestimable worth; as it has vision--it sees its own virtue and value reflected in the eyes of love.

The recovery of virtue

No one needs to teach a child that it possesses an essential goodness. This does not mean that the child is good in every thing, but that even in its disposition and actions which are self-centered and harmful to others, it is essentially good. Virtue is not an acquired character through the practice of moral disciplines, but the sense of one's own goodness as a spiritual being, albeit an imperfect one! The Bible tells us that we are born with the defect of selfish and sinful inclinations and that the grace of God is needed to redeem us from such. That is true, but virtue is the goodness of the spirit given to us by God in our creation not the result of our own good behavior! The fact that we need the grace of God to discover and uncover our God-created goodness does not deny that goodness but rather, esteems it. My children were never perfect, but they were always good. That is, by virtue of their being my children they were essentially good!

Abuse desecrates this innate sense of goodness. The child who is sexually abused by a caregiver begins to feel that he or she must be bad to deserve such treatment. After all, the caregiver is the only source of love and life. If one thinks that one is bad, that accounts for the bad thing that is happening.

A spouse who is abused by the one who provides the 'good' things necessary for life, begins to feel that she or he must be a bad person to deserve such punishment. When one who has been repeatedly abused by a spouse becomes compliant and obedient, the abuser may say, "You have been good for several days now. I haven't had to punish you for a long time." This reinforces the feeling of the abused person as not really being good, and as deserving the abuse. This is how abuse desecrates the spirit, by robbing the person of a sense of inward goodness. When the door to the self's sacred chamber of essential goodness has been broken through and every last shred of dignity and decency stripped away, abuse has done its work. The victim has become a slave, living off the few crumbs of affection tossed indiscriminately on the floor.

Virtue is not the good side of the self as opposed to the bad, but the integration of the self in such a way that the spirit recovers its sense of being holy and not defiled. The Bible speaks of both 'unclean' and 'holy' spirits, and both are aptly named! To live as though one's own spirit is 'unclean' is to be desecrated at the very core of the self. The picture of 'unclean spirits' invading a person and being driven out, as with the case of King Saul (1 Samuel 16), vividly portrays the condition of one whose own spirit has become defiled. David, after confessing to his own immoral actions and receiving God's grace and forgiveness, said, ". . . do not take your holy spirit from me. Restore me to the joy of your salvation, and sustain in me a willing spirit" (Psalm 51:11, 12).

Virtue is recovered when our desecrated and devastated spirits are renewed in holiness and goodness by the Spirit and grace of God. We are in recovery when we are able to affirm our own essential goodness as bearers of God's good spirit, created in his image and likeness. This is the spiritual work of healing that is necessary to recovery from abuse. We are in the place of spiritual recovery when we are with people whose own spirits are full of virtue. These people are open to God's Spirit through worship, prayer and shared life.

The recovery of value

Abuse not only desecrates the spirit of the self in violating its virtue, but in destroying its value. The victim of abuse, especially sexual abuse, can come to feel that one is 'damaged goods.' The abuser retains power over the victim by sending messages like this: "If you didn't have me, you wouldn't have anybody. Who would want you!"

Where virtue has to do with the essential goodness of the self, a quality like holiness, a sacred sense of the self, value has to do with the worth of the self, particularly to others. Virtue is something that the self is meant to possess as an innate quality of life. Value is a sense of the self's worth to others.

Abuse desecrates the spirit by devaluing the self as contemptible and undesirable by others. If one is made to feel worthless, then the abuser has power over the victim by pretending to give value and worth, even though it is not deserved. The abuser will stress how important and necessary the victim is to the abuser, giving the impression that the only source of value for the victim is to be found in relationship to the abuser.

The victim is thus placed in a double bind. Being made to feel worthless by the abuse, the victim looks to the abuser as the only one who seems to offer worth. In a strange and terribly twisted way, the victim's only value is found in meeting the abuser's need for someone to abuse!

When others attempt to intervene and affirm the worth of the victim of abuse as an argument to escape the abuse, the evidence of the abuse is a more powerful witness to the worthlessness of the self than the desperate entreaty of friends. Abuse can cause one to lose the capacity to feel valued by non-abusive persons. As one woman who suffered from abusive parents and an abusive husband in her first marriage told me, "I did not know how to live without pain. It did not seem normal." Feeling worthless can become a normal feeling for one who has suffered from abuse.

Recovery from the desecration of abuse to the spirit begins when the value of the self can be affirmed in such a way that it can be believed. We must remember that the negative value of worthlessness is created through actions that are abusive. This means that the value of having personal worth cannot be communicated through words alone, but through actions and relationships which are non-abusive.

The Apostle Paul wrote a brief letter to his friend Philemon, which later found its way into the New Testament canon. In this letter, Paul tells Philemon that Onesimus, a slave of Philemon, is being sent back. We do not know whether Onesimus had been sent by Philemon to serve Paul or had run away and was now being returned. In any event, Paul found Onesimus of great value to him, and in sending him back, said, "Formerly he was useless to you, but now he is indeed useful both to you and to me" (Philemon 11). The Greek name, Onesimus, means useful, or beneficial. Paul's play on words conveys the deeper significance of the fact that Philemon is now to view his former slave in an entirely different light. Onesimus discovered his true worth in serving Paul, who now asks Philemon to treat his slave as a brother.

The metaphor of slavery is an apt one with regard to an abusive relationship. Abuse makes slaves of those who are abused, treating them as having worth only as objects to be used for the abusers own gratification. Recovery from abuse is to move out of the abuser's power of deception into the truth and freedom of one's own worth and value. Abuse desecrates the spirit in the victim by perpetrating the lie that the victim is worthless except as a slave. Jesus of Nazareth, who treated all persons as having unique value, said, "The truth will make you free" (John 15: 32). "The slave does not have a permanent place in the household; the son has a place there forever. So if the Son makes you free, you will be free indeed" (John 15:35-36).

We are in the place of recovery when we accept the love and care of others as signs of our own worth, not merely as credit to their own goodness. We know that recovery is taking place when we feel the spirit within us responds to the spirit of truth and love in others who value their own life. We can trust that spirit, but it is the spirit of God leading us out of bondage into glorious liberty as children of God.

The recovery of vision

The spirit of the self is holy as it has virtue--it is essentially good; as it has value--it is of inestimable worth; as it has vision--it sees its own virtue and value reflected in the eyes of love. Virtue and value have no power in recovery until they are believed to be true of one's own self. Ultimately, recovery is self recovery. That is, the self must become the self that it really is despite the violation and abuse which has taken place. For all of the pain which the human spirit often must endure, it is indestructible. It can be bruised and broken, but not demolished. The terrible power of abuse is not that it can destroy the human spirit, but that it can blind it to its own virtue and value. When the vision of the self is obscured, it has lost its power of recovery. This vision must be restored.

"The eye is the lamp of the body," said Jesus. "So, if your eye is healthy, your whole body will be full of light; but if your eye is unhealthy, your whole body will be full of darkness. If then the light in you is darkness, how great is the darkness!" (Matthew 6:22-23). Abuse desecrates the human spirit by distorting the vision which the self has of its own virtue and value. Recovery involves the healing of this vision in order that new boundaries can be set and the inner life consecrated once more as good and worthy of care. Vision is a metaphor which suggests several aspects of recovery. Restored vision may require a corrective lens, the right amount of light, and a point of view.

How can we acquire these?

First, we need to have the right amount of light in order to have clear vision. The power of abuse is its secrecy. When the secret of abuse is revealed light has entered into darkness. In some cases, early childhood abuse has become a secret even to the self. Consultation with a qualified therapist can often uncover those secrets and shed light upon the abuse which has caused us to devalue ourselves. Where abuse is ongoing and recognized, it must be exposed to the light by breaking its secret.

It is the appropriate amount and kind of light that needs to be brought in to the abusive situation. Too much light, or light of the wrong kind, can cause its own distortion of vision. Unfortunately, some have disclosed abuse to persons who were themselves threatened by this revelation and whose reaction was one of denial, or even blame. In some cases, disclosure of abuse has caused some to suggest spiritual platitudes as a means of giving value to the suffering caused by abuse without making an intervention and stopping the abuse. There are twelve step programs available in almost every city. These are people who themselves are in recovery and often can provide a place with sufficient light to expose the evil of abuse while also shielding the self from the glare of over exposure.

Next, we need to have an eye examination! When we have problems with our eyesight, we go to a specialist who locates the distortion and prescribes corrective lens. When we have been the victim of abuse we need to go to specialists in non-abusive love and care. More than that, we need to ask them to conduct an eye examination by asking us what we see when we take a good look at ourselves. We need to trust their vision in order to correct our own.

Even as an ophthalmologist may write out a prescription for a lens that corrects our vision, we need a written prescription from those who have a more accurate vision of our own virtue and value than we do. It is not that others have not been saying these words to us, but that we have not believed them. We have trusted our own distorted vision of ourselves more than theirs. The written prescription of those who view us more accurately than we view ourselves can convey the authority of having the truth that will set us free!

Chapter 10

Bonding Without Bondage

Jesus cut through the casuistry of the legal squabbles represented by the various schools of thought concerning marriage and divorce in his own day by saying, "Therefore what God has joined together, let no one separate." (Mark 10:9). Marriage, in the eyes of Jesus, was not a mere social contract that could be dissolved on the occasion of evidence of fraud or failure on the part of one or both parties. Rather, it exists under a divine command through which a union created by humans is taken up, blessed and sustained by divine love. "Marriage," says Karl Barth, "may be defined as something which fixes and makes concrete the encounter and inter-relation of man and woman in the form of the unique, unrepeatable and incomparable encounter and relationship between a particular man and a particular woman."[107]

For Barth, this 'something' that determines the encounter is the command of God. However, this command of God is not primarily a rule of marriage and only secondarily a determination of cohumanity as male and female. Rather, the command of God that determines cohumanity to be concrete existence as male or female, male and female, finds its telos in the particular encounter that we have defined as marriage. The sphere of the male and female is wider than that of the marriage relationship. The fundamental ethical question for the relation of male and female is thus the question of how each man and woman lives obediently in terms of the divine command. Each man and woman is finally and therefore continually under the divine determination to experience his or her own humanity through the concreteness and uniqueness of being not only a person but a male or female person, The divine command is not an arbitrary rule but a direction and promise that each person discovers and fulfills for herself or himself. Marriage is but one instance of this divine command, even though it is a most significant and consummate instance.

It belongs to each person to be either male or female, but it does not belong to each person to enter into the state of marriage in order to be obedient to the divine command.[108]

What God Has Joined Together

Many people tend to equate the command of God with the Bible, or, more specifically, with the rules, regulations, or even principles that the Bible seems to teach. However, what we mean by 'the command of God' is the demand God himself places upon us through the concrete regulations and even words in the Bible. The command of God is a summons to think, act, and live so as to be accountable to God himself, not only to conform to an abstract principle or rule. When it comes to setting forth a theology of marriage this distinction is particularly important, As Geoffrey Bromiley has pointed out, "a law of marriage differs decisively from a theology of marriage." Thus,

> we should not conclude that all that is meant by a theology of marriage exists in biblical expositions of the topic. . . God reveals himself in and through the Bible. He speaks in and through it. Yet the Bible does not replace God. He has not just given us the Bible and left us to it. He himself is still the one with whom we have to deal. . .Even as we consult holy scripture, we are really consulting God himself in his self-revelation as he came and comes to us through holy scripture. God indeed says what scripture says, but this does not imply a direct equation of God and scripture.[109]

We must not misunderstand Professor Bromiley at this point. He is not suggesting that there is any other access to God than through the Holy Scripture. What he is arguing is the point that God holds humans accountable to himself, not merely to a law or principle that may be abstracted from God, even though that law is supported by biblical proof-texting. His point is that the biblical text is not merely an 'object' that can be used to formulate a principle independent of God's own relation to the text. In applying this argument more directly to a theology of marriage, Bromiley goes on to say that

> although an account of the biblical teaching on marriage may be a theology of marriage, it will not necessarily be so. Why not? Because no theology of marriage or of anything else arises if the teaching is abstracted from God himself, if God himself is not present at the heart and center in his own relation to the topic. A theology of marriage does not consist of a mere recital of what the biblical texts have to say about it. It consists of the relating of marriage to God, or of God to marriage, as he himself instructs us through the biblical texts.[110]

The command of God

This is why the command of God is the objective basis on which a theology of marriage is to be based. The command of God is a deep and demanding summons to be human. Thus, marriage is not the command of God by virtue of its legal or moral status as determined by society. Nor is marriage equal to the command of God by virtue of a religious law upheld by the church. To live under the command of God is to recognize and assume responsibility for one's own humanity in the concrete historical situation. Because humanity is cohumanity, and because cohumanity is a divinely determined order that includes human sexuality as male and female, male or female, marriage exists within the order of cohumanity as God's purpose for the full expression of human sexuality--what the Bible calls the 'one flesh relationship '(Eph. 5:31). Central to this purpose is also the establishing of the responsibility to bring children into the world in such a way that they are bound to the 'bonding' that exists between the father and the mother as the context of covenant love.

Clearly, the biblical teaching on marriage is that the bond of marriage actualized in the one flesh relation is not absolute. Rather, it is made relative by the eschatological truth that in heaven we shall neither marry nor be given in marriage (Mark 12:25). The bonding between parents and children is also made relative by this same eschatological reality. Thus, Jesus warns his disciples that they must be prepared to forsake husband and wife, mother and father for the sake of the kingdom of God (Luke 14:26). When one of his followers argued that he had filial obligations at home and thus should be excused from immediately following him, Jesus rebuked him and suggested that the demands of the kingdom come first (Luke 9:57-62). We should not conclude from this that marriage is thereby not to be taken seriously inasmuch as it has only temporal and not eternal status. This would be a mistake. The command of God under-girds temporal life and calls us to responsibility in our present situation. If one undertakes marriage as a calling of God for one's life, it stands under the command of God. If one remains single as a responsible life within the context of cohumanity, this life too stands under the command of God. That is, neither marriage nor celibacy can be absolutely equated with the command of God in such a way that one or the other has a higher status.

Nor can we spiritualize the command of God in such a way that it becomes disconnected from our actual existence in cohumanity as male or female persons. Paul warns the Corinthians not to attempt to live as husband and wife without consideration for the sexual aspects of the relationships, "Do not deprive one another except perhaps by agreement for a set time, to devote yourselves to prayer, and then come together again, so that Satan may not tempt you because of your lack of self-control" (1 Cor. 7:5). If there is marriage, then there must be consideration for the sexual relations that normally and naturally belong to the union. It must immediately be said, of course, that two people will ordinarily find their own way of expressing mutual sexual relationships within this union. The point is, one cannot deny or attempt to conceal sexuality as that which comes under the command of God as expressed in marriage. It can also be said that if there is sexual relation there must also be consideration for marriage. The command of God binds marriage to sexual union as surely as it binds sexual union to marriage. However, the apostle Paul gives pastoral counsel to the effect that there is a great deal of freedom to realize the command of God in one's own life without coming under some general 'law of marriage' or 'law of celibacy' (1 Cor. 7:27-38). The command of God is recognized and fulfilled within limits that are practical and possible for human persons.

Fidelity, then, as a mark of sexual integrity, is primarily fidelity to one's own sexuality as existence under the command of God. Because God has determined that cohumanity is fundamental to personal existence and that personal existence is in each case existence as male or female, male and female, one cannot evade the responsibility to be faithful to one's own sexual identity within the framework of coexistence.[111] Marriage too, says Barth, comes under the general category of the encounter and relationship of man and woman.[112] Therefore, the command of God is the objective basis for marriage. However, what is said of marriage in particular forms the original and primary criteria for all encounters between man and woman. In Genesis 2:24, the original determination of cohumanity is set within the context of the 'one flesh' relation. While this passage may not be descriptive of the first 'wedding,' it is the theological and creaturely presupposition of marriage and, therefore, of the determination of all humanity as male and female.

Thus, the indissolubility of the marriage relation is due to the absolute character of the divine command, rather than to a quality or intention of human love. Marriage is not subject to a universal 'law' that stands by itself on the basis of an ethical 'ought', rather, the law of marriage is the result of a divine determination understood by those who enter into the relation as a divine calling or vocation (cf. Matt. 19:11; 1 Cor. 7:17). "Therefore what God has joined together, let no one separate," says Jesus, as a reaffirmation of the absolute character of the divine command (Matt. 19:6). To this extent, marriage is not based on human love as its presupposition, but upon the divine command. Just what this means in the practical sense remains to be considered.

Marriage as a possibility, not a necessity

First, however, we must clarify the relation of the divine command to those who marry as well as to those who do not. Since the divine command does not relate primarily to marriage, but rather, marriage is a special instance of the divine command, we can see that marriage is a possibility, not a necessity. True, in the Old Testament marriage is presumed to be the primary duty of every person (i.e., every male). To remain unmarried was a disgrace, and to fail to have children (a son) was considered a bitter and tragic loss. The sexuality of man in the Old Testament, says Barth, "is considered almost exclusively in connection with the procreation of the holy seed and therefore the hope of Israel."[113] Barrenness was interpreted as God's judgment upon a woman, and failure to have a son tantamount to divine rejection of a man. For this reason marriage was considered sacred. In the New Testament, however, it appears that Jesus has made marriage relative, not only by his own example of celibacy, but by his many statements that gave priority to a person's relation to the kingdom of God over marriage and family (Luke 14:16; Matt 19:12). "The clamp which made marriage a necessity for man and woman from their creation is not removed," says Barth, "but it is certainly loosened. Marriage is no longer an absolute but a relative necessity. It is now one possibility among others."[114]

There is a valid point here for the emergence of a theology of the single person; not as a return to a call for spiritual asceticism that involved celibacy as a renunciation of sexuality altogether, but as a legitimate form of cohumanity in which one's own life as male or female is affirmed and authenticated. "The woman is the partner of the single man too," says Barth, "not woman in general, not an idea of woman, certainly not the Virgin Mary, but the concrete and definite form of woman encountering him in a particular way."[115] This partnership is not one of sexual love as in marriage, but it is no less a kinship, acquaintance, friendship, and vocation than that experienced by husband and wife. The context for this life of obedience under the divine command must surely be developed in light of the New Testament teaching concerning the entering into the present of the eschatological kingdom, where they "neither marry nor are given in marriage," and yet possess full humanity as male and female (Matt 12:18-27.[116] We will further elaborate on this when we consider the matter of the church as the new family of God.

Is every marriage is under the command of God?

We must now return briefly to consider, from a pastoral perspective, what it means to say that marriage is constituted by that which 'God has joined together.' Barth takes the somewhat curious position that not every marriage that purports to be a marriage, either by legal action or personal action, can automatically be assumed to be a union that God has 'joined together.' In these cases, Barth avers, the relationship is radically dissoluble because there has been no real union in the judgment of God.[117] Certainly it does give one pause to consider extreme cases where couples are married, in a civil ceremony, foolishly, incompetently, or capriciously. Surely some of these cases must be at best only caricatures of marriage. However, can one really seriously consider the possibility that many couples in marriages that appear to be real are not, in fact, joined by God? And does this mean that in cases where marriages apparently fail and result in divorce, that this is evidence the union was not joined by God?

Hardly, and Barth himself will not go so far. In the last analysis, Barth says, no one can know that any particular marriage has not really been concluded by God. If one does come to suspect that there has never really been a marriage, Barth says, this can only be accepted on the ground of certain "terrible indications." And no such indication is so terrible, he adds, that it might not be fallacious.[118] So what is the point? Just this. The absoluteness of the divine commandment can never be presumed on the basis of a human will or of human love. The undertaking of a marriage relation is meant to be a serious act of recognition and affirmation of the divine command. In like manner, the dissolution of a marriage can never be undertaken on the ground of mutual intention, nor even on the failure of human love.

However, Barth goes further to suggest that in certain cases the Word of God may contain a NO that powerfully and authoritatively expresses the final condemnation of a marriage, so that one is forced to conclude that the marriage itself no longer is under-girded (if it ever was) by the divine command. In this case, dissolution by divorce is a recognition of the fact that God has already brought the marriage under the judgment of non-existence.[119]

When a Marriage no Longer Exists

Thus Barth sees in the same divine commandment that makes marriage an absolute rather than a relative union, God's freedom to declare in his absolute sovereignty that a marriage is a non-marriage. This places the possibility of divorce under the condition that one can discern the will of

God in a specific situation such that the scriptural statements that condemn divorce as contrary to the command of God can also be seen to support the command of God that is the basis for dissolution. Hermeneutically, this can only be understood as a theological exegesis by which universal principles are subordinated to absolute determinations of God's will. In this case, no single text can be permitted to result in a universal law of marriage that prohibits God from acting in specific, concrete situations. We can compare this approach, taken by Barth, with one espoused by Brunner, who maintains that divorce can be supported in certain cases on the basis of the law of love, which stands above the orders of creation.[120]

It seems preferable, however, to assume that all marriages recognized by state and society in general are unions in which God has joined together two people in an indissoluble relation, even in their ignorance of the divine command. This avoids the casuistry of attempting to determine which marriages have a 'right' to annulment and dissolution and which do not. In this sense, no marriage can be assumed to be rightfully dissolved. However, it also confronts us with the theological reality of God's participation in and redemption of human events, including marriages.

If, in fact, a marriage relationship has utterly failed to be any semblance of a covenant partnership such that the integrity of human life is not sustained but rather is being destroyed, then we have to ask the question: What does God's judgment mean on such a relation? If one determines that the judgment of God is such that the relationship no longer exists in actuality, then it might be concluded that it no longer exists in the mind of God. For to assume that the commandment of God is a reality entirely separated from concrete human existence is itself a violation of theological method. It was the nature of the incarnation that conclusively united the being of God with concrete existence. Jesus himself expressed the command of God. And what he loosed on earth was loosed in heaven, and what he bound on earth was bound in heaven (Matt. 16:19). It seems to be the responsibility of the people of God not to break the words of Jesus free from his own being, and so to make out of his teachings a universal principle, but to continue to discern the 'mind of Christ' in obedience to the divine command through the reality of the Holy Spirit. Obedience to the divine command cannot circumvent the revelation of Scripture, but neither can it substitute the words of Scripture as an abstract law for the absolute command of God experienced in its binding and yet liberating grace.

Perhaps this will help us to understand the response of Jesus to the Pharisees' demand that he speak to the issue of divorce. In allowing no place for a 'rule of divorce,' Jesus was not merely taking the hard line as advocated by the school of Shammai as against the more permissive and softer line of those who followed the teaching of Hillel. He was not advocating one law of divorce against another law. Nor was he even arguing for one law of marriage against another law of marriage. He rejected the concept of a 'law of divorce' as not compatible with the divine command. When the Pharisees responded by asking why Moses stated that divorce was permissible in certain cases, Jesus answered, "It was because you were so hardhearted that Moses allowed you to divorce your wives, but from the beginning it was not so" (Matt. 19:8). Jesus presented the basis of marriage from the perspective of the command of God: "Therefore what God has joined together, let no one separate" (Matt. 19:6). In saying this, Jesus removed both marriage and divorce from the status of being under a law, and reminded his listeners that humans are accountable to God himself in thought, word, and deed, not least of all in the 'one flesh' relation of marriage. Viewed from this perspective, it is clear that there can be no rules by which marriage can be dissolved, any more than a marriage can be sanctified before God by observing certain legalities. If at times, for specific reasons, the command of God is expressed as a 'law of divorce,' such as Moses gave, it is immediately superceded by the command of God. Jesus, as the presence of God himself through the eternal Son, radically qualified all interpretations of the command of God by embodying it in his own person.

The irony of all this is that Jesus' very words have become abstracted into a new 'law of marriage and divorce.' As a result, pastoral decisions on how to minister to those who suffer irreparable breakdown in their marriage are complicated by a web of casuistry involving hermeneutical hair-splitting in handling the biblical texts. Rather than hold persons accountable to God himself, and rather than be accountable to God themselves, ministers often take refuge in abstract principles. If these principles can be supported by a biblical text, one can find an excuse for not acting on behalf of those who are in need of support when going through the breakdown of a marriage. At the same time, one can feel free to act in every case with little regard for the implications of one's actions. In either case, the result is to trivialize and render ineffective the commandment of God.

The command of God is always the work of God, even though it comes to expression through a regulation or rule. When the regulation or rule acts against the work of God, one is accountable to God himself, not merely to the regulation. This is what lies behind Jesus' statement

"The sabbath was made for humankind, not humankind for the sabbath" (Mark 2:27). This is all the more significant when we remember that the regulation for keeping the sabbath was enforced by no less a penalty than death by stoning (Exod. 31:15). When Jesus saw that to carry out this rule without regard for God's purpose for human healing and hope was itself contrary to the work of God, he brought to bear the commandment of God in such a way that the person caught in this 'legal trap' was freed and restored to life.

"For the kingdom of God is not food and drink but righteousness and peace and joy in the Holy Spirit," taught the apostle Paul (Rom. 14:17). Yet the Old Testament clearly set forth regulations concerning the eating of food that carried the force of being the Word of God (cf. Lev. 11). But in a pastoral situation, Paul saw that the command of God was directly related to the work of God. And therefore he admonished, "Do not, for the sake of food, destroy the work of God" (Rom. 14:20). Against those who argued that they were no longer under any regulations because of their freedom in Christ, Paul taught that they were still subject to the command of God, and the command of God is to 'walk in love.' Against those who argued that the regulations concerning food constituted the command of God, Paul taught that "those who eat, eat in honor of the Lord, since they gives thanks to God" (Rom. 14:6).

Is Remarriage a Possibility?

Is it impossible for God to work in the life of one who has suffered an irretrievable loss of the 'one flesh' relationship in such a way that he cannot or will not join this person together with another in a new marriage? Or, dare we suggest that the command of God can both put to death and raise again persons who experience dissolution of the marriage bond? Would it be too much to paraphrase the words of Jesus and say, "Marriage is made for humans and not humans for marriage?" If a theology of marriage insists that marriage is a work of God and exists under the command of God, there does seem to be a basis to suggest that in the situation where sinful humanity has experienced brokenness and loss, the commandment of God is the presence of God himself at the center of that person's life to effect new being and new possibilities. This would be to take the authority of Scripture seriously as directing us to God himself as the one who summons us in Scripture to acknowledge him as the author of life rather than of a 'law that kills.'

We can summarize the implications of what we have said here concerning marriage and the command of God as follows. Because God joins himself to the temporal social relationship consummated as a marriage and recognized by society and the church, that marriage is indissoluble on any grounds whatsoever other than the command of God. If a marriage comes to the point of utter breakdown so that it is a disorder rather than an order of human relationship, and inherently destructive to the persons involved, one can only seek to bring that relationship under God's judgment. For Christians, this means that the breakdown of a marriage to the point of utter failure is a betrayal of the covenant love that God has invested in that marriage, and is therefore a sin. To attempt to find legal or moral grounds on which to be excused from the marriage contract is to take a legalistic attitude to a relation of love. The scriptural teaching on marriage and divorce clearly brings the marriage under the judgment of God as the one who has the absolute right of determining its status. But this means grace rather than law.

If Christians, and the church, do not have a process to deal with sin and with grace as a work of God, then there will be little hope for those who become victims and casualties of hopeless marriages. But where the work of God is understood as his contemporary presence and power under the authority of Scripture to release those who are in bondage and create a new status where 'all things are new,' then the church as the community of Christ will have the courage to say NO to a continued state of disorder and YES to the forgiveness and grace of God that brings persons under a new authority of divine healing and hope. We are speaking here, by analogy, of a 'death and resurrection' experience as the work of God in the midst of human lives. To create a 'law of marriage' that would deny God the authority and power to put a marriage to death and to raise the persons to new life through repentance and forgiveness would appear to be a desperate and dangerous course of action. What God has joined together, indeed, let no one put asunder. But where God puts asunder as a judgment against sin and disorder, and therefore as his work, let no one uphold a law against the grace of God.

It would be misleading to end this chapter on marriage as the expression of love and sexuality on a negative note. The command of God by which marriage as a human, social relation is given the status of covenant partnership is a positive and rich resource of growth and renewal. What God 'joins together' he attends with love and faithfulness. This is a promise and commitment of God himself to the marriage relation as a source of love, healing, and hope. The Christian community participates in this work of God by providing a context of support and enabling grace for each marriage that belongs to the community.

Those who undertake the calling of ministry to families through pastoral care and counseling have as their first priority the ministry of encouragement and support for marriages, This is a constructive and positive reinforcement of marriage and prevents its deterioration into a shell of the love and commitment it is meant to express. God is faithful to weak and problem-plagued marriages--not merely angry at unfaithfulness. God is patient and loving to marriages where love has been lost--not merely angry at our own anger and lovelessness. God is hopeful toward marriages that are ready to crash--not merely angry at our incompetence. God never gives up on his 'joining together,' because God is himself the covenant partner of marriage. This produces a bonding that never is allowed to become bondage.

Chapter 11

Homosexuality: The Family and the Church

Running right through the center of human sexuality is the element of the tragic. When the beauty and promise of human love and intimacy are linked with the capacity for sexual desire and fulfillment, no experience will prove adequate and completely fulfilling. Whatever one's sexual orientation and practice, be it homosexual or heterosexual, the element of the tragic will always be present. The tragic can mean as little as the temporary frustration of sexual desire when there is no partner available or willing to share it. It can also mean the choice to live in a relationship where sexual relations are impossible, whether due to physiological, psychological or moral reasons. Redemption from the tragic does not guarantee perfect fulfillment of every capacity or desire. It does offer grace to bear with what must be borne, and to sublimate self-gratification in one area to self-fulfillment in another. Every human being is a sexual being and will experience some degree of the tragic in this area.

Theological assumptions concerning human sexuality, grounded in biblical revelation, must include an acknowledgment of the brokenness and tragic aspects of the human sexual experience as well as of the divine intention regarding it.[121] Where persons struggle to find meaning and value in contexts that are less than ideal and fall outside of what society considers normative, the family, and very often the church may be called upon to mediate compassion with conviction. This is not easily done, particularly in the situation where a family member openly discloses a homosexual life-style.

When Conviction Collides with Compassion: A Case Study

The following story is one shared with me by a student seeking pastoral as well as theological counsel with regard to a family crisis over the issue of homosexuality. The crises not only involved family members but also a conflict between the church's teaching regarding homosexuality and the family's relation with their son. The story has been written up for case discussion; the names have been changed for the sake of confidentiality. After reading the case, I will offer some comments as to what appear to be the factors that contribute to this family crisis, followed by some theological and pastoral reflection with the hope of providing a context for others who may be dealing with similar issues.

When Susan and Carl were informed by their 22 year-old son, Todd, an only child, that he was gay and had decided to come out openly, they were shocked and angry. Carl demanded that he talk with their pastor, as Todd had been an active member of the college age group in the church where the family had attended for years. Susan was an elder and Carl sang in the choir. "I have already discussed this with the youth pastor," Todd responded, "and he suggested that I see a psychologist as he thought that I may have some emotional problems causing me to have homosexual tendencies." "And did you," Susan asked? "No," Todd responded. "I had already talked with the counselor at school and it was in working with him that I decided to accept the fact that I needed to face my true sexual orientation honestly and to come out of the closet. Mom and Dad," Todd said, "I have finally come to terms with myself and, while I know that this is hard for you, it is important for you to accept me for who I am."

Both parents were too stunned to make a response at the time. In the meantime, Carl discussed Todd's situation with his pastor and was told that homosexuality was a perversion and not acceptable as a Christian life style. "You will have to confront Todd with this," the pastor told Carl, "while we must continue to love Todd we cannot condone his gay life style. Susan is an elder and knows that our church has taken a strong stand against homosexuality."

At the next meeting between Todd and his parents, Carl attempted to explain why they could not accept his openly gay life style. "We have no choice," Carl told his son, "We have always taught you to live by the Bible and we would be unfaithful to our own convictions if we pretended that your homosexuality was acceptable to us. This is a decision that you will have to make. If you expect to continue to have our support for your college tuition and be accepted as a member of our family, you will have to agree to renounce your homosexuality and seek counseling."

"I don't understand," Todd responded. "When you did not know that I was gay I was perfectly acceptable to you, even though I have been living as a gay person for several years secretly. Why am I not the same person today as I was a few weeks ago? When I kept that a secret you could accept me. Now that I have been honest with you, I am somehow unacceptable. I feel that God has accepted me as I never really had a choice about my sexual orientation. I guess for your sakes and the church I should drop out of sight."

Carl and Susan had long conversations following Todd's last visit. Carl felt that they had no alternative but to stick by the ultimatum given to Todd. Susan could not accept that. "I am torn between my theological convictions and my parental instincts," she told Carl. "If ever Todd needed our love and support it is now. If we abandon him for the sake of what our church believes about homosexuality, I could not live with myself. I can't see Jesus cutting him off over this issue. I shall probably have to resign as an elder, but I intend to tell Todd that he has the same place in our family as he has always had, with no strings attached." Carl was silent for a long while. "I know how you feel as a mother," he said, "but if I let go of my Christian convictions I don't know how I could live with myself."

What's a parent to do?

What appeared to be a conflict between the church's position on same-sex unions and one of their members suddenly has plunged the marriage of Todd's parents into crisis. Carl, Susan's husband, has not only taken a strong biblical position with regard to homosexuality but has issued an ultimatum to his son--renounce his gay life-style or be cut off from the family. Susan, who is an elder in the church and responsible to uphold the church's teaching is now torn between obedience to the church and loyalty to her son. She also finds biblical grounds for her sense of compassion and responsibility for her son as she looks to Jesus as one who took the side of the estranged and rejected. Her husband attributes her conviction in this regard to her maternal instincts-- "I know how you feel as a mother"--but apparently does not regard her feelings as based on 'Christian convictions.' If she resigns as an elder, that could removed the conflict with the church in her case, but only serve to intensify the conflict with her husband.

What are parents to do when confronted with what they are led to believe is a biblical teaching and a church disciplinary practice that could well break apart the family bond between parent and child as well as between husband and wife?

An intervention is needed in this situation. Ordinarily, one would expect the pastor to do this but, as the case suggests, this may not be possible. The Pastor has also issued an ultimatum based on his conviction that homosexuality is not only an immoral life style but that the church must exercise discipline by not allowing gay persons to be in fellowship. One is reminded here of a recent issue with regard to an army general who was quoted as supporting the army's policy of 'don't ask--don't tell' by saying that the reason why gay soldiers were not welcome in the military was that this life-style was immoral. A storm of criticism erupted, and the general apologized for intruding his own personal moral position regarding homosexuality into the army's official policy.

The pastor, in this case, can hardly apologize and retract his ultimatum because his view is both a personal and a theological one. Nor can Carl, the father, retract his ultimatum given on the basis of his 'Christian convictions' despite his sympathy for his wife's 'instincts as a mother.' Is compassion only a parental instinct? Even more important, is conviction without compassion a biblical truth?

What's a pastor to do?

If we put ourselves in the position of this pastor, assuming that an intervention must be made for the sake of this family, as well as for the church, what are his options? As stated earlier, he can hardly apologize by explaining that his teaching only reflected his personal moral view and not that of the Bible! Nor can he, if he understands his pastoral role to include ministry to families as well as members, abandon the marriage between Carl and Susan for the sake of imposing church discipline upon their son.

Perhaps there was a time when issues such as raised in this case were also kept under the unspoken rule of the church--don't ask, don't tell. We have all heard stories of family secrets kept for the sake of preserving one's role in a community, including the church. It is not an issue raised entirely by postmodernism, but by a progressive secularism that seeks to steadily and inevitably separate human values from religious doctrines and practices. Where one church attempts to resist this rising tide by re-affirming a 'biblical morality' along with traditional social values, other churches attempt to create a 'level playing field' with respect to how biblical texts are interpreted so as to include, rather than exclude. Carl and Susan, if they finally conclude that their relationship with their son takes priority over their own church's teaching, may well find another church where not only is their son welcomed, but affirmed in his life-style. After all, as Susan pointed out, Jesus invariably took the side of the ones who were rejected or scorned by the self-righteous religious authorities of his day. In addition, Jesus said nothing about homosexuality while he spoke clearly and emphatically about marriage, divorce, and responsibility for the neighbor.

The pastor knows this. And, if he has some better angels guiding him, will pause to do some theological reflection before swinging his sword and letting 'the chips fall where they may.' He remembered his seminary professor once warning the students that "Jesus was crucified on exegetical grounds!" The explanation was that when Jesus healed on the Sabbath, those who judged him to have violated the Sabbath and therefore was 'not of God,' probably did so on the basis of some Old Testament texts (John 9:16).

"Time out," says this pastor. Time to do some theological reflection and review the biblical data regarding human sexuality and, homosexuality in particular.

The Biblical Data

First, we need to be reminded that the ancient world had no word for or concept of 'homosexuality' as it is currently used today. The word 'homosexual' was not coined until 1869, when a Hungarian physician writing in German used it with reference to male and females who from birth are erotically oriented toward their own sex. The word first appeared in English in 1912, according to the Oxford English Dictionary, and its earliest use in an English Bible was in 1946, in the first edition of the Revised Standard Version rendering of 1 Corinthians 6:9.[122] Examination of the biblical texts must therefore take note of the problem of translation into English of the original Hebrew and Greek terms used.

Unfortunately, the question, "What does the Bible say about homosexuality?" has not led to answers upon which all can agree. Some have even argued that an appeal to Scripture cannot settle the issue at all as it is basically a moral and not a theological concern.[123] Same-sex relations are mentioned in the Bible, however, and so the biblical data must be taken into account in theological consideration of homosexuality as it relates to Christian faith and practice.

There is no biblical passage referring to homosexuality as a 'condition' or 'orientation.' The word 'sodomite' appears nowhere in the Hebrew text of the Old Testament, not even to designate a person living in ancient Sodom. The Hebrew term translated as 'sodomite' (*qadesh*) in the King James Version refers to a male temple prostitute (Deut. 23:17-18; 1 Kings 14:22-24; 15:12; 22:46; 2 Kings 23:7; Joel 3:3). Though the English word 'sodomite' is used twice in the New Revised Standard Version (1 Cor.

6:9; 1 Tim. 1:10), it is an incorrect translation of the Greek words *malakoi* and *arsenokoitai*.

The story of the incident at Sodom (Genesis 19:1-25), which can be read as an attempt to rape Lot's two male visitors by a mob of other males, is not often referred to in subsequent Scriptural references as a sin of a homosexual nature. In Ezekiel 16 the sin of Sodom is named as greed and indifference to those in need. In Matthew 10:12-15 and the parallel passage in Luke 10:10-12, Sodom's sin is described as inhospitality in general. In Matthew 11:23-24 the city's destruction is recalled as a reminder of what happens to those who rebel against God. The book of Jude, however, identifies the sin of Sodom as sexual immortality in which they "pursued unnatural lust" or, as the Greek puts it, "went after other flesh" (*sarkos heteros*, Jude 7). Much more was wrong with the citizens of Sodom than the sexual intent described in the story. But as David Wright points out, this consideration should not be allowed to eliminate the sexual element from the text and the moral judgment implied.[124]

Based upon the Levitical texts (18:22; 20:13), and the New Testament texts (1 Romans 1:26-27; Cor. 6:9; 1 Tim. 1:10), some have argued that homosexuality is an 'unnatural affection' and contrary to God's will. In this interpretation of the texts, an assumption is made that a male having sex with another male is forbidden in the holiness code of Leviticus 17-16, and thus homosexual practices of all kinds are forbidden, including contemporary homosexual relations between non-promiscuous partners.[125]

The context of the Levitical prohibition indicates that such an act by two males, where one takes the part of the female, is a violation of the maleness of both partners as the Hebrew text literally says, one partner is required to "lie the lying of a woman."[126] The Hebrews did not appear to make a distinction between same-sex practices and a same-sex orientation or condition. Rather, the emphasis was upon an objective act that violated the holiness code which separated 'clean' from 'unclean' actions and objects as a representation of Israel's separation unto the holiness of God.

There is no record in the gospel traditions of Jesus making any comments about same-sex relations, while he did offer clear teaching concerning fornication, adultery and remarriage (Mark 10:6-9; cf. Matthew 19:4-6). The silence of Jesus on this point, however, does not necessarily constitute approval. It would be unlikely that the practices which the Pauline texts forbid in the context of the Hellenistic Jewish community would have been unknown during Jesus time. It is more likely that the immediate context of Jesus' ministry amidst the Hebrew speaking Jews did not present situations demanding his response. Paul, and the Pauline text in 1 Timothy, make specific references to same-sex relations in three specific texts, and each with a negative connotation.

Paul's statement in Romans is explicit regarding same-sex relations and is descriptive in nature rather than prescriptive. In this text Paul does not state what Christians should or should not do, but rather, he describes the consequences of rebelling against God and turning to one's own passions as an object of desire and even worship (Ro. 1:25). At the same time, in reading Paul's statement in Romans 1:26-27, it is difficult to conclude otherwise than that Paul would say that those who are 'righteous' would not or ought not do these things. The word 'unnatural' (1:26) is a translation of the Greek phrase *para physin* which is standard terminology in other ancient texts for homoerotic acts. From this, it can be argued that Paul clearly identifies homosexual relations as sinful and contrary to God's purpose for men and women.[127]

The biblical concept of sin is not restricted to specific acts but addresses the fundamental structure of all that is human, including sexuality. This is the context of Paul's statement concerning homosexual relations. "The wrath of God is revealed from heaven against all ungodliness," Paul writes. Therefore, none are better than another, for all are "under the power of sin" (Ro. 1:18; 3:9).

At no point does Paul elaborate on his reasons for his negative view of same-sex relations. From other contemporary sources, however, scholars have discovered that homoerotic acts were viewed as 'willful' disregard for one's natural relations with the opposite sex and 'lustful' excess of sexual desire extending beyond what was 'natural' within the marriage relationship.[128] According to some theologians, the context of the biblical texts that appear to condemn same-sex relation are culturally determined. They suggest that what is forbidden is not consenting, committed same-sex relations grounded in love, but rather the use of same-sex relations in idolatrous worship, the sexual use of a boy by an adult male, and as a threat to what was considered to be 'natural' sexual relations between men and women. Consequently, some conclude that the Bible is silent regarding contemporary same-sex relations grounded in love and fidelity.[129]

I have debated this issue at several denominational assemblies with those who support ordination of homosexual persons to pastoral ministry. The claim was made that all of the biblical texts that appear to condemn same-sex relations refer to situations other than committed, same-sex relations in our culture, and therefore the 'Bible is silent' with regard to homosexual relations that are committed and based on mutual love. My response was to say that 'the silence was broken' in the creation texts of

Genesis 1:26-27, "In the image of God he created them, male and female
he created them." This, of course, was usually met by the response that
this text could not possibly be construed so as to forbid same-sex relations.
My response was, then we know where the debate must begin, not with
biblical texts regarding same-sex relations but with the creation text where
human sexuality is asserted to be grounded in the image of God a male
and female differentiation. Without some agreement on this basic text,
the discussion of same-sex orientation and relationship will be difficult
at best, if not impossible.

The purpose of this chapter is to present critical theological reflection
on the issues concerning homosexuality as both an orientation and practice within the contemporary Christian community. The following points
summarize my conclusions drawn from the above discussion and serve
to introduce the next and major concern of the chapter.

First, it is admitted by all that there are no positive statements in the
biblical literature regarding same-sex relations, regardless of what the
context may be. At best, those who argue that same-sex relations that take
place between committed and loving human partners are within God's
purpose, must argue from silence.

Second, the argument from silence requires that one dismiss the unique
and original appeal to nature in Paul's statement in Romans chapter one.
The allusions to nature in vs. 20, 25 suggest that Paul held to a divinely
created order with regard to human sexuality. Other statements in the
Pauline literature regarding the significance of the one-flesh heterosexual
relation (1 Cor. 6:16; 7:1-9; cf. Ephesians 54:31-33) make it inconceivable
that Paul would contravene that order by allowing for same-sex genital
relationships.[130]

Third, the distinction between homosexual orientation and homosexual
acts, as understood today appear to have been unknown or, at least, of
little concern to the Hebrew people. Indeed, the concept of a psychological or biological predisposition to homoerotic relations appears to be a
modern one quite foreign to a biblical worldview.[131]

Fourth, the moral issues relating to homosexuality are not determined
solely by whether or not homosexuality is an orientation or a practice
but by the way in which one's sexuality is related to the intrinsic nature
of human personhood as created in the image of God. This leads us to
the deeper issue of the nature and purpose of human sexuality itself as
taught by Scripture.

Fifth, a theological and pastoral approach to the issue of homosexuality within the church must take into account a wider spectrum of biblical

teaching than merely the few texts that condemn specific homosexual acts. The theological predispositions, I will argue, are more significant than discussion based solely on homosexual references in the biblical text.

Theological Assumptions

If the biblical texts that mention homosexual acts are read in such a way that the intent of the author is disregarded in favor of a reading that is relative only to the cultural context of its own time, this 'deconstructs' the text in such a way that no certain meaning can be gained that speaks to our present situation. If the biblical texts are judged to have no relevance for contemporary issues concerning homosexual orientation and practice, the use of such texts will only lead to a rhetorical standoff. The result will be an impasse that makes serious discussion of the moral, theological and pastoral issues involved impossible. There will remain differences, to be sure. But what is important is that these differences be grounded in the basic assumptions that are held concerning the nature of human sexuality itself as related to the image of God. The purpose of this chapter is not to resolve the impasse created by scholars who argue the fine points of linguistic exegesis, though that work remains to be done. What I attempt here is what might be called a theological exegesis of the biblical teaching concerning human sexuality, both in the original intention of creation as well as in its fallen and often tragic state.

Theologically, we only see perfection through the grace of God experienced through imperfection. We are not first of all concerned, then, with homosexuality but with human sexuality and specifically, with human personhood as bound to human biology.

The biblical teaching regarding human sexuality is linked with the statement that humans are created in the image and likeness of God, male and female. "Then God said, 'Let us make humankind in our image, according to our likeness; and let them have dominion over the fish of the sea, and over the birds of the air, and over the cattle, and over all the wild animals of the earth, and over every creeping thing that creeps upon the earth.; So God created humankind in his image, in the image of God he created them; male and female he created them" (Genesis 1:26-27).

I have chosen two modern theologians, Emil Brunner and Karl Barth as representative of two approaches to the theological question as to the relation of human sexuality to the image of God. Brunner separates the statement concerning the divine image from the statement concerning male and female. This interpretation allows for the divine image as constitutive of human personhood to be located primarily in the person as a spiritual and moral being without regard to biological sexual differentiation. Barth, on the other hand, links human sexual differentiation at the biological level with the divine image including both.

These two ways of relating sexuality to the image of God will account for differing views as to the relation of homosexuality to human personhood. Those who hold that sexual differentiation is not an essential aspect of the divine image will tend to view the moral issue of homosexuality as grounded solely in the quality of the personal encounter. Others, who hold that sexual differentiation is an essential aspect of the divine image believe that sexual orientation as well as sexual practice is part of the intrinsic order of human personhood. Let us consider each in turn.

Human sexual differentiation not included in the Divine Image

Figure 11.1 presents a schematic diagram of a contemporary approach to human personal and sexual relations based on the premise that human personal sexual relations are not grounded in created sexual/biological differentiation. In this view, the sexual identity of persons created in the image of God does not include biological sexual differentiation as determinative of human sexual relations. Same-sex relations are considered to be natural and normal in the same way that heterosexual relations are. The biological and the personal do not overlap, as shown in the figure below.

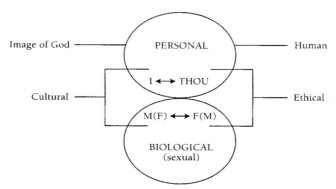

Figure 11.1 The personal and biological spheres

In this model, the personal I-Thou sphere is only linked with the male/female biological sphere by cultural and ethical structures of society. This understanding leads to the claim that sexual orientation and behavior are a matter of human and civil rights (ideological) in the same way that racial and ethnic aspects of humans are based on 'rights' rather than 'nature.' In this view, to judge same-sex orientation and relations as inappropriate or wrong, is to discriminate against the basic rights of individuals to express their personal sexual orientation freely and with the full social acceptance and affirmation as those of differing skin color or ethnic origin.

With regard to human sexuality, Emil Brunner held that the erotic sexual impulse is an "unbridled biological instinct" which can only be consecrated through marriage, or the ethical demand of abstinence.[132] While Brunner did not develop his view to the point that homosexual relations were appropriate, his only argument against them was an ethical one, grounded in human culture, and the use of the biblical texts as applying to contemporary same-sex relations. As we have seen, to the degree that his ethical position depends upon these texts, any argument against homosexuality will carry little weight with those who see the texts as quite unrelated to the kind and quality of homosexual relations under consideration in our contemporary culture.

When human sexuality is considered as primarily biological and in the same category as race and ethnic origin, the issue of discrimination, equal rights, and justice become the criteria for deciding the issue. There is ample biblical witness in support of such rights and equal justice if homosexual orientation and practice is considered solely from the grounds of human personal relationships with no biological aspect involved.

Human sexual differentiation an essential aspect of the Divine Image

Karl Barth argued that human sexuality is a manifestation of the image of God as co-relation (co-humanity) and that the mark of the human is this same co-relation grounded in sexual differentiation as male and female, male or female.[133] The only differentiation at the personal and social level with ontological (created being) status is thus human sexuality. The creation of Eve was more than a replication of humanity in the form of a numerical multiplication, suggests Barth. The solitariness of Adam would not have been overcome by another male for such a one could not confront him as 'another' but he would only recognize himself in it. Consequently, Barth considered homosexuality as "humanity without the fellow man."[134]

Barth's view leads to what one might call an 'ordered ontology' by which sexual differentiation as male and female is grounded in the personal being of humanity. By 'ordered ontology,' I mean that every human has an essential created structure which is sexually and personally differentiated, as male and female, male or female. In this view, sexual differentiation at both the personal and biological level is one aspect of the structured being (ordered ontology) of human life, while skin color and ethnic distinctions are related solely to the biological and cultural.

Figure 11.2 presents a schematic diagram of such an approach which grounds the personal and biological differentiation of male and female, male or female, in the image of God as created and intended by God and determinative of essential humanity. In this model, the personal sphere overlaps with the biological sphere so that the image of God as constitutive of humanity includes biological sexual differentiation.

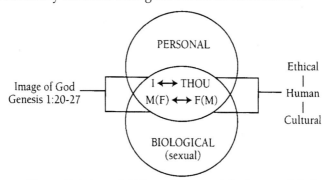

Figure 11.2. Sexual differentiation and the image of God

If one takes Genesis 1:26-27 as the foundational text for understanding human sexuality as rooted in the divine image, sexual orientation may be considered a personal and biological differentiation expressed through the 'ordered ontology' of male and female, male or female. A theological perspective on homosexuality thus does not rest alone upon biblical texts that speak against homosexuality, but also upon the foundational biblical texts that set forth a view of human sexuality as an 'ordered ontology' of personal and biological differentiation.

It can be argued, as Barth does, that there is an implicit semantic parallelism between the statement about the divine image and male and female sexuality, not only a formal parallelism. Barth protests that dividing the sentence in the text so as to separate the statement about the image from the statement about sexual differentiation is arbitrary and unwarranted. "Is it not astonishing," Barth exclaims, "that again and again expositors have ignored the definitive explanation given by the text itself [i.e., Genesis 1:26-27)], . . . Could anything be more obvious than to conclude from this clear indication that the image and likeness of the being created by God signifies existence in confrontation, i.e., in this confrontation, in the juxtaposition and conjunction of man and man which is that of male and female, and then go on to ask against this background in what the original and prototype of the divine existence of the Creator consists?"[135]

It is this basic theological assumption that led Barth to conclude that same-sex genital relations are prone to confusion and distortion of the divine image. I realize that this view presents difficulties, including some recent research that seems to point to the fact that at least some homosexual orientation is caused by genetic factors.[136] or, by psychopathological factors outside of the individual's control.[137] In the discussion that follows I will attempt to deal with some of these problems and develop the thesis that human sexuality is grounded essentially in the image of God and is a 'created order' represented by differentiation as male and female, male or female.

Following Barth, I suggest that theological criteria derived from biblical revelation concerning human sexuality is the basis for moral guidelines, and not the reverse. If the theological assumption is held that sexual differentiation is part of an essential order rooted in the divine image and expressed through each person's biological nature, it follows that homosexual relations cannot be affirmed as belonging to that order in the same way as heterosexual relations. As I will show below under pastoral considerations, the context of human sexuality under the conditions of fallen humanity is always less than ideal and that moral judgments concerning the sexual life of persons must be conditioned by compassion.

The Genetic Issue in the Homosexual Debate

Some have claimed that recent research seems to point to the fact that at least some homosexual orientation is caused by genetic factors or, by psychopathological factors outside of the individual's control, though conclusions drawn remain somewhat inconclusive.[138] Burr cites Hooker's attempt to correlate homosexual orientation to responses to the Rorschach test. Three eminent psychologists interpreted the results and concluded that no such correlation could be found. Her study, along with many others, led to the decision of the American Psychiatric Association in 1973 to remove homosexuality from its Diagnostic and Statistical Manual. By and large, psychologists today do not recognize homosexuality to be pathological and thus most do not attempt to change sexual orientation.

Research into possible hormonal and biological predisposition to homosexual orientation has been both promising and puzzling. Burr suggests that evidence of hormonal factors as a predisposition toward sexual orientation remains inconclusive, and fails to answer the question: If hormones influence sexual orientation, what influences the hormones?[139] The quest for genetic markers leading to sexual orientation has led to findings that appear to be more compelling, though surrounded by a host of unanswered questions as to the implications. The final irony, says Burr, is that if sexual orientation, like left or right-handedness, can be shown to be genetically determined, the conclusion will be morally irrelevant. If God made some persons gay, Burr argues, then the only thing that hurts them is hatred and ignorance.

It is not within the scope of this chapter to assess the validity of such scientific claims. At the same time, the moral issue remains, particularly for theologians and pastors who are now confronted with the person who argues that sexual orientation is not a matter of 'choice' but is rooted to some degree in genetic predispositions. If sexual orientation is not a matter of individual choice in every instance, then how can one pass moral judgment upon the sexual practice of homosexuals whose only sexual preference can be toward members of the same sex?

For those whose theological assumption corresponds to the situation depicted in Figure 11.1, the argument that condemnation of homosexuality is unfair, discriminatory, and a violation of human rights is quite compelling. Same-sex relations, many theologians assert, can have the same moral content and be as expressive of the divine image as heterosexual ones. Heterosexual relations may also fail to express the image of God where the personal aspect is absent or diminished. This has been argued from the Roman Catholic[140] as well as the Protestant perspective.[141]

The situation is quite different, however, if one argues that biblical teaching upholds heterosexual relations as God's designed and preferred order for human sexual orientation as well as practice, as Figure 11.2 depicts. Is it unfair and a violation of human rights to expect all persons to conform to this ideal, especially when some claim that their sexual orientation was determined by factors over which they had no control? The answer depends upon how we have determined what is 'right' and 'fair.' In a broken world, moral issues are often laden with such complexity and tinged with personal pain that abstract moral criteria when applied can sometimes offend concrete moral sensibilities. No one has a choice with regard to being born and certainly not with regard to the physical, emotional and social conditions and context in which one is expected to enter life. Some regard life itself as unfair and reject it.

Pastoral Considerations

Self-fulfillment and human sexuality are linked by a sense of the tragic. Not every desire nor every possibility can be fully realized in this lifetime. Heterosexual relations are not exempt from living with sexual unfulfillment for the sake of commitment to personal values and goals.

This is to live with a sense of the tragic. If one takes Genesis 1:26-27 as the foundational text for understanding human sexuality as rooted in the divine image, then sexual orientation may be considered a personal and biological differentiation expressed through the 'ordered ontology' of male and female, male or female.

A biblical / theological perspective on homosexuality thus does not rest alone upon biblical texts that speak against homosexuality, but also upon the foundational biblical texts that set forth a view of human sexuality as an 'ordered ontology' of personal and biological differentiation. There is ample Scriptural authority for establishing both God's preference with regard to human relationships and God's presence with persons in their struggle to fulfill God's purpose for them through the labyrinth of confusion, failure and brokenness that often attends such a struggle. The Old Testament is replete with God's expressed preference for his people, but also contains a multitude of examples of God's presence as one who graciously forgives, restores and empowers within the limits and constraints of consequences and conventions.

If one holds that God's preference for human sexual relationships follows the created order of male and female rather than same-sex co-habitation, this does not rule out God's gracious presence in the lives of those who find it impossible to live by that divinely created preference. The church as the body of Jesus Christ, expresses both divine preference and divine presence in the lives of its members. All members of the body of Christ fall short of God's preference, including homosexual Christians. The church must be as inclusive as Christ's outreach into human society and as clear headed as Christ's vision of the created purpose for humans as bearing the image of God. At the same time, it would be a source of great confusion and grave error for the church to make God's presence the only means of grace and God's preference as the law which died with Christ. Both preference and presence are grounded in the grace of God, and both alike must be upheld in the teaching and practice of the church's ministry.

If homosexual Christians are members of the body of Christ on the same basis as all others--how could we say otherwise?--does this not grant them the same right to be leaders and teachers along with others? Not necessarily. Discrimination within the body as to who should be set aside for the teaching office entails both wisdom and discernment on the part of the church taking into account many criteria, including maturity, domestic stability, personal integrity and spiritual giftedness. Might not these criteria also include sexual orientation as well as sexual practice measured by the responsibility to uphold both divine preference as well as divine presence?

So, What About Todd and His Parents?

Is God's presence and the reality of Christ evident in Todd as well as his parents? If so, then they are each welcome as part of the body of Christ on the same basis. Grace does not issue ultimatums, only invitations to receive grace and grow in it as members of the same body. Is it God's preference that human sexuality be defined and experienced as male and female, male or female? If so, then the teaching of God's preference does not nullify the practice of God's presence. Can Todd be empowered and encouraged to be welcomed into both the church and the family on this basis? One can only hope that Pastor and people understand and demonstrate this gracious spirit. Can Susan remain an elder? Of course, for elders and leaders are as responsible to mediate God's presence as to proclaim God's preference.

The church's ministry to families must embrace the tragic as Christ does. There is both healing and hope when his arms are open.[142]

Chapter 12

Death in the Family

The call came from the hospital. "Pastor, the doctor has just informed us that our mother, Emma, must have a feeding tube inserted if she is to survive, as she can no longer ingest food by mouth. My two sisters and my dad don't want to do this as they feel that this would be contrary to her own wishes. But I can't agree. Pastor, can you come over and talk with us, we need help."

I knew the family well. They were members of the church of which I was pastor at the time, and each professed vital Christian faith. I had made several pastoral visits to the mother in the hospital. Emma was a 68 year-old grandmother who had two operations for cancer and prolonged chemotherapy treatment following her last surgery, It was her son, Joe, who called me. He was emotionally upset and angry with his siblings for even considering taking their mother home to die by slow starvation. "To do this is like killing her," he told me over the telephone. 'I think that we must just keep her alive so that there may be a chance that God could heal her in answer to our prayers."

At the hospital, in consultation with the doctor, it became clear that Emma was suffering from incurable cancer and that at best, even with a feeding tube, she could live only a few months. I learned one other thing; while she was barely conscious and unable to converse at this point, she had made it quite clear to her husband that the one thing that she did not want was to 'just become a vegetable' tied to a machine. "If I am to die," she told him, "I want to do it with dignity."

I now use this case as a basis for discussion with my students, some of whom are preparing for pastoral ministry and others for the practice of psychotherapy from a Christian perspective. What emerges in our discussion is that there are three overlapping spheres demanding mediation and decision. The physical sphere has become predominate with regard to her medical condition. The social sphere has become critical with regard to the family situation. And the spiritual sphere looms in the background, brought to the forefront by her son Joe's appeal for divine intervention.

A Biblical Paradigm

In reflecting on this case as a practical theologian, I look to the biblical story of creation for clues. The Bible is primarily written as a narrative of God's interaction with human beings from the story of creation through the drama of sin and redemption leading to a final vision of healing and hope. The book of Genesis describes the creation of the first humans in dramatic narrative form: ". . . the Lord God formed man from the dust of the ground, and breathed into his nostrils the breath of life; and the man became a living being" (Genesis 2:7). From this account the formation of humans from the dust of the ground points to the physical sphere in which personal being comes into existence and on which it is dependent for life itself. A second spiritual sphere of life is indicated by the 'breath of life' that appears to come directly from the divine Creator. Of no other creature is this said in the biblical account. The 'living being' which we call human being is essentially spiritual being.

The narrative does not end here. There is something missing. "Then the Lord God said, 'It is not good that the man should be alone; I will make him a helper as his partner'" (Genesis 2:18). What is lacking cannot be found through any of the other creatures that the Lord brought forth out of the ground (2:19-20). Only when the Lord has fashioned another human along side of the first (out of the rib!), is there human speech and human life: "Then the man said, 'This at last is bone of my bones and flesh of my flesh; this one shall be called Woman, for out of Man this one was taken'" (2:23). From this account, we can determine a third sphere of human life that is essential to being complete and whole, the social dimension. Only when there are two humans can it be said that it is 'good.'

We can look again at the drawing used in Chapter Seven of the three ecological spheres.

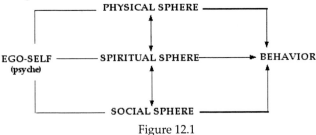

Figure 12.1

These three spheres--physical, social, spiritual--seem to constitute all of the possibilities in describing humans. Each sphere represents an ecological matrix in which humans exist. I use the term 'ecological' to indicate that the three spheres, while each has its own unique content, interface with each other so as to affect the condition of each.

Obviously the physical sphere includes the brain and whatever mental processes that emerge out of cerebral activity including emotion. The physical sphere also relates humans to the external world (including nonhuman creatures) while the social sphere relates persons to all other humans. The spiritual sphere then includes all that is meant by self-transcendence and openness to the spirit of others, including but not limited to other human persons. I will argue that no other sphere can be suggested that is equivalent to these three and one could not think of any aspect of human life and existence not included in these three.

The fact that these three spheres are derived from the biblical account of creation is not intended to suggest that knowledge of and access to these three are dependent upon any particular religious conviction. Instead, what is suggested is that any attempt to oppose a secular versus a sacred (religious) view of humanity is overcome by this ecological model. The model that I present is intended to function in a wholistic rather than a partial way. The fact that I have found a theological basis for this model in Scripture does not mean that it cannot be discovered and affirmed as an essential structure of humanity itself.

Reviewing the situation of Emma

The relevance of this model to the case presented at the beginning of this chapter can now be seen. The physical condition of Emma has produced a crisis in the social sphere of her relation to the family and of the members of the family to each other. By suggesting that divine intervention in answer to prayer be sought rather than suspending medical treatment, her son, Joe, focused on the spiritual sphere as a way of avoiding what appeared to be an inevitable and unacceptable outcome in the physical sphere. I realize that some families in the same situation might disregard the spiritual sphere and attempt to mediate the situation through only the physical and social spheres. At the same time, many of those who provide mental as well as physical health care are becoming increasingly aware of the significance of the role of prayer and other spiritual resources in just such situations.

For example, Claudia Wallis reports:

Some scientists are beginning to look seriously at just what benefits

patients may derive from spirituality. To their surprise, they are finding plenty of relevant data buried in the medical literature. More than
200 studies that touch on the role of religion have been ferreted out
by [Jeffrey] Levin of Eastern Virginia and the late Dr. David Larson, a
research psychiatrist formerly at the U.S. National Institutes of Health
and more recently at the privately funded International Centre for
the Integration of Health and Spirituality. Most of these studies offer
evidence that religion is good for one's health.[143]

In the case described above, Emma, the mother, is experiencing a devastating and debilitating loss of her physical strength that has already sup-
pressed the expression of her ego-self. The social sphere, represented by
her family (and the attending medical staff) are concerned and distressed.
At the same time, despite the lack of expression by the ego-self due to the
physical deterioration, Emma is considered to be as much present in a real
sense as when she could talk and express her feelings. We are reminded by
those who care for those who appear to be unconscious due to a comatose
situation, that we should always speak in their presence as though they
can hear, even though they cannot respond. This is to reinforce the fact
that the ego-self as representative of the personal life of each individual
is fully present in each of the three spheres, even though one or more of
the spheres may be virtually dysfunctional.

This is what Joe felt so strongly and why he expressed the hope that
divine intervention through prayer could reverse the physical deterioration and restore her to a degree of health sufficient to function once again
as part of the historical life of the family. As I counseled with him, it became apparent that it was not so much his faith in a miraculous healing
that caused him to resist the idea of allowing her to die, but rather his
emotional need to hang on to his mother's life even though she was unable to respond to him. I helped him to understand that she was indeed
fully present as the person that he loved despite her lack of physical
response. In addition, he acknowledged some guilt over not being able
to do anything to preserve her life, which he projected upon God in the
hope of a miraculous healing.

I reinforced the feelings of love that he had for her while, at the same
time, leading him to see that the reality of love is also vulnerable to the
loss of that which is loved. He had fused his love with the need to protect and preserve her life by any means. His faith was expressed through
the hope that the power of God through prayer would do what neither
he nor the doctors could do. It was actually his love for his mother that
empowered him to release her to God's power and enter with his family
into the sacred space where pain and suffering, even fear of death, can

be transformed by divine presence.

A Christian response to suffering and death

The reframing of the relation of love and power by reflecting on the presence of God in human pain and suffering is a way through our powerlessness rather than seeking to move away from it. Arthur McGill makes this clear, "As Christians we know how terrible and degrading is the anguish of bodily pain, of social rejection, of the silence of God." There is something almost demonic about such suffering. At the same time, McGill reminds us, "They also know that God's grace is moving them toward a world from which the demonic will have completely vanished."[144]

As my own father was dying of cancer at our home our family gathered around him to attend to his final hours. While he was unable to speak, he gave indication that he could hear and understand what we were saying by the movement of his eyes and small gestures with his hands, as if to punctuate sentences which were in his mind but impossible to express with the tongue. Within a few hours, even those responses ceased and he lay motionless, except for an occasional raising of his hand to rub his lower lip, a ritual familiar to us and so common to him that it required no conscious thought. At the end of 36 hours or so, there was no response and the doctor who made a brief visit said that the end was not far away.

It was on a Sunday morning. The Lutheran minister came by following the morning service and walked straight to his bedside. After only a brief greeting to the family he began to recite the 23rd Psalm. 'The Lord is my shepherd, I shall not want. He makes me to lie down in green pastures; . . . ' My father who had not moved a muscle for several hours, suddenly raised his hands and folded them across his chest! Those words, placed in his heart so many years ago, brought forth a response that confirmed for us that God was already beginning to lead him beside the still waters to restore his soul. Here too we experienced the ecological dynamic of the three spheres. Until his last breath he was fully present in the physical, social and spiritual reality of embodied human existence. He died with dignity, as was the expressed wish of Emma to her own family.

The case of Emma and her family with which we began this chapter reminds us that the spiritual sphere must not become a solitary refuge for our own pain and sense of loss. For her son, Joe, the reality of his mother's impending death was too great to bear. It may be that he had not yet dealt realistically with the fact that being physical beings, we are also mortal beings. What was normally a comfortable equation of physical, social and spiritual life in times of health, has now split apart and isolated him from the reality of his mother's condition as well as from his siblings and father.

In his grasp for spiritual hope through divine intervention he slipped into the kind of false hope against which Christian Beker professor of biblical theology at Princeton Seminary, warns when he says:

> When such perceptions of reality become too threatening or are deemed too pessimistic, we create forms of hope which are simply false hope, a result of our unwillingness to see the real world as it is. Thus they are based on the foundation of an illusion. Hope which is nourished by repression, illusion, blindness, or self-deception becomes false hope. Indeed, expectations and hopes which separate themselves from the realities of suffering in our world become demonic hopes; they cast a spell over us and mesmerize us. They are as destructive as the illusory hopes engendered by a drug trip. It is indeed characteristic of the apocalyptic climate of our time that just as the question of suffering numbs us, so the question of hope is divorced from any meaningful relation to suffering.[145]

What then is my task as a pastoral care giver in such a situation? First, I must provide a framework or gestalt of understanding by which Joe's emotional pain, perhaps guilt at not being able to sustain his mother in her need, and desperate reach for a divine solution can be disarmed and brought within an ecological context. By meeting him at the level of his own feelings I could assist him into gaining insight into his mother's feelings. Her expressed desire to die with dignity, clearly communicated and accepted by the others, is too threatening for him to grasp. When he is led into what his mother might be feeling, even at this very moment, about her own physical condition, he can re-enter the ecological matrix from which the shock of her impending death has expelled him. A decision to take Emma home and attend to her through the painful and yes, terrible, process of dying will tax the physical, social and spiritual strength of the caregivers. The fact that this family was finally able to make this decision and carry out this task in a fully human way gave Emma the dignity that she requested. In such times we discover the dignity and strength of our own humanity in upholding the humanity of another.

Theological Perspectives on the Value of Human Life

Human life is not 'sacred' in the sense that there is intrinsic 'holiness' in the psychical/physical organism that constitutes the natural life of the person. While humans are created in the image and likeness of God, we are creaturely beings with mortal bodies and subject to the dust from which we came (Genesis 3:19). Only God is holy, humans are not holy in the same sense as God. Theologian Otto Weber suggests that if holiness is to be attributed to humans, it is derived from relation to God and not an intrinsic value. "For the other creatures and for his fellow man, man is for God's sake and because of God not a thing but something holy (*sacrum*). This is also the background of 1 Corinthians 7:11f. But that 'holiness' is not inherent in man but resides in the special relationship to himself which God the Creator has granted."[146]

The value of human life is, however, an intrinsic value due to this divine image. What distinguishes the human from all other creatures is a spiritual orientation to and personal relation with God as Creator. One way of pointing to this distinctive is to recall that the texts that speak of the 'image and likeness of God' refer only to humans and not to non-human creatures (Gen. 1:26-27; 5:1; 9:6). While it is true that animals also were created as 'living souls,' there is no reference in Scripture to animals being created in the divine image and likeness (Gen. 1:20, 21, 24). In this regard, Old Testament theologian, W. Eichrodt says in his reflection on Psalm 8:4, "Ultimately, therefore it is a spiritual factor which determines the value Man sets upon himself, namely his consciousness of partnership with God, a privilege of which no other creation is considered worthy."[147]

Human life is not attached to a biological form of life as the only source of value or meaning. Quality of life cannot be determined solely by extending the biological life of human persons. The New Testament concept of human life is expressed more directly as *zoe* rather than *bios*. Zoe refers to a person's life made abundantly full, and this life is inseparable from Jesus Christ as the source of life (cf. John 10:10; 1 Tim. 6:11, 12, 19). Robert Nelson suggests that we might better speak of 'zoe-ethics' rather than bio-ethics.[148] In 1984, in Melbourne, Australia, the world's first baby developed from an embryo that was frozen, thawed and then implanted in her mother's womb was born. The baby was named 'Zoe'--gift of life![149]

Human life may often be experienced under 'marginal' conditions

Not everything that comes from the body of a human person is human--but some things are. Children conceived through a human sexual act are considered to be as fully human as their parents. The divine determination that constitutes humanity is, as far as I can see, joined to the human process by which children are conceived and born into this world. Because the biological process has a 'margin of error,' there is a certain marginality that accompanies the possibility of being human, at both birth and death. Most Christians would agree that at some point the creaturely (biological) form of human existence loses the power to determine the state of human personhood. A corpse that shows some remaining evidence of cell division due to chemical processes continuing, is nevertheless not still 'a person.' Otherwise an autopsy would come under the same category as surgery, for life in this case would be reduced merely to a biological process. Decisions must be made, and some are more difficult than others. Identifying human personhood with sheer biological existence is dangerously close to "worshipping and serving the creature rather than the Creator" (Rom 1:25). There is a semblance of idolatry in the glorification of the creature as an object of technological fascination. As technological competence proliferates, the line between 'nature' and 'technology' becomes blurred.

The 'marginal' condition of human life results from an insufficient or pathological form of life at the physical level. In a sense, all human life is marginal due to the fact that the physical sphere is liable to 'error' (for example, genetic abnormalities), to sickness and trauma, and finally, to death. In the face of the ambiguity of human life in such situations, some are tempted to determine the value of life as solely residing in the maintenance of the physical organism. In so doing the freedom and responsibility for making decisions with regard to withdrawing life support mechanisms are denied to the person as well as the community. From a biblical perspective human life is not an absolute value in terms of survival as a mere physical organism. This does not mean that such creaturely existence has no value; it has the full value of human life as long as there is the possibility for human life as determined in its total ecological structure of reality. The ethical implications of such issues as suicide, abortion, and euthanasia all bear upon this question of quality of life.[150]

The 'right to life' is qualified by the gift of life

Human life may be characterized as being both 'gift' and task.' Otto Weber says: "It is generally characteristic of the Old Testament that it does not make statements about 'nature' and 'being' but statements about 'the task' or a 'relationship.' As the being who is like God, man is supposed to do something. . . . [The image of God} endows him with a 'gift' and a 'task' (*Gabe* and *Aufgabe*)." [151] This means that no individual has an absolute right of disposal over one's own life; this 'right of disposal' or 'right to determine' one's own life violates the ecological structure of life. For example, in the biblical story Adam receives his own humanity as a gift in the form of the woman who is created out of his own 'not-yet-human being;' he has no right of disposal or determination over her being for her life in its concrete form represents the possibility of his own. Nor does he now have the right to absolute disposal or determination over his own life, for her humanity is now also contingent upon his existence as the 'gift' that constitutes her humanity.

Quality of life is qualified by the social as well as by the physical aspect of the self

This means that disorder at the 'I-thou' level of the self is capable of diminishing the quality of life as much as at the 'I-it' or 'I-self' dimension. Even as it could be a violation of the value of human life to be forced to live merely at the biological level, so it would be a violation of the value of human life to be forced to live in a role structure (economic, social, or political), which has as a consequence the deprivation of life as a gift to be with and for the other in a relationship of parity and reciprocity. Human rights are thus grounded in the ecological construct of humanity itself, not in an abstract principle mediated through self-determination; the other person has a right to my responsible action in upholding her own humanity; but not the right to kill me for failing in this responsibility. The 'right' to be free from a person or persons who diminish my own quality of life is qualified by my need of persons to uphold the gift of life which constitutes my humanity.

However, it must also be said that the meaningfulness of human life is more related to life as task than as gift. Life can lack meaning for the self while still possessing value as personal human life. For example, a sense of despair, or a period of depression, can produce suicidal thoughts where no sense of value is seen from an existential perspective. In this case, therapy must seek to restore the ecological construct of the self as a functional reality. Appeals to value of life in the face of existential meaninglessness will have little positive effect.

On the other hand, a sense of meaningful existence through a perception of life as a purposeful task carries with it a strong sense of value. For example, severe disability at the physical level for some persons appears to be compensated for by meaningful task orientation. The social and spiritual spheres of the self are the most direct source of meaning through a task orientation toward life. An example is the 'logo therapy' approach of Victor Frankl, where 'will to meaning' is experienced as the key to survival and function of the self under affliction, severe distress, and some level of incapacity at the psychical/physical level.[152]

From a Christian perspective faith can be understood more as the task of life in its orientation to the world, to others, and to God than as an existential experience and value. The 'task' of believing in God includes the task of living in real symbiosis with the world as creature and in real 'sym-zoesis' (to coin a word!) with others as a gift of life to life. Faith exists as a task of life in opposition to our experience and is often under attack by experience; for this reason, the meaningfulness of life is not an empirically derived value, nor is it susceptible to loss merely through empirical or experiential resistance. Otto Weber reminds us of this when he says,

> The voice of our own heart is as such not the voice of faith. That "I" am the person in the new constitution of existence is an immediate given of experience just as little as the reverse, that I cannot deduce from experience that "I" am a sinner. This opposition, which certainly exists in Christian experience, can only be understood on the basis of the Word addressed to us, as the opposition of our existence before God. [153]

So, the Apostle Paul, when contemplating the alternatives of continued life on earth under distress as compared with life with Christ (which, he stated, 'is far better'), found his answer in his life as a task of living out faith for the sake of others, and 'fruitful labor' for Christ (Phil. 1:19-26; cf. 2 Cor. 5:1-10). The biblical perspective of resurrection of the body answers to the question of the ultimate and real value of the physical aspect of human personhood. The transformation of the physical through resurrection provides continuity of personhood while, at the same time, allows the discontinuity of the physical to occur without violation of the integrity of personhood. Human life is an inviolable endowment. Because it is a contingent form of life and not determined solely by creaturely nature, it is not destroyed by the destruction of the flesh, though what torments the flesh afflicts the person in a real sense.

Assessing the criteria for determining quality of life

- The life of persons has value to the extent that it can be willed to survive in its concrete situation by the self and others as a totality.
- The value of life in its physical existence is relative to the degree of health and/or trauma to the total self as a result of biological incapacity to support life.
- Upholding life as personal value may entail a decision to release persons from the torment to the total person by the trauma to the body; in any case, a decision that death has occurred is a decision for and not against the value and dignity of persons.
- The so-called 'right to die' is not absolute, any more than is the 'right to life.' Living and dying take place as events which involve the whole person in an ecological structure of humanity.
- The 'border-line' of human existence can never be reduced to absolute boundaries on which abstract principle and technological capability

can be squarely placed; the criteria by which quality of life is to be assessed can be found in the human community's self-understanding as life endowed with a meaning and destiny beyond its creaturely power and potential.

- Decisions on this 'border-line' of human existence are not decisions which attempt to 'play God,' but rather, are decisions which seek to uphold God's purpose for this life and his provision for human life beyond death.

The Role of the Community in Upholding Quality of Life

The determination of humanity is a function and therefore a responsibility of human persons. But human persons do not first of all exist as discrete individuals with an ethical conscience. They exist first of all as co-humanity, in a polarity of relation through which the image and likeness of God is discerned as responsible love. The differentiation essential to humanity is knowledge of oneself in terms of the other. While the Genesis creation account does not refer explicitly to the term 'covenant' (berith), it does make it clear that existence in community (as co-humanity) is actually and logically prior to existence as a discrete human individual.

The biblical concept of covenant gives historical meaning to this fundamental order of humanity. Consequently, the people of God come into being as a covenant community and as such they are responsible for serving as the custodian and steward of the mystery of human life. Cain protests that he is not his 'brother's keeper,' but he surely is his brother's brother (Gen. 4:9). He is responsible for Abel's life, because both bear the imago Dei as a concrete and social structure of their human existence. The killing of Abel is also a moral outrage, but it is first of all an act against the imago Dei that cannot be destroyed in one without damaging the other. Cain has suffered damage to his own personhood before he comes under ethical guilt.

The ethical and the human

The rituals by which the covenant community enacts its own existence are anthropological rather than ethical or religious. The community knows what it is doing in bringing forth and sustaining life before it knows what it ought to do. It is responsible to be human, to be what it is determined to be. Thus the contingency of human existence as an occasion that occurs on the broad field of creatureliness is preserved, and the continuity of human existence is maintained at the same time. The human community under the determination of covenant love acts responsibly to recognize and preserve human life with a knowledge that is hidden to creaturely existence alone. At the margins of human existence, when the contingency is exposed most nakedly, the community undertakes the determination of whether human life is present or not, and it does so humanely (that is, theologically), not merely ethically.

Even the disorder of human being through sin does not destroy the covenant basis on which the human exists. Indeed, the covenant becomes even more explicit as the gracious provision by which human life is supported. When Cain kills Abel he comes under the universal and ethical principle of being a murderer. Under this principle some might have warrant for exacting vengeance in the name of justice. But the divine covenant love, concerned to uphold humanity anticipates this ethical absolutism and neutralizes it. The 'mark of Cain' is a gracious act by which the Creator upholds Cain's humanity and forbids those who would attempt to destroy him as a 'favor to divine justice.' One cannot use human sin as an excuse to transfer the responsibility for stewardship of the mystery of life from persons to abstract principles. Even as sinners, the community of God's people are a human community. As such they are responsible to recognize and exercise that humanity in obedience to God. Thus faith becomes the source of obedience, not conformity to ethical principles--though it must be added immediately that ethical principles are entailed in faith. It is just that faith is not entailed in ethical principles, nor is obedience to God.

The original contingency between true humanity and creatureliness, experienced as differentiation (co-humanity) was resolved into creaturely determinism at the fall. But divine reconciliation reintroduces the contingency and thus liberates humanity from this fate. Through the covenant love now expressed as reconciliation, humanity is once more set within the limits of divine determination as a creaturely order of being. The Ten Commandments are premised upon the law of covenant love (Rom. 13:8-10) and are themselves based on a divine act of reconciliation which restored the humanity of Israel through the Exodus (Exod. 20:2). The Commandments reflect the two-fold law: "You shall love the Lord your God with all your heart, and with all your soul, and with all your mind . . . and your neighbor as yourself" (Matt. 22:37, 39; Lev. 19:18). Love of God entails love of neighbor. This has never been repealed in favor of a more abstract principle of human responsibility. Accordingly, the people of God became the custodians of the mystery which represents human life.

Embracing the mystery

At an earlier stage of human knowledge, sheer naiveté about the process of life permitted more tolerance with respect to locating human personhood in the life process. Life and death were once primarily observational, de facto determinations. But today we know too much about the biological process that sustains life, and how to either initiate or prolong the process to allow this kind of tolerance. Since human life has been demythologized more precision is required. Naiveté permitted mystery to be embraced as a ritual of community, where decisions regarding personhood were made on non-technical grounds. But with the loss of naiveté came also the banishment of mystery. Modern science knows too much about life to entrust it to the rituals of community. A new order of priests has arisen, who are pledged to serve the laws of natural life. But there are encouraging signs of change. It is now customary for the sterile environment of the delivery room to be open to parents to experience the mystery of birth together. So also the experience of dying has come to be recognized as a ritual appropriate to a hospice setting, if not a home.

The very nature of human personhood is linked to the human community as determinative of its existence. This determination is not arbitrary, but accords with its understanding of the divine determination by which human life is in conjunction with but not ultimately determined by creaturely existence. The conception, embryonic existence, gestation, and birth of a human person is as much a ritual of the human community by which it is responsible to recognize and affirm humanity as it is a biological process. It is both, of course, but here is precisely the mystery that the community can grasp in a knowing and responsible way. The loss of naiveté does not entail the banishment of mystery.

The organic death and expulsion of an embryo is not an event in the process of human existence that can be determined to be either human or anti-human on the basis of either ethics or biological science alone. Both must participate in providing insight and information, but neither can fully grasp what is at stake with regard to human personhood. For neither can comprehend contingency and mystery as a state of being. The claim that an individual has a right over his or her own body and is therefore free to decide for or against the beginning or ending of human personhood does not accord with the theology of human personhood outlined above. This concept of 'human rights' is alien to a biblical understanding of human life. Human personhood is a determination of creaturely being in such a way that co-humanity is the fundamental structure of personal existence. What is called a decision in regard to particular case situations in which human personhood is at stake is actually a theological determination which the community is prepared to support and enact as an affirmation of the true order of personhood. The role of the community,

whether immediate family, or extended family, is charged with the task
of upholding the life of its members so far as possible.

Human rights as liberation

In a certain sense this constitutes a limitation on human rights expressed in the form of autonomous, individualistic actions. Yet at the same
time, it liberates the person from the tyranny of a deterministic morality
that measures the personal against an abstract principle. There is liberation also from the tyranny of a naturalistic ideology by which the personal
is subordinated to an impersonal technocracy that measures human life
in terms of electrical impulses on a scope. Recognizing the mystery that
clings to the contingent relation by which humanity exists in creaturely
form, the human community will not surrender personhood to unrelenting disorder. Instead, it claims its responsibility to affirm the true order
of personhood by liberating persons from sheer disorder--for example,
existence as a mere 'vegetable' connected to a machine.

However, the determination to permit the termination of creaturely life
for the sake of personhood by removing extraordinary means for survival
is a responsibility that can only be rooted in a theological understanding
of human existence as co-humanity. Such a determination must be rooted
in a profoundly 'liturgical' act of the community itself, by which its own
existence is determined by the reality of God.

Only here can fear and trembling lead to faith and conviction. Legal
and ethical concerns are by no means irrelevant in critical cases where
human life becomes marginal. But these concerns are insufficient to safe-
guard the mystery of human existence when it is subjected to situations
that jeopardize not only its existence but its dignity.

The concerns of which we speak ought not to be excluded in determining the fate of human life in extraordinary situations. And on occasion
only the community of God's people will have the courage and faith to
do what must be done, even at the risk of becoming an accomplice in
ethically ambiguous actions. Here again we must be reminded that this
involves an (ethical) judgment against that which is disobedient and in
disorder as well as a summons to repentance and faith.

Were the community of Christ to assume that it can merely act for the
'good of humanity' in general, it would fail to understand its own theological structure as a community also under judgment which, through faith
and the gift of the Holy Spirit, exercises a true knowledge of God and thus
of real humanity. The ancient liturgical acts were actions of community
before they became religious acts. These acts are not merely primitive,

they are deeply human. And as such, express deeply human needs and longings as well as penetrate the mystry of divine reality.

A liturgical act of a father's faith

One Sunday afternoon the father of a four-year-old boy called me as his pastor. The boy had been struck by a car and was in a coma. The father--who was also a medical doctor--was at his side in the hospital. I joined the vigil, waiting for some sign of hope that the boy's life would be preserved, despite a crushed skull and the resulting swelling of the brain under the effects of a serious contusion. After thirty-six hours, the father spoke to me quietly. "I am going to take one more EEG reading," he said, "and if that shows no sign of life then I would like to disconnect the machines which are keeping him breathing. We can keep the body functioning for a few more days, at least, but I believe that we should release him to be with God if that is his will."

This father was not asking for my opinion. He was seeking a confirmation that what he believed about the nature of human personhood is true. To allow a person to die, even a four-year-old boy, was not the end of his life but the beginning. Should we prolong or hinder that transition, or accept it with faith? As a minister of Jesus Christ and a representative of the community to which the family belonged, could I affirm a truth in that situation in which the mystery of that boy's life could be sustained even through death? Was I willing as such a representative of the community of Christ to become an accomplice of this event, or would I abandon the father to his scientific training and his tormented love? In prayer and faith, we agreed that extraordinary measures to prolong the mechanical functions of breathing were beyond that which was demanded by the dignity of the person in that boy. There was a deeper sense of the dignity of honoring the sovereignty of God, even in death. And so together we began the processional which led to the grave.

This is an 'awe-ful' responsibility, and it can only be done with fear and trembling. The church as the community of God's people must have the theological nerve to enter into such an act on the part of one of its members. One could speculate endlessly on the ethical implications of the act without coming to a conclusion that would guarantee the innocence of those responsible to decide the issue. Perhaps ethical innocence is not even an option when human existence becomes marginal. One is responsible to do the will of Christ, which is ordinarily not for the individual to decide, but for the community itself, or for its members who act in complicity with each other.

At the graveside service for this little boy, the father asked that the casket be opened. He drew a letter out of his pocket, placed it reverently on the breast of his son and said "I have written a letter to Gary telling him of what we have done and what we believe." This was a liturgical act not required by the professional pastor's funeral manual. But it was an authentic act in respect of the humanity of Gary as well as a sacrament of life beyond death. Who am I to challenge that? On what grounds would anyone wish to challenge it? I allow Abraham to ascend Mount Moriah, though I cannot explain to others why I do not try to stop him. His act of faith is too terrible for me to comprehend, yet I bow before his act as a manifestation of the power and reality of God in his life. Being human is no easy task, for our own humanity is at stake when another's is called into question.

Being human is ultimately a theological form of existence. It is one thing to have delineated the form of the human, and quite another to grasp my own humanity in the concrete moment in which it is put under trial. It is one thing to have outlined the reality of being human under the various aspects of the theological curriculum; it is quite another to become human through the labyrinth of errors that confronts us without and within. The community that serves as the context of human personhood must define itself in accordance with the theological and liturgical framework of its own existence as the people of God. To be part of such a community is the core of our humanity.

Addendum

The issue of prolonging life with the insertion of a feeding tube in the case of person with a terminal illness is discussed by Joanne Lynn and Joan Harrold (M. D.s) in a book titled, *Handbook for Mortals*.[154] The following are some excerpts from this Handbook.

"Why is it sometimes so hard to let a patient go without eating? In all cultures and throughout all history, offering food has been a sign of caring and hospitality. Our mothers made sure we were well fed. Most people enjoy eating with family and friends, especially on special occasions. In most religions, food is part of sacred rituals. It is no wonder, then, when someone we love is unable to eat and drink naturally, that we feel compelled to 'feed' them in some way It seems to be basic caring. But, as death approaches, you will not 'keep up your strength' by forcing yourself to eat when it makes you uncomfortable. If eating is a social event for you, or providing food is one of the common ways of expressing caring in your family, loss of appetite may be distressing to you and your loved ones.

You might enjoy small amounts of home-cooked food, dishes that mean something special to you. However, you should also know that a decrease in appetite is natural and eating less may increase, rather than decrease comfort. Because most dying people are more comfortable without eating or drinking near the end of life, forcing food or liquids is usually not beneficial, especially if restraints, IVs, or hospitalization would be required. Not forcing someone to eat or drink is not letting him 'starve to death.' The truth is, for those who are dying, the times come when it might be more compassionate, caring, even natural, to allow a natural dehydration to occur. Forcing tube feedings and IVs on dying patients can make the last days of their lives more uncomfortable."

"Many people can be supported with artificial feeding even though they do not seem to be conscious. Some stroke patients may never again respond to any stimuli. Many young people have suffered head trauma and are also permanently unconscious. . . . The courts and medical practice have ruled it acceptable to withhold or withdraw tube feedings from such patients. This not taking an action to kill the patient; rather it is allowing a natural death to occur. Again, all the advantages of dehydration in any dying patient will benefit these patients in their last days. They can die a comfortable and peaceful death. The real struggle for the families of these patients is an emotional and spiritual one. Can we let go? Are continuing the artificial feeding for us or the patient? If the patient could make his or her own choice would the choice be to withdraw treatment and allow a natural, peaceful death?"

The web site for the Division of Church in Society, Evangelical Lutheran Church in America provides a Christian perspective on this issue.[155] The following are some excerpts:

"When medical judgment determines that artificially administered nutrition and hydration will not contribute to an improvement in the patient's underlying condition or prevent death from that condition, patients or their legal spokespersons may consider them unduly burdensome treatment. In these circumstances it may be morally responsible to withhold or withdraw them and allow death to occur. This decision does not mean that the family and friends are abandoning their loved one. When artificially administered nutrition and hydration are withheld or withdrawn, family, friends, health care professionals, and pastor should continue to care for the person. They are to provide relief from suffering, physical comfort, and assurance of God's enduring love."

Chapter 13

Ministry to the Family
in a Postmodern Culture

The shift from a modern to a postmodern view of reality challenges the basic assumptions which form a Christian perspective of moral and spiritual values as the foundation of family life. The emphasis on diversity rather than uniformity, and relativity rather than certainty with regard to what is true, appears to confuse if not threaten the mission of the church to a multicultural and pluralistic society. My purpose is to develop a core social paradigm out of the creation story in Genesis which identifies essential components of human existence underlying all cultural forms and practices. Cultural diversity can thus be allowed as expressive to some degree of the essential components of the core social paradigm without relativizing true moral and spiritual reality to cultural perceptions and practices. A biblical theology of the family then can be developed based on the core social paradigm that defines family as image of God, as a social context for identity formation, as a moral context for character formation, and as the domestic context of spiritual formation.

The Gospel of the Kingdom and the Gospel of the Family

The first century Christian community came into existence where the social and political orders were largely determinative of family life. The traditional Jewish social structure bound family life to the rigid requirements of the law as interpreted by the scribes and enforced by the religious authorities. For the Gentile world, the secularizing of sacred myths and concepts were used to provide stability and continuity. In the face of these structures which demanded loyalty and conformity, Jesus taught a radical gospel of the Kingdom that challenged the priority of these older structures and which appeared to set aside family relations as dispensable. "And everyone who has left houses or brothers or sisters or father or mother or children or fields, for my name's sake, will receive a hundredfold, and will inherit eternal life" (Matt. 19:29, see also, Luke 14:26; Mark 10:29-30)

The gospel of the Kingdom was itself thought to contribute to the breakdown of these essential social constructs of marriage, family, parental obedience, and even the economic and political structures. The radical demands of the Kingdom were indeed couched in terms which challenged these structures as having a prior claim upon men and women. Yet, when we observe the actual practice of Jesus, we see that he affirmed the validity of these very structures, even though they were relativized to the demands of the Kingdom of God. What is questioned in the sayings of Jesus concerning the radical demands of the Kingdom is one's captivity to these domestic and social relationships, not their role in upholding human life. The coming of the Kingdom of God means the end of the absolute hold, the 'spell' which the social and natural order has over the person who is first of all determined by God to be free to love him and also to love the neighbor. The Kingdom of God values love as the core of discipleship. There is a gospel of the family included in a gospel of the Kingdom.

In his letter to the Ephesian Christians, the apostle Paul drew out the implications of the gospel of Christ in such a way that the basic structures of that society were to be 'humanized' through the activation of the Spirit and law of Christ. Paul did not seek to replace their culture with a concept of a 'Christian culture.' Rather, he called for the liberation of authentic human life within the culture as a freedom from the 'magical' as well as from the mythical.

In this context, Paul provided a criterion of Christian community which is grounded in the identification of Christ himself with those in whom his Holy Spirit dwells. Here too, both Jew and Gentile must learn to shift their obedience and loyalty from traditional concepts of authority by which they sought stability and order, to the structure of social life regulated by the community as the body of Christ (Eph. 2:11-22). The foundational social structures of family, marriage, parents and children, as well as the existing political and economic structures are basically affirmed as good and necessary. Yet, all of these structures are radically qualified by the 'humanization of humanity' which occurred through Jesus Christ (Eph. 5, 6).

In drawing persons around him Jesus re-created humanity in the form of a community of shared life and common identity. Even this narrower circle, defined by the specific calling of the twelve, was structurally open to the 'unclean' leper, the tormented demoniac, the self-righteous Pharisee, and the women of ambiguous reputation. In contact with Jesus humanity was liberated from the blind and capricious powers of nature and disease, as well as from the cruel and inhuman practices of the social and religious tyranny of the powerful over the weak. In the real humanity of Jesus we see the humanization as well as the socialization of humanity.

The Incarnation and the Humanizing of Human Social Structures

For Christian theology the event of the Incarnation of God in Jesus Christ is understood as a social paradigm by which human nature and destiny is defined and determined. A Christian anthropology does not begin with the 'humanity of man' in seeking to find relationship with God. Rather, a Christian anthropology begins with the 'humanity of God' as observed in the historical person, Jesus Christ, and with the social structure of the new human community within which he himself is known.

This approach does not deny the empirical form of humanity as we know it in our own experience, but makes possible the perception of humanity within its own social and cultural setting without confusing the social and cultural form of humanity with the core social structure of humanity itself. At the same time, this allows the particular form of humanity in its cultural setting to retain its distinctive.

If there is a culture which belongs to the Kingdom of God and which transcends all other cultures, it is a culture of true humanity as the gracious power and presence of Christ in a structure of human social and personal relations. This culture of the Kingdom of God has no other language and no other custom other than that of the particular people and society who become its manifestation. Yet, these existing social and cultural forms are relativized to the real humanity of Jesus Christ as expressed through the embodiment of the gospel in the lives of Christians. One culture is not relativized to another culture, as has so often tragically happened in the missionary expansion of the church. Rather, every culture is related to the critical construct of real humanity through the power of the gospel. And to that extent, every culture can bear in its own social structures the reality of the Kingdom of God, and make manifest the humanity of the Kingdom through its own forms.

One of the most devastating effects of social chaos is the breakdown of existing structures within any culture that are assumed to provide social stability and moral authority. Being human means living as this specific person belonging to these particular people who speak the same language and participate in the same rituals of community life. All human self-perception is thus culturally conditioned and socially approved. Not to have the social approval of one's own people is to suffer estrangement, if not derangement. Jesus himself experienced this powerful social judgment when he was thought to have an unclean spirit by the standard of the self-perception of the Pharisees (Mark 3:30). Even his mother, brothers and sisters sought to intercept his ministry and remove him from public exposure because they concluded that "he is beside himself" (Mark 3:21).

The effects of human sin and the fall, as recorded in the third chapter of Genesis, were experienced as the breakdown and confusion of the core social structure which bound the first humans to each other and, together, to God. From that point on, the social and cultural patterns of human life reflected to a certain degree distortion, alienation, and conflict. The moral and spiritual integrity of human life is bound up in the social structures particular to each society and culture. Humans cannot exist apart from some social structure, even those that are less than perfect and, in some cases, actually corrupt. The Kingdom of God exposes sin and seeks to overcome its effects through the liberation of humans from the sinful structures which stand as an authority over them, as well as from the inner motives of pride and self seeking that tend to undermine all authority.

The effects of sin are overcome, not through a more rigorous form of spirituality, but through a renewed structure of sociality. Love is defined as living peaceably in a domestic setting, as clothing the naked and feeding the hungry, and as loving the neighbor as oneself.

Concepts of human rights, of justice, of concern for the unborn and the aged, are not ethical perceptions subject to cultural modification. Rather, they are constraints upon individual and collective actions that would violate the very structure of humanity itself. When Jesus healed on the Sabbath, ate with publicans and sinners, and asked a Samaritan women to minister to his thirst, he penetrated through all racial, sexual, social and cultural barriers to restore true humanity to others. Indeed, his own humanity could hardly have been the true humanity that it was if he had drawn back from the real humanity of others. Nor did Jesus institute some new ethical concept of the good as a kind of 'Christian ethic.' He merely reinstated the criterion of goodness that belongs to true humanity as the ethical foundation for all of the laws and commandments.

This same criterion was quite clear to the prophet Micah: "He has told you, O mortal, what is good; and what does the Lord require of you but to do justice, and to love kindness, and to walk humbly with your God?" (Micah 6:8)

The Core Social Paradigm and Family Formation.

Human beings are defined by the social structures of their behavior as well as by the ritual forms of their culture. Hidden within every culture lies an implicit social paradigm of humanity. This implicit social paradigm is the pre-critical mass out of which social theories are developed and with which cultural anthropologists and philosophers work. All humans exist essentially in concrete social relationships or what I have called a core social paradigm. Herbert Anderson helpfully points this out:

> A theology of the family is shaped by two similarly contradictory principles. First, the family is a necessary component of creation. Despite wide diversity of form and function throughout human history, the family has fulfilled God's intent to provide a context for creation and care in order to insure the continuity of the human species. . . There is no known human community without family in some form.[156]

Experience of family is indispensable to the development of personhood; it is the 'world' of the child, as the Berger's put it.[157] In this sense, family can be said to be that 'locale,' or 'world' where this socialization takes place. No cultural form of the family can completely conceal or deny the nature of humanity as it confronts us in the sheer objectivity of core social relations. We know humanity in the concrete form of its being humanity; this is discovered in the core social paradigm. All theories as to the nature of persons in the generic sense of human being are culturally relative. If it is also accepted that a social paradigm of humanity lies behind each particular culture, then it is possible that the social structure of humanity contains elements of a common denominator, or essential core, which is recognizable to some extent in every culture, race and ethnic community.

The core social paradigm that determines the basis for all human life regardless of the cultural context has at least three components. These can be drawn forth from the creation story in Genesis 1-2. Humans are related to the concrete world--taken from the dust; are related to each other--this is bone of my bone, flesh of my flesh; and related to a transcendent spiritual reality--made in the image of God.

First, as created originally out of the dust of the ground we are creaturely beings, which makes all of us dependent upon basic needs related to our earthly environment. Second, our personal existence and identity is grounded in the quality of life we experience with others in community as social beings. And thirdly, as spiritual beings our quality of life is grounded in the ultimate reality which gives hope and meaning to life in the face of frustrations and failures life, and the finality of death.

The core social paradigm is sub-cultural, existing within every human culture and society as the hermeneutical criterion for evaluating family roles and relationships. The depiction of this core paradigm (Figure 13.1) parallels to some degree Maslow's 'hierarchy of needs' but is meant to be more developmental than hierarchical.

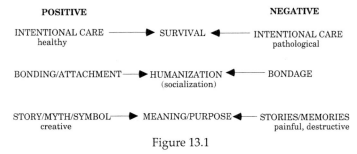

Figure 13.1

The core social paradigm depicted in this model begins with the basic human need of survival as do other creatures who need food and drink, as well as other 'creature comforts' in order to live. Humans are born 'premature,' as it were, with each infant totally dependent upon others for the kind of intentional care that is necessary for survival. Every human society, regardless of its cultural patterns, must provide this intentional care in order to survive. It is on this basis that social customs and cultural patterns must be judged as either leading to healthy human development or as pathological.

Second, the core social paradigm includes some form of socialization that becomes the formative process of human development. Here, the bonding or attachment rituals and practices particular to a culture perform this task, either in a positive or negative fashion. It is possible that the need for bonding as a form of human development can become a form of bondage, which cripples and deforms the human spirit. Every culture is thus accountable for the moral development of its members by holding in check and exposing the tendency for traditional and culturally approved rituals and practice to become bondage.

Thirdly, the core social paradigm depicted above fulfills its mandate by providing meaning and purpose for those who are subject to the authority and influence of those responsible for the development and maintenance of the community's life. The stories, myths, and symbols used by a culture--and all cultures have them--provide this function, often mediated by priests, elders, teachers and parents. Where these stories and symbols enhance and liberate the human spirit by inspiring sacrificial love, abiding faith, and sustaining hope, they are creative and enriching. Where the stories and symbols produce negative effects, they are painful and destructive.

What is more important than who fulfills the role and provides the function at each level of the paradigm, is that it is done effectively. Cultures have a way of identifying and mentoring persons who are charged with the responsibility of filling these roles. But there is a danger here. Those who carry the role responsibility can wrongly assume, or be expected to believe, that it is their role that gives them their moral and spiritual authority. When this occurs, the authority vested in one who fulfills the function needed can become authoritarian and tyrannical, if not abusive.

There is no single cultural form of the family that carries the moral authority by which all others can be judged. When abuse occurs, we must look deeper than the cultural form of family and hold up the core social paradigm as the basic moral basis for accountability. I have argued that the core social paradigm is rooted in a biblical account of the creation. A biblical theology of the family must build on this model and take into account the redemptive purpose of God as related to family. This must be done in the context of the social and cultural patterns and practices which determine the actual form of family structure and relations in a fallen and sinful world.

Recovering a Biblical Theology of Family.

When we look again at the Bible we see that, while certain cultural role patterns are viewed as the means by which the core paradigm is carried out, it is the actual function and the result that God values and expects, not who it is that performs the role. The people of God in the Old Testament were basically a patriarchal society, with some forms of polygamy accepted as common practice. The twelve sons of Jacob who became the founders of the twelve tribes were born to four women. And yet, this same tradition, as later expounded by Moses, clearly taught a monogamous form of marriage as reflective of the divine image (Genesis 2:23-24). Working from within the cultural form of the 'family' as it existed in the choosing of Abraham, God revealed a deeper core of human dignity and integrity which showed polygamy to be inherently degrading and inhuman.

We fail to find in the Bible a single, unambiguous form of the family which we can with certainty call the 'Christian family.' At the same time, the content of the word family is unambiguous and carefully contoured with moral and spiritual authority when grounded in the core social paradigm. I like the way that Herbert Anderson expresses it:

> A theology for the family begins by identifying themes from the whole

of the Christian tradition that are of particular significance for understanding the family. Such an approach seeks to avoid absolutizing either
the family or the theological tradition. It allows for the possibility of
a lively interaction between Christian texts/traditions and common
human experience. A theology for the family begins by exploring
general theological principles--order, change, uniqueness, mutuality,
justice, forgiveness, diversity--in order to understand first of all what
it means to be live in a family. The pastoral theologian's agenda is not
to identify a 'Christian family' but to help people find ways of being
Christian in families.[158]

This is why my former colleague, Dennis Guernsey, used to say, "we
should speak of 'familying' rather than of 'family.' Family is a verb before
it is a noun." Being family is grounded in the core social paradigm rather
than in any particular cultural pattern and practice. All things being equal,
there are certain social forms relating to marriage and family that serve
more effectively and efficiently to fulfill the mandate of the core social
paradigm. Monogamy, rather than polygamy has already been mentioned.
Yet, there are many monogamous marriages that are abusive, destructive
and close to being demonic. For this reason we cannot lodge moral law
and biblical authority with the form of marriage alone.

Given the confusion and uncertainty in our present culture, even
among Christians, we need to clarify and give fuller expression to a
biblical theology of the family in our postmodern world. Based upon the
argument that I have developed thus far, I offer these suggestions as a
tentative step toward such a task.

The family as Image of God

Contemporary attempts to define a biblical theology of the family
come to grief when they begin with the role relationships within marriage
and family life rather than with the quality of life that persons experience within these roles and cultural patterns. Because the Bible does not
present a single, unambiguous model of marriage and family structure,
one form or another of a contemporary cultural form is assumed with
Scripture texts chosen to make it a 'biblical' model.

When we look at the biblical account of creation we can discern the
contours of family life revealed in the core social being of human life.
The statement, "It is not good that the man should be alone" (Gen. 2:18),
precedes the statement, "Therefore a man leaves his father and mother
and clings to his wife, and they become one flesh" (2:24). This latter statement is often taken as a reference to the first marriage, and thus discussion of family is based on the social institution of marriage rather than
on the essential core of human social existence. Marriage, as it becomes

clear in the New Testament, is a possibility, not a necessity for persons to find fulfillment as created in the divine image. Social being, however, is a necessity, as the Genesis 2:18 text makes clear.

The first human was not deficient because he lacked a wife, but because he lacked a human counterpart, necessary to his own personal existence. The divine image is not grounded in a social or cultural pattern, but in a core social relation. Biblical theologian Phyllis Trible draws out of this story the exegetical point that this first 'man' prior to the creation of the woman was not described as a male but merely as 'adam--the Hebrew equivalent of 'earth creature,' which is a term closely related to the Hebrew word for 'earth' (ha-adama). Trible, therefore, concludes that the creation of human persons as 'male and female' ('ish and' issa) occurs only after both are present, simultaneously, not sequentially.[159]

The mutual existence of the first humans constitutes the essential core of what the Bible means by family--mutual care--where development into self identity, personal maturity, acquiring of moral values, and spiritual formation take place. Because the reproduction of humans takes place through sexual relation, marriage becomes the social institution that binds parents one to another prior to their bonding to offspring. It is not, however, marriage that constitutes the essence of the image of God, but mutual, creative, and spiritually enriching social existence.

The family as a social context for identity formation

"In every hour the human race begins," wrote Martin Buber.[160] Biologically this may be true. All creatures begin anew with the perpetuation of their own species through the reproduction of their individual components. With humans more is needed than biological reproduction to be human persons. Human personhood is certainly a mystery--not only a question of why there should be persons at all, but a fundamental mystery in the experience of one's own personhood. Without the mystery of personhood, love and relationship would be little more than instinct and drive. Biological creatureliness is a necessary but insufficient condition for human existence. Personal existence, with a specific sense of self-identity derives from existence in relation to other humans.

Social scientist Clara Mayo says that ". . . this dependence of offspring is much longer than in animals and is guided by more than the biological heritage. Only sustained social contact enables the child to develop a sense of self and a capacity to cope with the tasks that the environment presents."[161] The development of self-identity, therefore, is not only based upon being created as persons in the divine image, but in becoming persons through the socializing process of experiencing bonding and attachment to other persons.

The failure of human care and love as a social context where self-identity is formed is a deprivation of personhood, not merely an ethical fault. Ordinarily it is assumed that the biological parents will provide this essential matrix of social relation, but often it also includes extended family members or, in the case of foster parents or adoption, others who assume this responsibility. Again, a biblical theology is not so concerned with who provides the context of care, but that it is provided. Whatever definition we give to the word 'family,' it is the context of primary social relations that, for better or for worse, contribute to the formation of self-identity and moral character.

The family as a moral context for character formation

The shift from a modern to a post-modern view of reality has raised the question of the status of values with regard to marriage and family. If moral values are no longer held to be universal principles binding upon all persons, regardless of their social institutions and cultural patterns, then where do we look for moral guidance in a multi-cultural society? If cultural diversity and moral ambiguity have replaced uniformity and certainty in our postmodern world, does each community determine its own moral standards? And what does this mean with regard to a biblical view of moral character?

The moral foundation on which commandments are given in the Bible is not in abstract principles, but the core social bond of love. Jesus taught that the two great commandments--love of God and love of neighbor--are both based on love (Matthew 22: 37-39; Deut 6:5; Lev. 19:18). The apostle Paul wrote that all of the commandments of God are grounded in the law of love.

"Owe no one anything, except to love one another; for the one who loves another has fulfilled the law. The commandments, 'You shall not commit adultery; You shall not murder; You shall not steal; You shall not covet'; and any other commandment, are summed up in this word, 'Love your neighbor as yourself.' Love does no wrong to a neighbor; therefore, love is the fulfilling of the law" (Rom. 13:8-10).

Family is the context of primary relations responsible for the care and development of persons in the image of God. This is an intrinsic moral responsibility, with moral character determined by quality of human life grounded in the core social paradigm. All moral principles and all commandments, as Paul has indicated, are ultimately grounded in the moral

structure of human life as life lived in mutual care and common commitment to the development of the human potential of each person.

Because parents are considered to be the primary care givers, the Bible
places responsibility for the development and formation of moral character
on mothers and fathers. "Hear, my child, your father's instruction, and
do not reject your mother's teaching; for they are a fair garland for your
head, and pendants for your neck" (Proverbs 1:8-9)

At the same time, parents do have not have ultimate authority, even
over their own children, for parents are accountable to the larger community in their responsible to develop moral character in their children.
Failure at this level required judgment and discipline by the elders in
the community. Parents could not shield their delinquent and disobedient children from the community's ultimate responsibility to discipline
(Deut 21:18-21).

Within the extended context of the community in which parents and
children live, moral development and character formation is delegated
to the primary unit of family, but ultimately belongs to the community
itself. Yet the community is not free to base its moral standards on cultural patterns relative to its own tradition and ethos, but is to derive its
moral criteria from the core social paradigm that lies behind all cultures
and every social institution. It is in this way that the core social paradigm
places the responsibility for moral character formation within the community itself. Moral values are acquired within each core social unit of
family, without making them relative to the diversity of each community's
moral culture.

The postmodern emphasis tends to be placed on each community's
narrative of its moral perception of reality. In this perspective, it is hard to
avoid the charge of moral relativism. The core social paradigm overcomes
this problem by lodging moral values and character in that which is essential to the full expression of human life in faithfulness to the biblical
mandate. This means that the core family unit is the critical context for
moral values and character formation. This grounds the criteria for moral
character in the human social core that underlies all cultures. Abuse of
children, for example, is a moral transgression cutting across all cultural
attitudes and patterns.

The temptation to impose moral imperatives in the hope of engendering spiritual conformity to biblical principles is hard to resist on the
part of pastors and therapists. Some, in their zeal to justify their role as
a Christian counselor find it necessary to speak of moral values and imperatives as a way of avoiding the appearance of offering only secular

psychology. Others, who are often anxious about their own spiritual life, may feel morally compromised by clients who exhibit immoral behavior or attitudes. As a result, they impose moral imperatives on others as a way of reducing their own moral anxiety. The effect is the same. To offer moral imperatives to one in need of empowering grace is to give a stone when one asks for bread.

What is normative in biblical teaching is not a certain structure or form of family, but acting and living in ways that create, nurture and support persons within their social structures, including marriage and family. This is what I earlier meant by speaking of 'familying' as a verb rather than a noun. Being family is a process of spiritual formation, even as living in the power of the Spirit redeems and restores family.

Spiritual formation is a process of spiritual empowering more than it is a program of moral development. The contemporaries of Jesus were scandalized by his apparent tolerance of the lack of conformity to the moral law on the part of those to whom he brought the good news of the Kingdom of God. What concerned Jesus were the personal and social disorders and derangements which marginalized and minimized the significance of persons. "I came not to judge the world, but to save the world," said Jesus (John 12:47).

Spiritual formation, as one aspect of family ministry, cannot afford to use moral judgments as a qualifying standard attached to healing presence. God's moral freedom is the basis for God's moral law. Unconditional grace mediated through the spiritual power of forgiveness is itself a moral quality of love. Moral imperatives without spiritual empowerment only cripple and condemn. To moralize under the guise of Christian ministry is itself a form of spiritual abuse.

The Family as the domestic context of spiritual formation

Persons are not only intrinsically social beings but human spirituality is located at the essential core of social being. Spiritual formation is thus an essential component of self-identity and competence in human social relationships. An approach to a biblical theology of the family that fails to take into account spiritual formation as the essential core of each person's growth toward personal maturity is reductive, partializing, and lacking in therapeutic insight. We are reminded here of the insightful thesis of Dietrich Bonhoeffer that the social structure of human personhood is intrinsically spiritual.[162]

The reality of spirit is first of all a social reality rooted in the nature of human personhood. Social spirituality reflects the divine image and

likeness constitutive of human personhood. The individual person exists
as structurally open to the spirit of another person as well as structurally
open to the Spirit of God. Authentic spiritual life is learned in the context
of primary relationships--it is a domestic skill. Every person speaks with
two languages when expressing the deeper pain of the soul. There is a
psychological as well as a spiritual voice with which clients speak their
pain. The counselor who does not have 'bi-lingual' competence will tend
to reduce symptoms to either psychological treatment or spiritual instruction. An integrative approach to counseling is one that has multi-level
competence in recognizing and dealing with persons as physical, social,
psychological and spiritual beings.

On one occasion, Jesus was confronted by a man who not only was
possessed of demons, but who had become a maniac, running naked
and wild among the tombs, mutilating himself. After the demons were
cast out, we are told that the man from whom the demons had gone, was
found "sitting at the feet of Jesus, clothed and in his right mind" (Luke
8:35). The casting out of a demon was relatively easy. The self-destructive
behavior was stopped. But the ministry of Jesus went beyond modifying
behavior. The fact that the man was clothed, sane and spiritually open to
the Kingdom of God as offered by Jesus is a paradigm of what all Christian ministry should have as its aim. In this case, the result was systemic,
hygienic, ecological and integrative. The clothes did not come with the
casting out of demons. Someone in the community, his family we hope,
reached out to him and reclaimed him.

While we may be attracted by the dramatic exorcism, it was no shortcut
to spiritual formation. We may not always know what demonic powers
lie hidden in the pathology of mental illness. Nor should we attempt
to develop a diagnostic category of demonic disorder as a therapeutic
technique. In removing the effects of demonic disorder we have, in effect,
practiced a kind of exorcism without naming the devil. Spiritual formation
restores and rebuilds the life of persons from the inside out.

I accept the shift from a modern to a postmodern view of reality as
closer to a biblical perspective as represented by the core social paradigm
that underlies all cultural forms and practices. Cultural diversity can be
allowed as expressive to some degree of the essential components of the
core social paradigm. At the same time, I argue that the moral and spiritual
values that determine authentic human life as endowed with the divine
image are not relative to any particular culture but are intrinsic to the
quality of human life as God intended. The mission of the church thus
seeks to bring the good news of the Kingdom of God to all people as a

redemptive and healing ministry to people within their own cultural and ethnic identity. Cultural sensitivity begins with respect of persons. The culture of the Kingdom of God restores the moral and spiritual character of persons in the context of their primary social relations. In this way, culture too is redeemed and brought into conformity to authentic human life as created by God.

Chapter 14

The Church as Family of Families

It was Dennis Guernsey, in the class that we taught together on marriage and family, who first spoke of the church as a 'family of families.' [163] His thoughts on this theme seem more relevant than ever as the church faces new challenges in the context of the postmodern emphasis on relationality along with a distrust of institutions. The concept of the church as a family of families can only be viewed as a metaphor in somewhat the same way as the Bible speaks of the body of Christ as a 'household' of God, or the 'temple' of God.

Historically in our Western culture the transition from a society whose economic life was largely supported by 'cottage' industries and extended family units to a more highly industrial and technological one is significant for our understanding of family. The new industrial economy tended to create more of an emphasis on the marital, or conjugal unit than on the extended family. The industrial society required mobility and a fluid population (work force). In this kind of society, the marriage relationship, and especially the so-called nuclear family unit, becomes more prominent as a primary social construct. Placing the emphasis on marriage became a social ideal, and thus a religious one as well.

The focus of the church on the marriage unit as the core of the family led to a systematic exclusion of the non-married, or formerly married from the center of congregational life. Even the terminology referring to family units reflect this transition. With the death of a spouse, or a divorce, the result is a 'single parent' family where children are involved. Even the phrase a 'broken home,' or 'broken family' crept into the literature where the ideal marital unit was dislocated. Blended families came to be more commonplace than original nuclear family units, as I discussed in the first chapter of this book.

As a result, the church tended to reflect these social changes in terms of is own emphasis on ministry to families. Church members who were not part of a 'couple' (husband and wife) were relegated to the sidelines, not only in church social functions, but in terms of the church's focus on family ministry. Larger churches, recognizing the existence of the growing number of single adults (non-married) members, began to develop special programs such as 'divorce recovery,' and 'single adult' ministries as an attempt to include at the edges what had been excluded at the center.

Researches into this phenomenon discovered that when the single adults in the church community are pushed to the side, it tended to produce life-styles that were itinerant, casual, and temporary.[164] Churches that become largely 'marriage-centered' create two classes of membership, with those who are not married often viewed as second class.

Alternative models have been suggested that focus more on 'consensual' relations rather than conjugal (marital) ones. In the sociological literature, relations that are based primarily on choice (consensual) come under the category of voluntary associations. These kind of relationships constitute 'clubs' or 'associations' rather than family units. In this way of thinking, purely voluntary association and families are mutually exclusive. Thus, the attempt to define the church's life primarily in terms of consensual relations breaks apart, rather than reinforces family units. There is a paradox here. For in our contemporary culture, except for churches that tend to view baptism as a sacramental union with the body of Christ, persons 'join' the church as individuals even though they are members of families. Adult member of families often join the church (by way of a voluntary association) leaving their younger children to join at a later time. A husband or a wife may join on the basis of a personal confession of faith leaving the spouse to be a 'non-member' until such time as a personal confession of faith can be produced.

In one church, I was told that when the current pastor came to the church there was a list posted in the church of 'non-member' spouses with the exhortation to pray for their conversion so that they could also be 'members!' The new pastor immediately caused this list to be removed, much to the relief of some who had been attending well aware that they were on the 'list!' It is hard to think of a more dreadful approach to the evangelization of non-believing spouses, not to mention the violation of the spiritual integrity of a 'household of faith' in the sense that the Apostle Paul viewed such relations--"The unbelieving husband is made holy through his wife. . . " (1 Cor 7:14). Paul's argument is that even as children are 'consecrated' through relation to parents who believe, so are unbelieving spouses. From the Apostle's Hebrew background, this would have been a customary way of thinking of the integrity of the 'household.'

In considering how the church can be a 'family of families' as an expression of the Kingdom of God as Jesus taught, we need to take another look at his teaching and draw from it some insights for the church in our postmodern culture.

The Kingdom of God and the Family

What is Jesus proclaiming in his pronouncements concerning the radical claims that the kingdom of God makes on every natural order, including the institutions of marriage and family? Certainly it is not a proclamation that dissolves the basic social relation between people. On the contrary, Jesus teaches that the commandment to love your neighbor as yourself is of equal importance with the other supreme commandment to "love the Lord your God with all your heart, and with all your soul, and with all your mind, and with all your strength" (Mark 12:28-31). He does not dissolve the natural order of family, though he qualifies it as an absolute and brings it into the service of the new order, which is itself the original order.

This does not question the relationships between husband and wife, parents and children, brothers and sisters as such. What is questioned in these sayings is one's captivity to these relationships. Family structures can be a clannish imprisonment of the person no less than material possessions or worldly fame. Jesus' proclamation is a message of liberation from these relationships as an absolute demand over the Christian disciple. Thus the excuse of the invited guest, "I have married a wife, and therefore I cannot come," is to be seen precisely on the same level as those whose purchases of land or oxen claimed their prior interest (Luke 14:18-20). In a similar situation, Jesus gives a remarkable answer to the man who was considering discipleship: "Leave the dead to bury their own dead; but as for you, go and proclaim the kingdom of God" (Luke 9:59-60). To this series of teachings belong the other provocative sayings about 'leaving,' 'dividing,' 'disuniting,' and even 'hating.' If a person loves father or mother, son or daughter more than him, Jesus says this person is not worthy of the kingdom of God (Matt. 10:34-38). When Jesus requires one to 'hate' his father and mother, even his own life, he warns against setting out to build a tower or go to war without taking stock of what the cost will be. Those who are preoccupied with entanglements that will eventually cause them to abandon the kingdom of God have not really been liberated by the kingdom of God. Love of neighbor is the other side of the coin from love of God; it is not a coin with its own realm. The coming of the kingdom of God means the end of the absolute hold that the natural order has over the person who is first of all the object of God's love and determination.

We can conclude, therefore, that rather than there being a contradiction between the family and the kingdom of God, there is a correlation and even a symbiotic relationship. The demands of the kingdom preempt the demands of filial and family relationships indirectly, not directly. The same God who has established family as the basic unit of human social existence is the Lord to whom each family and each family member owes worship and obedience. Jesus came preaching a gospel of the kingdom of God (Matt. 4:23). There is also a gospel of the family, which Jesus proclaimed through his own participation in and upholding of the filial and domestic relationships in his own life. One of the last words from the cross takes account of this filial relationship, wherein Jesus made provision for his mother by designating the beloved apostle, John, as her son, and her as his mother (John 19:26-27). There is a gospel of the family as well as a gospel of the kingdom.

The creative tension between covenant and creation

What we see in the teaching of Jesus is not an essential contradiction between family and kingdom but rather a tension that takes two forms, positive and creative or negative and destructive. The first point of tension between family and kingdom, which is positive and creative (even re-creative) is grounded in the original tension between the sixth day of creation and the Sabbath as God's day of rest. The six days of God's creating are reflected in the command "six days you shall labor. . . but the seventh day is a sabbath to the Lord your God" (Exod. 20:9-10). The structure of family life is linked closely with the sixth day, but the quintessence of family life is linked with the seventh, which represents the paradigm of covenant as the quintessence of family. Thus, a creative and positive tension exists between family as a social reality of the sixth day and family as a covenant reality of the seventh day. The family is not an 'order of creation' in the older sense of having its own natural order and laws that give it independent status over and against the kingdom of God. To the degree that family is also a part of the 'created orders,' it has its own place and purpose within this created structure. But the created order does not yield any law of the family that is not superceded by the Lord of the family.

We see this tension reflected at certain points in the New Testament.

For example, when the apostle Paul suggests that it might be preferable not to marry and thus to assume the responsibilities and duties that accompany such a relation, he has in view the impending dissolution of all created orders by the new order inaugurated by the resurrection of Christ and hastening to its consummation at his return. In Paul's mind, the "appointed time has grown very short" and consequently one should live with a view to serving the Lord with undivided attention (1 Cor. 7:29-31). This frees marriage and family from bondage to a natural or biological determinism, while at the same time, placing it within a new context of covenant love and responsibility.

The redemptive tension between order and disorder

The second level of tension is between order and disorder, and this cuts right through both covenant and creation as humans experience them. The effects of the fall and the consequent disorder that infects every personal form of existence from Adam to Christ (but does not include him) brings defeat, frustration, destructiveness, and bondage into human relationships. It is this latter distinction between order and disorder that is absolute and lies behind the polemics of both Jesus and Paul against 'nature' and even natural institutions. For under the tyranny of sin and disobedience, the natural becomes unnatural and even demonic. The liberation of creation from disorder so that the covenant order may be reestablished is often convulsive and uncompromising. When the family becomes an autonomous social structure in society it tends to become cultic, demanding loyalty to its own existence. Cut off from responsibility to and for others, such a family can become a 'terror cell' within the larger society. Stanley Hauerwas makes a telling point in this regard:

> Ironically, . . . the family is threatened today partly because it has no institutions that have the moral status to stand over against it to call into question its demonic tendencies. The first function of the church in relation to the family must, therefore, be to stand as an institution that claims loyalty and significance beyond that of the family.[165]

The church as a family of families, notwithstanding its own proclivity to disorder, can and ought to function as a community of redemption amidst structures of disorder.

Failure to distinguish these two levels of tension leads to the confusion between renunciation and redemption. The creation order is redeemed, not renounced. The Sabbath is for the benefit of humans. That is, God seeks the true creaturely order as he determined it to be. So then, marriage and family life are first of all qualified by the relation between covenant and creation, and second are brought under the redemptive and mediating work of Christ. Because Jesus represents the presence of the kingdom of God as the eschaton, or the end of the old order, there is an eschatological tension as well in his proclamation. In light of the new order that is inaugurated by the kingdom of God as present in Christ, a radical judgment is pronounced upon existing orders that seek to bind humanity to the old.

Was Jesus disloyal to the institution of marriage and family? Of course not. He continues to be the Lord of the family, who desires that each family experience and embody the righteousness, joy, and peace that belong to those who have received the kingdom of God. What remains for us is to trace out the way in which the church, as the new family of God, enhances and upholds family life by exorcizing the destructive and demonic disorder that threatens it, and by re-creating it into the new order of God's covenant community.

The message of the good news, which became the hallmark of the New Testament church from its very inception, is the announcement of the new covenant community being formed in Christ. The corporate life of the church immediately following Pentecost experienced a communal life with a domestic character. In describing those first believers, Luke recalls that "day by day, attending the temple together and breaking bread in their homes, they partook of food with glad and generous hearts" (Acts 2:46). This commitment to each other as brothers and sisters in a new community of love and faith captures exactly the import of Jesus' own teaching.

"Who are my mother and my brothers," Jesus asked? And looking around on those who sat about him, he said, "Here are my mother and my brothers! Whoever does the will of God is my brother, and sister, and mother" (Mark 3:33-35).

New filial relations are created between those who were once strangers and unrelated. Paul properly calls Christ the 'head' of this new community, his Body (Eph. 1:22-23). And yet, Christ is himself the Body in which the individual's new personal identity as one who has experienced the salvation of God is formed through a common existence in Christ's Body. This commonality, or koinonia, binds each person to Christ and one to another. As a consequence, failure to love the brother or sister is to break fellowship with Christ himself (1 John 4:20).

The Church as a Family of Families

Turning now to our task of giving positive content to the concept of the church as the new family of God, I will set forth three aspects of the church as family. These aspects will relate to the developmental model of personal and spiritual formation that we presented earlier. The church as the family of God sets forth a new criterion of worth, a new form of parity, and a new context of belonging for each person in the kingdom of God.

A new criterion of worth

Why a new criterion of worth? Does not one's existence in family give sufficient self-worth to each other? Yes--and No. As the foundation for family love, covenant love is not based on merit but on belonging. It was not because Israel was greater in number than other nations or had greater merit when compared to others that God chose and loved her. But, we are told, the Lord set his love upon Israel and chose her to be his own people "because the Lord loves you" (Deut. 7:7). Covenant love creates worth and is itself the criterion of worth. It is not erratic or idiosyncratic but comes to expression as a bonding of God to his people, and of them to each other and to him through the social, religious, and political structure of their life as a people. The Israelites grew up in this social context knowing first of all that each belonged to this structure, and that each person's identity is grounded in this belonging.

It is the responsibility of parenting to reinforce this self-worth, ordinarily in a context where consanguinity is the fundamental criterion for acceptance. Infants ordinarily experience the 'flesh and blood' or kinship ties first. The church as the new family of God, however, is not formed by consanguine bonds (not everyone is biologically related!), nor by mere consensuality (it is more than a voluntary association). Through spiritual rebirth we each become a brother or sister of Jesus Christ through adoption into the family of God. Consequently we are brother or sister to each other. This new criterion of worth has a transcendent source and thus a permanent status. Husbands and wives are first of all brother and sister in Jesus Christ before they are husband and wife. Sons and daughters are also brother or sister to their father and mother before they are sons and daughters. This precedence is logical, not always chronological. Nevertheless, because it is theological, it does constitute a real precedence in each relationship. Unlike the human consanguinity that comes to an end with the temporal order, this new consanguine relation, which is constituted by divine election in Jesus Christ, builds self-worth on that which will abide in and through life's changes as well as life's losses.

Each member of the Body of Christ receives the Spirit of Christ and is given a new standing with God in Christ. This does not happen merely individualistically or privately, but corporately and publicly. Baptism is a community event as well as a personal and individual one. Yet the church as community does not become surrogate parents for young people nor does it replace the family as a social and domestic unit. In extreme cases it may appear to do so, but this is not its calling; if indeed it must do so, it must also prepare for that function to be one of expediency. Individual members of family units as well as those who for one reason or another remain single, become peers in the Body of Christ as brother or sister. When this criterion for self-worth has become internalized prior to any critical point of change in family status, the individual can experience the transition with minimal trauma. "For my mother and father have forsaken me," says the Psalmist, "but the Lord will take me up" (Ps. 27:10). Yahweh asks, "Can a woman forget her sucking child, that she should have no compassion on the son of her womb?" and then answers, "Even these may forget, yet I will not forget you" (Isa. 49:15). The Hebrew child grew up with a criterion for self-worth that was not yet revealed to those outside the covenant. Thus, in all of our parenting there must also be weaning. Even the extended family, where grandfather and great-grandmother are part of the household, can become a sentimental attachment that provides no permanence in the midst of change. Brother and sister may be the only names we will need in heaven.

Here on earth we have many names, and we wear many faces. Having been baptized into the new family of God, we are adopted into the filial relation that exists between God the Son and God the Father. We are brother and sister to God in Christ. And when we call each other brother and sister this is more than an affected characteristic of a certain Christian life-style--it is a new criterion of our worth, and one that will survive.

A new form of parity

This is not a word that we use frequently in terms of family relations. We should not confuse it with equality. By parity I mean equivalence of share rather than equality of role in a relation. In other words, parity means having full equivalence of partnership and value without having to have the same functional roles. Marriage relationships are meant to express parity between husband and wife who share equally in the benefits of marriage (we hope), even though their respective roles may differ. Children equally are 'family,' with parents, though they are to obey their parents and parents are to instruct and discipline their children. In these cases, parity is related to equal status despite differing roles and responsibilities. Thus, parity is grounded in the commonality, or koinonia, that characterizes the life of the family.

As we know, not all social relationships are included in marriage and family life. The single adult who has left the parental home will not experience parity in social contracts alone. One's intrinsic worth as being a member of a healthy functioning family has no 'cash value' when becoming just another member of society. In other words, social contracts will not provide a bonded relation in which the personal being of one is sustained and affirmed by the other(s). Parity in the sense that I mean it is a determinative of covenant love, not of contractual and performance-oriented social relations. An employer/employee relationship, for example, has no essential parity in terms of life-enhancing and person-reinforcing benefits. It is not that such contractual relationships cannot also express some dimension of parity, but parity is not the essential purpose of the relation between employer and employee as expressed in organizational line relationships, financial remuneration, or share in the company's profits.

The church as the new family of God, however, does offer a new form of parity--or at least it ought to. Not every member of the body has the same function and not always the same honor, says Paul. But there is still absolute parity: "If one member suffers, all suffer together; if one member is honored, all rejoice together" (1 Cor. 12:26). The church often fails, precisely at this point, because it tends to segregate members on the basis of married and single persons. A 'ministry to singles' within the church is no more valid than a separate ministry to racial or socioeconomic segments of the church family. The church's unique gift is its inclusive and transcending order of family life, which gives each member full parity in the fellowship of the body of Christ.

Can the church promote stable marriages and healthy family life in society without abandoning the non-married and relegating them to the status of second-class citizens? It not only can, it must. And it will, if it teaches and practices a proper theology of family. It will be difficult, to be sure. The church family carries with it the strengths and weaknesses of the society in which it exists. It will be all too easy to assume that family life as the fellowship of the Body of Christ is identical with the social life of its members. It is not. The true fellowship of Christ is not only intergenerational but intramural as well. Not only are all parts of the body to function, but they are to function together. If it should happen that momentarily, and even frequently, members of the Body of Christ forget that they are single or married, parents or children, and rejoice and suffer together as brothers and sisters, this will not damage or destroy homes and families! Instead, such experiences of parity liberate the organizational, administrative, and social role functions from having to carry the entire weight of personal worth.

Within the New Testament the mandate for parity within existing social and domestic structures and role relationships is a judgment against the power of the old orders, but at the same time it is a power to experience the full measure of belonging and grace that belongs to each one in the kingdom of God. Thus the apostle Paul can urge parents and children to live within constraints, slaves and masters to make their relationship work for the highest good, and husbands and wives to find liberation from practical role requirements through mutual submission and full partnership in the benefits of love and life (see Eph. 5-6). Quite clearly, the essential parity that exists as the very structure of the church as the new family of God seeks to overcome and transform all roles and relationships that belong to the old order, which is passing away. This, of course, creates a new form of social and domestic life that must be practiced before it can be credibly taught. And this leads us to consider a third aspect of the church as the family of God.

A new context of belonging

The third aspect of the church as the new family of God is experienced as a new context of belonging as members of God's family. This may be one way of understanding the somewhat quaint New Testament expression 'family of faith.' In his letter to the Galatian church Paul urges the believers to "work for the good of all, and especially for those of the family of faith" (Gal. 6:10). In this case, the word 'family' (household) is a much broader term than what we ordinarily mean by a nuclear family unit. It includes not only parents and children but other relatives who live with them, as well as servants or even slaves. The household is a microcosm of society itself, and provides a certain self-sufficiency as well as mutual interdependence to all who belong to it. Thus salvation is experienced not only by individuals; it "comes to a household" (Acts 16:31; John 4:53; cf. Gen. 7:1). The 'household'--or family of faith--in this sense, is the social and ecclesial contextualization of one's personal life. It is in this context that worth and parity become real.

It is noteworthy that the renewal movement in the Roman Catholic Church following Vatican II strongly emphasized the domestic aspect of the church. Pope John Paul II, addressing a group of bishops from the United States in one of his few public speeches before his death, said that "the Christian family is so important, and its role so basic in transforming the world and in building up the kingdom of God, that the Council called it a 'domestic church.'[166]

Commenting on this, David Thomas writes,

> We are invited to make present the love of God in human form. This takes place in the relationships in the family and in the relationships of the family to outsiders. These can all be sacramental relationships .... These are charisms, extraordinary gifts given by God, that qualify the recipients as ministers of the Lord, true disciples of the living Lord who remains alive especially through their many expressions of generosity, care, and service. [167]

What does this mean for us? Will this become another church program that promotes marriage as the cure for the loneliness and alienation of the unmarried adult? Or will the church as the family of God contextualize both the married and the unmarried, both the parents and the children, in the form of a 'household of faith'? We hope the latter will be the case. But how is this possible in the contemporary social order where household means, in IRS language, the smallest sociological unit with a single wage earner at the head? It would be desperate enough if we were to consider the more typical nuclear family unit a household, but 'parents without partners' also constitute a sizable number of households under this definition. "One of the problems of family life in contemporary society," writes Thomas, "is the isolation felt by the individual nuclear family."[168] Rather than view this as the ideal of the domestic life of the church he suggests that the church will need to reconstitute family through the facilitating of a 'domestic church' as a basic cell of the larger ecclesiastical unit. These cells, or 'block units,' will begin to function like 'households of faith.' They will perform many functions, including some aspects of education, stabilization of economic existence for members of the group, prayer and liturgy, and even the evangelization of the larger community in which they exist.[169]

Setting up priorities

- The health of the church as the community of Christ is the source of healing for the members (families) of the community. There is a priority of ministry to the family as a family of families.
- The effectiveness of the church as a community of reconciliation is measured by the function of its members in primary personal and social relationships. There is a priority of social relatedness in setting the criteria for spiritual and personal maturity.
- The unity of the church as a community of ministries through its programs and services is grounded in its congregational life. There is a priority of congregational life in determining the status of indi-

vidual members in the Kingdom of God.

• The nature of the church as a family of families is to provide stability and order through the social and cultural transition in the forms of family life. There is a priority of the rules for loving in adjusting the roles for living.

On Being a Family of Families

These are not new concepts, of course; various sectors of the Christian church have attempted on an experimental basis to create new forms and models of the church through the cell-group process. It would probably be a mistake, however, to substitute the concept of a small group for that of family, and it most certainly would be a mistake to break down the precarious structure of family life as it presently exists in the nuclear family unit. Thus, the question I would ask is this: To what family, as a domestic unit (or household of faith), does the nuclear family belong? In one sense, each adult who no longer lives with an original family unit has experienced a 'broken household.' We tend to think of children whose parents have divorced, and of the divorced parents themselves, as coming from 'broken homes.' But this is only half the truth. The man or woman who leaves a parental home to set up his or her own home, whether with a marriage partner, a roommate, or alone, has experienced a 'broken household.' The original filial unit is designed for self-destruction when children leave home and strike out on their own. It is easy (relatively speaking) to set up housekeeping by renting a room or an apartment, and easier still to create a new home through marriage (even at $100.00, the cost of a marriage license is the smallest obstacle to the setting up of housekeeping). But even a so-called Christian marriage is not yet a 'household of faith.' And how much less than a household of faith is a room with a single person, or even one shared with a roommate?

Marriage is not meant to be the sanctification of the human disorder of solitary existence. Rather, it needs to be sanctified itself by belonging to a 'family of faith.' Far too many family units, as defined by the latest census reports, are actually islands of quiet despair in the sea of humanity. And this is often at their best! More often, life in these families is demeaning and destructive to human personhood itself. No, it is the household of faith that is the sanctification of marriage and family, as well as of the unmarried and non-family persons.

For the ancient Israelite, the covenant community constituted the household of faith, and consequently also sanctified families and individuals. Even as the covenant community had its origin in the tribe, and the tribe

188	SOMETHING OLD / SOMETHING NEW

in the household of Jacob, so the household of Jacob has its consummation and ultimate meaning in the covenant community. The breaking up of one family unit in order to form another did not constitute the breaking down of the 'household of faith.' The covenant community contextualized both individual persons and family units in the eschatological reality of being people of God. In this context, the worth and parity of each person were assured, despite the injustice and tyranny of the old order.

I will rephrase the question: To what family, or household of faith, does the family belong without losing its character as a domestic community where ordinary and daily life is affirmed and supported? Does it belong to the church as the family of God? Does this not mean then, that the church itself must become the 'family of faith?' And if so, will this not mean that the church becomes both the sanctification and celebration of that commonality (koinonia) that exists between people who are the friends of Jesus and who exist for and with each other? Should not these 'families of faith,' by whatever definition or form they take, be the center of the liturgical life of the people of God, even as they are the source of nourishment and support for the daily and ordinary life of the members?

Ought not Christian baptism be baptism into a 'family of faith,' where one is immediately joined with other 'brothers and sisters,' and should not the eucharist be celebrated by and with those who have a stake in each other's daily bread? Until this takes place how can the church be the true people of God? And how can renewal of the family take place without the renewal of the family of faith itself? We cannot rightly pray 'forgive us our trespasses' and 'give us this day our daily bread' until we have prayed 'thy kingdom come, . . .on earth as it is in heaven.' And when I pray this prayer, I surrender my right and privilege as husband or father, and I ask for and positively seek the right and privileges of my brothers and sisters to sit at table with me and so make visible the kingdom of God. Here there is no room for a separate ministry to 'singles', for they are my family of faith"--we are each from broken homes, and in need of a family where there is belonging and healing. I am reminded again of Eugene O'Neill's great line: "We are born broken. We live by mending. The grace of God is the glue."[170]

The church as the family of families is the place where effective mediation of God's grace not only is a spiritual means for healing, but touches the very core of the human self, enabling it and assisting it in the integrative task of becoming whole. What the Apostle Paul calls the 'works of the flesh' as contrasted with the 'fruit of the Spirit,' are symptomatic of negative and pathological social spirituality-- enmities, strife, jealousy, anger, quarrels, dissensions, factions (Galatians 5:20). These are some of the diagnostic categories by which the Bible identifies sin; not first of all violations of an abstract moral law, but the breakdown of the social spirituality which is necessary for healthy marriage and family life, as well as other social relations. The therapeutic effects of the indwelling of the Holy Spirit are likewise described in terms of healthy social spirituality--love, joy, peace, patience, kindness, generosity, faithfulness, gentleness, self control (Galatians 5:22-23). In being and doing this, the church grasps whatever is broken and brings it toward wholeness. It touches whatever is orphaned and creates family. It saves families by saving husbands and wives from destroying each other through impossible ultimatums. It saves parents from having to determine their children's destinies, and it saves children from having to enshrine their parents in their own goals in order to carry them with them. Jesus calls each to be his brother and sister and so makes brothers and sisters out of all who come to him. God is family.

Chapter 15

The Role of Grandparents
in Modern Families

The rapidly changing dynamics and demographics in American family life over the past 50 years provide a new frontier for grandparenting. There was a time when grandparents lived in close proximity to their adult children and were considered a normal part of extended family life. Grandparents were often relied upon by their adult children for their experience and wisdom in the rearing of children.[171]

Where grandparents were once looked to for intergenerational stability and identity, they are today more likely to be expected to provide childcare for working mothers. Some grandparents have had to become parents again. There are 3.2 million grandparents raising their children's children. These grandparents have stepped in to rescue their grandchildren from the incapacity or inability of their sons or daughters to function effectively as parents. These grandparents have had to make radical adjustments in their own lives and take on responsibilities for which they have more wisdom but less energy.

According to a survey by the American Association of Retired Persons (AARP) 31 percent of adults are grandparents. Of that number, 8 percent are providing day care on a regular basis, and 3 percent are rearing a grandchild. The 2000 U.S. Census reports that 6.3 percent of US children under 18 (4.5 million), live in grandparent-headed households. There are no parents present in the lives of about one-third of these children. This isn't something that just happens to a particular race or area or social class. It happens in all socioeconomic groups due to divorce, neglect, teen-age pregnancy, the death of the parents, incarceration, unemployment, abuse, alcohol or drug usage, or abandonment. It can happen to any couple.[172]

When grandparents take on a parental role it affects many aspects of their married life. There are many stresses that can severely damage a marriage, and studies show that it takes about a year for a couple to adjust to the many changes that result from caring for grandkids on a full time basis. They feel more stressed due to concerns about their own health and finances. Housing may be an issue if they are living in a senior citizen complex. The issue of medical care for the children is difficult. There is the loss of time for themselves and their dream of retirement dies. Their social life and circle changes drastically. There is also an emotional toll. Feelings range from fear, anger, exhaustion, resentment, grief, and shame to thankfulness and joy. This type of stress can damage a marriage. Even with these many stresses in their lives, many grandparents report that through it all, they feel a greater purpose for their lives. Caring for their grandchildren makes them feel young and active. They say that the sacrifices are worth it.

Perhaps the most difficult challenge for grandparents in today's society is to observe the radically different life styles and parenting dynamics practiced by our adult sons and daughters with our grandchildren. Today's parents tend not to look to grandparents as mentors and models for their own parenting and family life. Often, they will intentionally break with a family tradition of parenting as a way of establishing their own independence.

Their adult sons and daughters are more independent, less open to advice and more involved with their own peer group than with their parents. Anxious about their own financial burdens and stressed by the fast-paced life of their children and the cost of their education, parents find it hard to include the grandparents in the family life cycle. When they cannot be physically present, grandparents often lavish grandchildren with gifts as a way of staying in touch. In 1992 grandparents spent $8.3 billion on gifts for their grandchildren.

In our contemporary society the mold for grandparenthood has been broken. Grandparents today are, on average, younger, more mobile, more active, and less involved in the day-to-day activities of their adult children and grandchildren. The structure of family life has undergone radical change. And along with those changes the role of grandparents in families has also taken on a new perspective. Child rearing experts have replaced grandparents with new scientific theories as to parenting. Increased mobility in the work force, migration from rural to urban and suburban centers, and the high rate of divorce, has meant that grandparents are often less involved in daily family living.

Divorce creates new problems for grandparents. Not only does divorce separate children from one of their parents, it also can create a problem for grandparents. With remarriage, children often acquire a new set of grandparents, resulting in 'top heavy' family structures. This can be confusing for the children and awkward for the grandparents. When grandparents divorce, a new set of problems emerge. Who receives 'custody' of the grandchildren?

Conflict between parents and their married sons and daughters can also lead to alienation with the result that grandparents are denied access to their grandchildren. Some grandparents have sought legal recourse in their attempt to have relationship with their grandchildren. A grandparents 'bill of rights' has even been proposed in support of those who have been denied contact with their grandchildren. While these situations are unusual, they reflect the fact that grandparents may be the neglected casualties in the disintegration of the family structure.

All of this can leave grandparents sometimes anxious, confused and helpless. Participation in parenting decisions is often taken as unwanted intervention. The culture gap widens the generation gap, and many a grandparent has retreated, wounded and hurt. Because being a grandparent is a form of love, there will be risks and hurts, as with all loving relationships. Grandparents learn to live with what is possible in order to create room for what is potential.

First time grandparents find themselves thrust into a new role without preparation and without a traditional context in which to fit comfortably. How does one shift gears from becoming a parent to a grandparent? It is not as though being a grandparent comes naturally, with a set of basic instincts along with gray hair! For most of us, entering into the role of being a grandparent is uncharted territory. The exhilaration of having the first grandchild is often accompanied by a shock of dismay at suddenly being called 'grandma' or 'grandpa!'

However fulfilling it is to see one's own adult children hold their own newborn child, we sense immediately that our relation with this son or daughter who has now become a parent is significantly changed. The arrival of a child is the beginning of a 'new family' and marks a generational transition more sharply defined than having an adult child leave home and marry. The father or mother of a married son or daughter is still a father or mother with the addition of a daughter or son-in-law. But when an adult child becomes a parent, our role as parent is displaced and we have become grandparents

There are pitfalls as well as pleasures in being a grandparent. What used to be advice when given to one's own child may now be received as criticism when offered with respect to a grandchild! Learning to give advice, whether asked for or not, with practiced indifference as to whether or not the advice is followed can be the key to effective relationship with the parents of one's grandchildren. By respecting the rights of parents, the privilege of being a grandparent is preserved.

The number of grandparents is on a rapid increase. In the last twenty years, the number of grandparents has risen from 58 million to more than 76 million. Nearly half of these grandparents will come from the present population of baby boomers. The need for grandparents is greater than ever! What grandparents need to discover is how to meet this need and what shape their role should be in the family life of their children and grandchildren.

First of all we must understand that grandparents represent a valuable and rich resource for the contemporary American family. This is a resource not available through social services, community support groups, and professional experts. Grandparents perform an important task for some of the following reasons.

Grandparents Are a Repository of Values and Beliefs

The task of being a grandparent is not that of being a religious teacher as much as it is living a consistent life of personal faith that embodies the teachings and practice of the Judeo-Christian tradition. Where grandchildren are brought up in a religious tradition different from that of the grandparents, this task becomes more difficult. There is often a temptation to make an issue of the differing religious tradition and belief system with the result that a conflict and division arises in this area between the grandparents and the parents. While this can be viewed as a form of adherence to one's own religious convictions, it can become an obstacle and even a deterrent to the spiritual development of the grandchildren.

When the Apostle Paul sought to encourage the younger man, Timothy, he reminded him of the faith that "lived first in your grandmother Lois and your mother Eunice and now, I am sure, lives in you" (2 Timothy 1:5). Here we have an instance of a three generational religious faith within the very first century of Christianity. More than an allusion to a historical fact, Paul's reminder to Timothy of his grandmother's faith was meant to be a source of inspiration and encouragement for his own faith in a time in which there was a great deal of opposition, confusion and uncertainty.

Grandparents need to be reminded that their first priority is to live out their own religious beliefs in such a way that the value of having faith is transmitted to grandchildren through the conduit of a shared family story.

What grandparents can provide is an on-going narrative of life lived with assurance of God's faithfulness toward us in such a way that grandchildren can take up that story in their own faith tradition. Even where the religious tradition of the parents is the same as that of the grandparents, it is the shared family narrative of God's faithfulness based on the biblical stories that provide a resource for grandchildren in their own discovery and pilgrimage of faith.

Grandparents are Living Symbols of Family Continuity and Stability

What children need today are family icons, not cultural heroes. An icon is like a figure that is familiar and yet carries a kind of transcendent, luminous quality. Some software programs use icons as a user-friendly way of accessing the mysterious and hidden power of the computer. In somewhat the same way, grandparents can make the hidden wisdom of life user-friendly.

For the small child, a grandparent is viewed in a different way than is a parent. Grandparents are the nearest that a child comes to experiencing a reality that stands outside of their daily life and yet is approachable and familiar. Parents are bound into the child's small world as extensions of the child's needs for survival and security. Grandparents move back and forth across that boundary, shedding their light upon the family and at the same time, providing for the child a luminous icon extending into the past and pointing to the future.

The task of the grandparent is to preserve that role by not attempting to become another parent to the child while, at the same time, capturing the life of the child in a relation that is as free as a fairy tale and as cozy as a warm hug. When adult sons and daughters become parents and have their own family, they need grandparents as icons of continuity and stability as much as do their children. More than good advice as to how to raise their children, parents need from grandparents a 'river that runs through' life which provides a sense of continuity and stability amidst change and uncertainty.

Grandparents are a repository of stories, anecdotes, and ancestors that must be remembered, told, and recorded. But relationship with grandchildren must go beyond stories about the 'good old days!' It is not easy to fulfill this task. Grandparents often find that an effective way to communicate with their children and grandchildren is to share in their activities and interests. While this is important, even more important, is for grandparents to find ways to interest their grandchildren in their family history. This may be done by making sure that the oral history that grandparents carry with them is recorded, in writing, tapes, pictures, or other means, so that it will be available when there is more interest in such information.

Grandparents need to remember that their role is often an invisible and unrecognized one. As grandparents, we are providing a scaffolding for the building of lives we may never get to see. When we remember our own grandparents, we see that this is true.

Grandparents Are a Source of Unconditional Love and Acceptance

Everyone needs someone who believes in them and loves them unconditionally. Grandparents can do this in a special way. While it is true that parents often accuse grandparents of spoiling their children by giving expensive gifts and 'breaking the rules,' children have need of someone who mediates pure grace. Self-worth is not like a safety deposit box, locked up and sealed to prevent any loss. Rather, self-worth is more like a bucket of water that we carry every day with some holes in it, some larger than others! We need our bucket constantly refilled and, when it can be done, have some of the holes plugged or at least made smaller.

The self-worth of a child is constantly under assault. Failures come by the dozen, at school, with friends, and at home. Without expectations, a child has no sense of motivation. But with every bright expectation there is a shadow of failure. Parents are caught in the cycle of behavioral problems and the need do discipline. Grandparents have a different role, equally difficult, but clearly essential.

Grandparents face the difficulty of supporting parental rules and discipline while, at the same time, offering the child a special relationship. It is in the special relationship, not in breaking the rules, that a grandparent provides the kind of love and acceptance that a child needs. Without playing favorites, grandparents can give each grandchild the feeling of being a 'favorite' person.

When children receive attention and affirmation from grandparents, it comes as unmerited favor, rather than as a reward for some performance. This is the same quality of love that is conveyed by the theological word 'grace.' We all need to learn to receive grace in order to live 'grace-filled' lives. Grandparents have a special role in developing the capacity to receive grace in children and thus prepare them for the grace of God. This is especially important when so many children today suffer from lack or loss of parental love. Grandparents can provide a window of grace that opens up the child as both the object of God's love and as a person who receives and appropriates the grace of God.

Grandparents Are Mentors in the Task of Facing Life and Death

In former years, when grandparents spent their last years and some-times their last days in the family home, children were initiated into the reality of death as part of the structure of life. The death of grandparents put a human face on death for the child, as it were. The passing of a gen-eration was a ritual that embraced all members of the family, preparing each for their own journey.

Today, few people die at home, and children rarely experience the dying of a family member. People simply disappear from the child's world when they die, leaving the child to cope with a loss that has no formative power in shaping their own encounter with mortality.

One important role of grandparents is that of mentoring their children and grandchildren in the task of entering into life with both a vision for living meaningfully and dying with dignity and hope. I well remember as a boy, going with my parents to the local rural cemetery near the farm where we lived to walk among the grave-sites and read the names of my grandparents, with stories told that brought them to life again.

One of my earliest memories as a small boy is that of my grandmother lying in her coffin in the parlor of our farm home during the two or three day interval between her death and the funeral service. At that age I had little sense of what death meant. But I understood that this too was part of our family life. Grieving a loss without surrendering to despair and hopelessness is a capacity that must be learned. Who better to mentor us in the crucial passages of life and death than grandparents?

Preparing to be a grandparent and acquiring the skills of being an ef-fective grandparent begins with the intentional formation of rituals and rites of passage in which grandchildren can participate. This is a life-long task. The benefits begin immediately and the rewards accrue to the gen-erations that follow. The fifth commandment exhorts us to "Honor your father and your mother." It is the first commandment that carries a promise for this life and, by implication, for generations to come (Ephesians 6:2). Grandparents are also fathers and mothers; to honor such is to find the glue that can bind our broken families together. This is a promise![173]

Chapter 16

The Future of the Family

Living in a postmodern culture, one is asked to look in two directions at the same time. Ironically, living toward the future requires that the past be kept in view in order to escape being caught in its shadow. At the same time, there is something immobilizing about being obsessed with the past and as happened to Lot's wife, end up as a pillar of stone on the highway out of town (Gen. 19:26). But then we must also listen to Søren Kierkegaard who once sagely observed, "Life must be understood backwards but lived forwards."[174] Too often we take just the opposite approach. Failing to understand the future or, perhaps in fear of the future, we live in the past in hopes of avoiding 'future shock.' In the race toward the future, the worst fear is that one has become so disoriented that fleeing the past makes one a fugitive rather than a freedom-fighter. The nineteenth-century philosopher, J. G. Hamann, himself something of a maverick, wrote: "In a world of fugitives/One who moves in the opposite direction/Will appear to run away."[175] It is often hard to discern whether those who are moving forward in the flow of postmodernism are merely fugitives from their own past. The purpose of this chapter is to better understand the past in order to live in the future. We may end up with a strained neck!

The nuclear family is a fragile organism. Created for the Industrial Age, it has been viewed in economic terms as a mechanism whereby the husband's wages subsidized the unpaid support services provided by his wife. Today this subsidy has been withdrawn. Vulnerable to the stresses of the Information Age and no longer financially viable, for better or for worse the two-parent/one wage earner family is no longer a major component of our society. What will replace it? What should replace it?

It is not just alternative forms of marriage that create ethical and theological issues today. Alternative models of becoming a parent present new challenges for families in the future. Modern technology now provides a way for a woman who wishes to conceive a child a means of doing so with a biological sperm donor but not a father! This raises enormous ethical as well as practical questions. Reporting on this in the *Los Angeles Times*, Kay Hymowitz says that as long as a medical doctor performs the artificial insemination of donated sperm, "the donor is not a father. This doesn't simply mean that the child is fatherless in the way that, say, an orphan is fatherless. Rather according to the law, the child never had a father at all." She goes on to say that intentionality has now supplanted biology, by pretending that nature does not exist. When is a sperm donor a father? Can his mother be the child's grandmother even though he did not intend to become a father? Can a child have two mothers and no father?[176] The spirit of modernity challenges humans to pursue whatever is possible. There is a deeper spirit that reminds us that not everything possible for humans is good for humans.

Ask a group of conscientious parents what kinds of conditions are optimal for raising children today. They will unfailingly mention plentiful, unhurried time with nurturing adults, lots of love and physical affection, freedom and space to roam and presence of extended family or other caring adults. Any reasonable person who gave the matter sufficient thought would agree that these should be our design criteria for the 21st century family.

The majority of today's adults were raised in nuclear families where Dad was the breadwinner and Mom was the homemaker. Imperfect, yes, but at least it provided most children with a full-time, committed caretaker. With less than seven per cent of today's children growing up in this kind of family, who will fill the roles of housewife and mother? Current socioeconomic conditions have not been kind to families. Neither have they benefited children, who now comprise the largest class of people living below the poverty line. These days, time is money, and time spent with children rarely produces much in the way of dollars.

But have things really changed so dramatically? Despite the changing face of the family, it is still the way in which most people live. The family remains an institution that plays a key role in the way society is organized and controlled, and which adapts, not to the whims of individuals, but to the conflicting priorities placed upon it by the world at large. In fact, the major shift in modern Western society has been not in the family itself, but in the culture surrounding it. While it is accepted that the family does, and should, play a central role in nurturing individuals and raising children, there is a growing ambivalence about people's capacity to succeed at this task.

You Can't Go Home Again

The Southern novelist, Thomas Wolfe, in his poignant probing of the longing of the soul for life as it once was, spoke for all of us when he wrote, *You Can't Go Home Again* (1942). Dietrich Bonhoeffer, writing from prison to Eberhard Bethge, his former student, reminded him that we now live in a 'world come of age.' It is no use trying to 'leap' back to the middle ages, he wrote, when life seemed so certain and predictable. "It's a dream that reminds one of the song, 'If only I knew the way back, the long way into the land of childhood.'" Much as we might long to return to our adolescence, he said, the world has reached a more mature age, and we must realize that the day in which religion could be viewed as the source and solution for what unravels humanity at the core is over. However much we might now question his optimism concerning the 'maturity' of the world, Bonhoeffer was surely right in recognizing that secularism and pluralism has opened a Pandora's box that can never again be closed.[177]

In light of the rapid changes affecting marriage and family structures in a postmodern society, some have called for a return to the values represented in traditional structures of marriage and family.[178] Can we recover the values that we cherish by returning to former patterns of family life? Or must we 'reinvent' family in new forms that fulfill the same promises and yield the same results in the investment of our lives in the task of creating a new generation that will honor the old?

Social theorist Robert Bellah and his research team, in their book, *Habits of the Heart*, suggest that our contemporary culture has reached a profound and critical impasse:

> Modern individualism seems to be producing a way of life that is neither individually nor socially viable, yet a return to traditional forms would be to return to intolerable discrimination and oppression. The question, then, is whether the older civic and biblical traditions have the capacity to reformulate themselves while simultaneously remaining faithful to their own deepest insights.[179]

The key phrase in this citation is in the last sentence. Can the "older civic and biblical traditions have the capacity to reformulate themselves while simultaneously remaining faithful to their own deepest insights?" It may be difficult for postmoderns to realize or even comprehend the fact that the older, more traditional forms of marriage and family life, despite their sometimes distorted and even oppressive forms and practice, contained authentic insights as to what is quintessential to human life.

Surely Bellah is correct when he warns of the intolerable discrimination and oppression (usually of women and children) of some previous forms of marriage and family, especially in light of contemporary culture. Liberation of children from exploitation in both the home and workforce, as well as women from oppressive and dehumanizing roles in marriage and family is not a 'postmodern' ideology, but an authentic biblical theology. Even within the biblical narrative, where unredeemed social structures, such as polygamy, became part of the tradition, there were deeper impulses that pointed to the liberation of persons from those structures as part of God's design and purpose for humanity. Thus there is need for a 'hermeneutic of insight' in reading some of these texts, as in the case where the Apostle Paul makes an accommodation to a traditional cultural practice--male headship in a marriage--with an accompanying exhortation for 'mutual submission' in the spirit of Christ (Eph. 5:21-24). The 'insight' in this text is mutual submission; mutuality is the quintessence of a marital relationship, submission of wives to husbands was a practical expedient dictated by culture and subject to cultural transformation. In the same way, while children are commanded to obedience, the parent child relationship is under the command of God by which both parents and children are under the 'discipline' of fulfilling God's promise (Eph. 6:1-4).

There is no 'biblical' model of marriage and family that can be drawn out of the patterns found in the biblical narrative apart from the insights contained in these patterns. The theological task in assessing the future of the family is thus a hermeneutical task, that is, the task of rightly discerning the deeper insights of the biblical texts pertaining to marriage and family while, at the same time, accurately interpreting the deeper instincts that control the urges and desires of persons in our contemporary culture.

Reinventing Marriage and Family Life in a Postmodern Culture

Every generation must 'reinvent' marriage and family in our postmodern society. It was not always so. The roles and structure of my family of origin were carried over to the 'new world' from the 'old country'--in this case from Norway and Denmark. My mother's role in her marriage and family was not much different from that of her ancestors in Denmark, going back for centuries. My father's family of origin was Norway (Sweden on his father's side!). In any case, whether it was one Scandanavian country or another, the roles and form of marriage and family were handed down from one generation to another largely in a predetermined way. The language spoken and the food served survived the transition for one generation, but even when those became obsolete in a new culture, the family structure and marital roles continued virtually unchanged.

My own children belong to a new generation where marriage and family must be reinvented in the context of rapid and sometimes chaotic social and culture changes. Here is where Bellah's challenge strikes home: Can our children 'reformulate' the essence of the biblical and traditional forms so as to remain faithful to the insights that were contained within the older structures in the process of reinventing new roles and patterns for their generation? More importantly, can we help them in this task without imposing upon them models that worked well enough (we think!) for us? We can if we interpret correctly the key insights that were embedded in the older tradition and reformulate them in contemporary forms and structures of family life. What are people looking for today when they think of family?

Individuals in search of families

Predictions made a couple of decades ago concerning the demise of marriage and family now seem premature and lack the conviction they once had. Two opposing forces struggle in the psyche of our contemporary postmodern culture. One is fueled by the remnants of a romantic, but tragic, love affair with modernism's greatest achievement--the emergence of individualism out of the roving masses of a medieval tribal mentality. Alongside of this primal urge is another force, a wistful, nostalgic longing for what novelist Thomas Wolfe spoke of so eloquently: "Which of us has known his brother? Which of us has looked into his father's heart? Which of us has not remained forever prison-pent? Which of us is not forever a stranger and alone? . . . Remembering speechlessly we seek the great forgotten language, the lost-lane-end into heaven, a stone, a leaf, an unfound door. Where? When?"[180]

In their research, Bellah and his team discovered what they feel is a deep ambivalence at the core of contemporary North American culture. It is the ambivalence resulting from the social forces of individualism combined with the personal longing for belonging and community.

Therapists see a need for the social ties that they cannot really com-
prehend--they cry out for the very community that their moral logic
undercuts. Parents advocate "values" for their children even when they
do not know what those "values" are. What this suggests is that there
is a profound ambivalence about individualism in America among its
most articulate defenders.[181]

I think that we can view this ambivalence as a creative tension rather
than a crucial tear in the social fabric of our contemporary culture. Behind
the search for individual meaning lies a longing to be a person as well
as a performer. Solitary personhood is finally impersonal and existential
bankruptcy. When God declared, "It is not good for the man to be alone,"
it was the beginning of a creative act that resulted in a communal union,
"This at last is bone of my bone and flesh of my flesh" (Gen. 2:18-23). This
was the first experiment with individualism and the beginning of personal
humanity as we know it. There were no roles in the creation story, only
human beings, male and female. Husband and wife, father and mother,
emerged as creative living merged into cultural roles (see above, Chapter
Three). Reading the text through a 'hermeneutic of insight' yields a promising clue for a theology of the family in a postmodern culture. Which is
to say, in whatever form, family is necessary to be a human person, not
a cultural artifact.

If the contemporary quest to become an individual and to preserve
personal autonomy ends up with an existential and cosmic loneliness,
such as Thomas Wolfe describes, will there be family in which to find
refuge? If the more traditional forms of marriage and family are allowed
to disintegrate in a postmodern culture where freedom from confinement
in social constraints is viewed as a kind of moral freedom from oppressive
institutions, what will quench the thirst for communion and community?
Will the ambivalence that Bellah describes drive our souls downward into
despair where stimulation replaces edification? If the church only offers
another form of stimulation by adapting its worship to capture the idiosyncratic and homeless passions of individuals broken from their roots at
the core, will it not bring the virus of ambivalence into its own soul?

We are told that in our postmodern culture we are seeking meaning
rather than truth. Further, that meaning is embedded in our communities,
not in abstract concepts. If this is the case, then the forces that drive us toward individualism and away from community are not merely sociological
dynamics but epistemological demons. Epistemology means having to do
with what we know and how we know it. The commitment that moves
an individual into community and therefore into truth, is conditioned at
its source by the evidences of the person's truth-in-belonging. This is a

rational, not merely emotional commitment, for it is the will to belong in truth. "Our believing is conditioned at its source by our belonging," wrote Michael Polanyi years ago.[182]

Without family, can there be community? And, it might be asked, without community can there be family? In this sense, the postmodern culture in its departure from the more abstract and universalizing concept of truth might turn out to be more congenial to the biblical concept of truth as embodied in story, community, and lived experience.

Being-in-community means being in the presence of others in a personal way. It also means being present in such a way that our own personhood is allowed to develop and take form as social / spiritual being. Is the postmodern culture a friend or foe to family in this regard? In thoughts that were remarkable prescient, Ronald Gregor Smith, former professor of theology at Glasgow University in Scotland, mused:

> But how is the Presence known? How tested? And what is this life with which man then is dowered? In the midst of a world constantly, sullenly, willfully, despairingly denying this life of persons as the one historical reality, where is this community of which you speak? And how, even if there is such a community, may it possibly continue in life amid such hostile and perverse circumstances?[183]

To speak of *presence* without also speaking of the form in which it exists is, of course, impossible. Whether we think of community in the larger sense or family in a more local sense, we mean that to which we, as individuals, belong and in which we have both our individuality and need for community met. This is why the church must answer the question as to whether it is basically 'hostile' to such presence in community or can be a formative force in facilitating 'family' both in terms of its corporate life and in the lives of its members.

The 'future of the family' thus is also a topic that has to do with the future of the church. For the church, not only must be a 'family of families' as discussed above (Chapter 14), but also a positive force in creating and supporting healthy families. In this way, the church also must become active in the reinventing of family in the postmodern culture and contribute to the discussion of what constitutes 'familying' in the midst of changing forms of family life.

The question facing us is not whether or not the concept of family is becoming obsolete but whether the kind of family we experience leads us to be more or less human. Regardless of the form that family takes, there are 'ground rules' by which persons living in families must abide in order to develop their own humanity and personhood.

Rules for loving control roles for living

One of the maxims coined by Dennis Guernsey when dealing with the issue of the biblical teaching concerning marital role relationships was: There is a priority of the rules for loving in adjusting the roles for living. The rules for loving are biblical mandates, unambiguous and applicable to all situations and every role relationship. All human relationships create roles by which the relationship functions. Friendship may be the only relationship without clearly defined roles, though even here maintenance of the relation depends to some extent upon one or the other assuming responsibility for interaction to occur. But what is noteworthy about friendship is that it is the only human relationship that depends for its existence upon the mutual affirming and upholding of the personhood of each. This, of course, is what constitutes the inner core of love.

One can be a good neighbor, a good employee or employer, and even a good husband or wife as long as 'good' means fulfilling one's obligations, without the virtue of love. What I mean is that the absence of love does not immediately dissolve the form of the relation though it may affect the quality of the relation. With friendship, it is entirely different. Love is the glue that binds friends together. If I should humiliate a friend, be insensitive to the feelings of a friend, cause unnecessary harm or hurt to a friend, or in any way treat a friend as an object that I use for my own pleasure and gratification, the friendship dissolves. There is no reason why a person should want to continue a friendship where there is no love, other than we use another to meet other needs. And in that case it is not a true and healthy friendship.

In a marriage relationship, for example, husbands and wives often take the liberty of saying hurtful things to each other and act with rudeness and carelessness toward each other, without regard to their effect. This kind of behavior would end a friendship quickly unless there was repentance and forgiveness leading to restoration of the relation. Why does it seem easier to show kindness to a friend than to one's marriage partner? When persons who are married do not show kindness as a consistent pattern, the marriage is no longer a caring and loving one. Such a marriage has failed the litmus test of love. For love is not a relation where one only takes care *of* the other, but where both take care *for* the other. When one becomes incapacitated and unable to care for oneself, taking care of the other become the deepest expression of love. The promise of love includes the commitment to the care of each other should the need arise. But mutual care *for* each other is what keeps lovers friends and the relation healthy. Part of the reinventing of marriage in a postmodern culture is not redefining marriage itself but rediscovering and reaffirming personhood amidst the roles of marriage.

In one of our class sessions my teaching partner, Dennis, drove home this point with stunning effectiveness when he told of a turning point in his own marriage. He and Lucy were driving home one evening after teaching in a local church on maintaining healthy marriage relationships. As they drove, Lucy began to share her desire to do more than be a homemaker and wanted to get a job. Dennis found this somewhat unsettling, by his own admission. While he could lecture on the responsibility of husband and wife to affirm each other as persons (which had actually been the content of that evening's talk!), he disclosed the fact that he found himself so threatened by the thought of his wife going to work outside the home that he attempted quietly to convince her that he was able to make enough money to support them both and that he wanted her to be free not to have to work. It was a long discussion. As they drove into their driveway and stopped the car, Dennis said, "what shocked me to the core of my being was the realization that despite the fact that I considered myself not the stereotypical 'head of the household type,' I was defending my own personhood at her expense." Instead of getting out the car, Dennis told us, Lucy sat with her head in her hands, rocking back and forth, saying, "But I'm a person too. I'm a person too!"

The impression made upon all of us in that moment was deep and lasting. In his own way, Dennis could be transparent with respect to his own struggles while, at the same time, create a space where it was safe to expose our own hidden insecurities and begin the process of realigning our own motives and methods of relating to the law of love. When the rules for loving become instinctive, the roles for living become flexible and fluid. Insightful hermeneutics have to do with interpreting the forces that fuel our own intentions and so gain insight into the effect that our actions have on others. Marriage roles, in particular, are changing, not always in such a way as to overcome the ambivalence of which we have been speaking. Here too we need to turn the ambivalence into a creative and positive enhancement of human personhood.

Viewing marriage as creative partnership rather than mere companionship

Diana and David Garland suggest that the hierarchical model of marriage as a traditional form, while still advocated by some, has largely given way to other models.[184] Some modern couples tend to form companionship type of relationships, where each partner seeks equality. For the man it may mean an adjustment in terms of control over his wife's life with some kind of rotation in domestic roles in order to achieve equality in functions pertaining to the home and parenting role. For the woman, it may mean a great deal more in order to achieve equality in the world outside of the home. The failure of the companionship model of marriage as an alternative to the hierarchical model, according to the Garlands, is based on its excessive preoccupation with self-development in a mutual sense.

> The goal of the companionship model is the individual growth and self-actualization of the partners and the growth of the relationship. The question that comes to mind is, "Growth toward what?" The assumption is that the purpose of growth in the marriage is to achieve deeper intimacy with each other--the process is the goal. Wife and husband are to develop their gifts as individuals in the larger world outside the marriage and then use this greater maturity to deepen the intimacy and sharing of the marriage. The marriage has no major function except to meet the spouse's interpersonal needs and to enable the individuals to accomplish their own tasks and personal goals. Other functions of the marriage, even procreation, are less significant than the emotional nurture of the partners.[185]

The companionship model, say the Garlands, eventually becomes a consumer model, where the needs of each for fulfillment and satisfaction deplete the emotional resources of the couple and reveal their basic lack of interpersonal skills to fulfill each other's needs. For example, when the tasks relating to the marriage roles are viewed as a unit of 100, each seeks to maintain at least 50 of those units as a 'fair share' of the marital responsibilities. This leads to constant negotiation and arguments in attempt to achieve the 50/50 division of labor. Equality is sought in terms of how the tasks are divided. The same is true with regard to meeting each other's needs. If one expects the other to meet 100 percent of personal needs, failure on the part of one is judged to be a lack of equality in being 'companions.'

This is why the Garlands suggest that partnership is a much better concept than companionship. Equality is an unrealistic goal, they argue. It is itself more of a carryover of modernity, where abstract measurement of subjective qualities of life was sought as an attempt to be 'objective' and avoid these kind of disputes. Whereas in fact, they say, such an approach leads to more dissatisfaction and conflict. We need to move beyond hierarchy and equality as two different models and strive for a third, that of partnership. Partners in a task may have different levels of responsibility, but both share equally in the process and goal.

Being a partner is more fulfilling than being an equal

The goal of marriage based on partnership is not the relationship in and of itself, but pursuit of the purposes of the marriage as the couple has identified them in the will of God. Partnership marriage does not focus on itself, an earthly institution, but strives to transcend itself by focusing on a joint task.[186] Companionship marriage addresses power distribution; partnership marriage is concerned with the relationship's purpose. Companionship marriage is primarily a focus on structure and process; partnership marriage is primarily a focus on content and intention. Another way of looking at the companionship model is to see that the quest for equality is a striving for symmetry in the relation rather than complementarity.[187] A symmetrical type relation is one in which both are alike in as many aspects as possible--the two peas in a pod concept. Here, the effort is equal distribution of power, function and payoff. A complementary type relation is one in which the differences mesh so as to create a field or force of energy and effort which neither could do alone. I have attempted to put this in the form of a quadriplex (figure 16.1), showing four possible types of relationships related to how tasks are viewed in a marriage both from symmetrical and complementary dynamics.

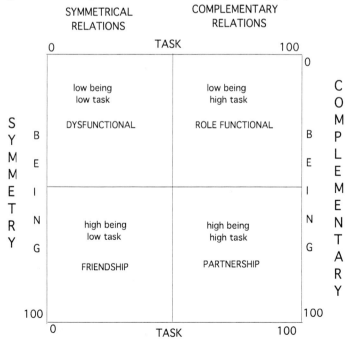

Figure 16.1

In the above figure, I have placed personal being as one dimension and task at the other, with symmetry and complementary types of relationships representing two options. When personal being and task are both at their lowest (upper left quadrant), we tend to see a dysfunctional relationship represented as symmetrical rather than complementary. In other words, the relationship is not only dysfunctional but there is no mutuality of interaction. In the lower left quadrant, where there is very low task but high being, it represents friendship; because there is no task, the interactions between each are more symmetrical, sharing the same feelings, experiences and desires. In the upper right quadrant, where there is low being but high task, the relationship is primarily determined by the role function of each. One person's work complements the other. I have worked together with faculty colleagues on tasks with virtually no interchange of personal experience, where we each do our tasks and work efficiently in our roles. The lower right quadrant represents, I think, what the Garlands mean by a partnership marriage, high task and high interchange of personal being. Here there is more of a complementary role for each that may not be equal in many ways, but both have an equal share in the outcome of the task. Creative partnership can overcome both the traditional hierarchical and the modern companionship type without necessarily denying the form of either one. This is the basic thesis of Garlands' book

The quest for equality through a drive toward symmetrical relationships, while it overcomes the perceived unfairness of the hierarchical type of relationships, becomes the goal of the companionship model. But both the hierarchical and the companionship model struggle over the issue of equality, one based on structural inequality the other on the struggle for perfect equality. Partnership in a common task, the Garlands, argue defuses the hierarchical model from the effects of its structural inequality and frees the companionship model from its conflict over equality. In other words, what made the more traditional hierarchical model work (such as in my family of origin), was the fact that both of my parents received equal benefit of the shared task of their marriage, regardless of the disparity in role definition.

A shared task orients the marriage toward the future

A shared task, or purpose, is what orients a relationship to the future, and causes it to endure. Stanley Hauerwas says this in a forceful and helpful way.

> Unless marriage has a purpose beyond being together it will certainly be a hell. For it to be saved from being a hell we must have the conviction that the family represents a vocation necessary for a people who

have a mission and yet have learned to be patient. Marriage and family require time and energy that could be used to make the world better. To take the time to love one person rather than many, to have these children rather than helping the many in need, requires patience and a sense of the tragic. Indeed such activities remind us of how limited we are, but at least we in the Christian tradition claim that it is only through such limits that we learn what it means to be free.[188]

The Garlands identify the primary task and purpose that offers creative partnership as a calling of the marriage partners to seek and find God's will for the marriage. They tend to define this as something above the task and purpose which marriage itself has in contributing to the community of which it is a part. "The marriage relationship," they suggest, following the model of Christ and the church in Ephesians 5, "has a transcendent purpose in God's scheme of things."[189] To the extent that they mean that the marriage itself has a purpose or task beyond that of each individual, and beyond the role of each person in the relationship, I would agree. They give five suggestions as a basis for thinking of the task concept of marriage:[190]

• Marriage is a unity, with a task and purpose of its own beyond those of the individual partners;
• the task or purpose of each marriage is unique and cannot be imposed by a standard definition of the function of marriage;
• the task or purpose of a marriage is often not explicitly defined but can be found in the structure of the relation rules and values that define the couple's life together;
• the task or purpose of a marriage varies over time;
• a significant source of meaning in marriage comes from the partner's roles as co-creators; marriage requires creative use of space, structures of relationships, and their own history, or their own story.

The 'promise' that becomes a vow in the creation of a marriage relationship, is thus related as much to the task of partnership as to the relation itself. A promise that binds persons together is the source of the moral worth of the relationship. When the promise is dead, the relationship is dead. There are no good rules for living in a relationship that no longer has a shared promise. The roles in a relationship have ethical value through participation in promise; without shared promise, the role has no moral imperative. Craig Dykstra says, "A culture without liturgies that make promises secure by the promises of God, is a culture that allows our promise-acts continually to be open to question, and thus continually unstable."[191]

What has contributed to the instability and lack of moral character for our modern society is not the loss of traditional roles and family structure, but the loss of binding promise-acts which overcome the slipperiness and ambiguity of human intentions and actions grounded in self-fulfillment. The greatest threat to the family for the future is not poor marriages, or conflicted family structures, but the freedom not to be bound by promise. An unresolved issue is the status of non-married adults who have freedom and autonomy, but no shared promise. The early church legitimated the single life style as a vocation alongside of marriage. But as Hauerwas says:

> Singleness was legitimate, not because sex was thought to be a particularly questionable activity, but because the mission of the church was such that "between the times" the church required those who were capable of complete service to the Kingdom. And we must remember that the "sacrifice" made by the single is not that of "giving up sex," but the much more significant sacrifice of giving up heirs.[192]

If the church is to be a 'family of families,' it must provide a language and liturgy of promise by which both the married and the unmarried can be bound to the Kingdom of God and to each other. If family, including marriage, is not first of all an institution of the church it is an indispensable element of the Kingdom of God. The Kingdom of God cannot be equated with the church; it is instead the rule of Christ that includes the church but is larger than the church. The Kingdom of God is the invisible sphere of Christ's power and reign into which we enter through the Holy Spirit and faith. In this way, Paul viewed the Kingdom of God as not primarily concerned with material things and political realms, but rather as a personal and social reality--righteousness and peace and joy--the fruit of the indwelling Spirit (Rom 14:17). Kingdom-living in the present time, according to Paul, begins with our reception of the Holy Spirit as the 'down payment' (*arrabon*) of our inheritance (Eph 1:14). The word signifies the promise of what lies in the future, not merely a promise, but the present reality of living in that promise. The future of the family thus is part of the future of the Kingdom of God, a present reality that points toward future fulfillment.

Thy Kingdom Come, On Earth as it is in Heaven

While there may be no instinct for marriage, there is a natural instinct for family.[193] Human infants are born premature when compared to the young brought forth in the animal world. The need for care and nurture is a physical and even personal need and therefore becomes a moral imperative. There is no moral imperative requiring marriage while there is one that requires family. The unmarried are not morally bound to marry, but they are morally bound to honor and respect their parents.

The abandonment of the new-born child on the part of those who brought it into existence is a violation of the humanity of each and thus binds the sexual act to the social act. The conception of a child is an 'ethical event' because it is the act of human persons, intentionally or accidentally, and as such, brings ethical responsibility for the protection and sustaining of human life. This is the origin and purpose of the human family.

From the beginning of the human race, the social construct of family was grounded in this 'natural instinct' for preservation and perpetuation of human life. This is what family is and thus what is determines what ought to be. Postmodern ethics was anticipated by Dietrich Bonhoeffer in this regard when he turned on its head the 'modern' basis for ethics as advocated by Kant, when he wrote: "In the sphere of Christian ethics it is not what ought to be that effects what is, but what is effects what ought to be." [194] Attempts to devise principles that determine the form of marriage and family as abstract, universal concepts, and use these concepts to form and shape marriage and family as a matter of public policy will inevitably fail in a postmodern period. But all is not lost, because in going back to what family is as an indispensable construct of human social being, we can trace out both the moral and practical 'shape' of family for the future.

As I have said above, while there are natural instincts for family that are grounded in the biological/social construct of what it is to be a human person, marriage as a sub-set of family has no natural instinct that determines either its necessity nor form. What is unique about marriage in Western societies in particular, is that since the Protestant Reformation, church, state and civil laws have worked together in promoting and sanctioning marriage relationships. Martin Luther broke with the medieval concept of marriage as a sacrament controlled by the church, viewing it as an institution willed by God through creation and thus basically a secular, not a sacred, institution. The church, Luther held, could only bless a marriage union, it could not create it. [195] In contemporary Protestant churches, marriage is ordinarily held to be a union established by mutual consent of the couple (man and woman), confirmation by family and friends, registration before the state, and the blessing of the church. As an order of creation, marriage thus was not viewed as a source of salvation but, if undertaken as a solemn vow, carried religious significance in the same way that being a good citizen, responsible parent, and honest worker were under a divine commandment.

From the beginning, it is apparent that human societies have viewed marriage as part of its economic and communal structure with more emphasis on the communal than the personal. Historically, the emphasis has gradually shifted from the communal to the personal with the result that in our day marriage as an institution has lost favor. Marriage is more and more being viewed as essentially a private, mutual arrangement only incidentally sanctioned by church or state.

More recently, the very concept of marriage as involving one male and one female has come under attack as a violation of the rights of persons who wish to establish same-sex marital relations and thus gain the legal, financial, and social benefits and privileges of a more traditional marriage. If one follows Luther's stipulation that marriage is not a sacrament of the church, there still remains the question as to whether or not as an 'order of creation' under the command of God, marriage is an expression of the divine image by which humans were endowed at creation as male and female, male or female (Genesis 1:26-27). One could argue that this indeed was the view of the Apostle Paul, who considered marriage between a man and a woman to be grounded in the creation account (Genesis 2:24), in some way reflecting Christ's relation to the Church (Eph. 5:31-33).

Since there are no marriages in heaven (Matt. 22:30), this may qualify at least to some degree our insistence as to what constitutes marriage here on earth. But if there is family in heaven--and there is!--then the future of the family here on earth is something we better be concerned about!

Despite all of the confusion about what form the family should take for the future, there can be no uncertainty about what is required of us with regard to the future of the family. We are to care for the weak and vulnerable, become advocates for the oppressed and victims of neglect and violence. There are thousands of children dying of hunger every day, others who are subject to violence and abuse every day. There are women who are suffering exploitation and abuse every day from someone in their family. The future of the family is the future of our children--and the elderly. If we wish to know what God's concern is for the family, it is clear from Scripture that it is not so much for what *comprises* family, as for what *happens* to persons in family. When the church prays, "Thy Kingdom come, on earth as it is in heaven," it is praying for "every family in heaven and on earth" (Eph.3:15). There is no statute of limitations with regard to being family. We better make it work!

Endnotes

[1] I have drawn some of the above from, "Postmodernism: A Primer for Pastors," Bill Kynes, *The Ministerial Forum*, Evangelical Free Church of America, Fall, 1977, Vol. 8 No. 1

[2] Brigette and Peter Berger, *The War Over the Family* (Anchor Press, 1983), 90

[3] *The War Over the Family*, 59

[4] Thomas Aquinas, as quoted in Stephen Clark, *Man and Woman in Christ* (Ann Arbor: Servant Books, 1980), 64

[5] *The War Over the Family*, 60, 63, 89

[6] Stanley Hauerwas, *A Community of Character* (Notre Dame: University of Notre Dame Press, 1981), 155

[7] Ibid., 155-6; original source: "Family Time and Historical Time," *Daedalus*, 106/2, Spring, 1977, 58

[8] *The War Over the Family*, 153

[9] C. Marshall Lowe, *Value Orientation in Counseling and Psychotherapy* (Cranston, R. I.: The Carroll Press, 1976; second edition, 1969), 2, 3

[10] *Habits of the Heart*, Robert Bellah, et al (San Francisco: Harper and Row, 1985), 144

[11] Stanley Hauerwas, *A Community of Character*, 160

[12] *A Community of Character*, 171, 172-3

[13] Ibid., 161; original source: "The Dilution of Fraternity," *Encounter*, October, 1976, 30

[14] Ibid., 173

[15] Stephen R. Covey, *Principle Centered Leadership* (New York: Simon and Schuster, 1990), 103

[16] *Person/Planet* (New York: Anchor Press, 1979), 163-64; 16

[17] Real encounter of the other, says Barth, means 1) "a being in which one man looks the other in the eye;" and consists in the fact 2) "that there is mutual speech and hearing;" and in the fact that they 3) "render assistance in the act of being;" and finally in the fact that 4) "all the occurrences that we have so far described as the basic form of humanity

stands under the sign that it is done on both sides with gladness." *Church Dogmatics*, III/2, 250-265

[18] Cited in his essay, "The Role of Parenting in the Development of Persons," in *On Being Family: A Social Theology of the Family*, Ray S. Anderson and Dennis B, Guernsey (Grand Rapids: Eerdmans, 1985), 74

[19] "Different Voices, Different Genes: 'Male and Female Created God Them'," in *Christian Perspectives on Sexuality and Gender*, Adrian Thatcher and Elizabeth Stuart, eds. (Grand Rapids: Eerdmans, 1996), 98-103

[20] Phyllis Trible, *God and the Rhetoric of Sexuality* (Philadelphia: Fortress, 1978), 98-99

[21] Ibid., 103

[22] Karl, Barth, *Church Dogmatics*, III/1, 186f

[23] Otto Weber, *Foundation of Dogmatics* (Eerdmans, Vol I, 1981), 575-6

[24] John Macmurray, *Persons in Relation* (London: Faber and Faber, 1961), 62

[25] Hans Urs von Balthasar, *A Theological Anthropology* (New York: Sheed and Ward, 1967), 87

[26] *The War Over the Family*, 174

[27] Macmurray, *Persons in Relation*, 44-45

[28] Clara Mayo, "Man: Not Only an Individual, But a Member," *Zygon* 3 (March 1968), 21

[29] *On Being Family: A Social Theology of the Family*, Ray S. Anderson and Dennis B. Guernsey (Grand Rapids: Eerdmans, 1985), 90; the citation from Barth is from *Church Dogmatics* III/4, 200

[30] *A Community of Character*, 172

[31] Karl Barth, *Church Dogmatics*, III/1, 312-315

[32] Ibid., 316

[33] This is a point discussed by Herbert Anderson: "A theology of the family is shaped by two similarly contradictory principles. First, the family is a necessary component of creation. Despite wide diversity of form and function throughout human history, the family has fulfilled God's intent to provide a context for creation and care in order to insure the continuity of the human species. . . There is no known human community without family in some form. . . Second, the importance of the family is qualified by the teaching of Jesus. From the perspective of discipleship, the family cannot be an end in itself. The metaphor of the realm of God is used here to point to God's intervention in history for purposes of continuing a process of transformation begun in creation. We are invited to participate in that process. Being a disciple in God's realm means being a subject who is willing to function as a sign to the world of God's vision for creation.

The realm of God is both gift and task. It comes to us by God's grace, not by human effort, and it sends us on a quest for justice, peace, and freedom in ever-widening human communities." *The Family and Pastoral Care* (Philadelphia: Fortress, 1984), 31

[34] *A Community of Character*, 55; 166

[35] Aristotle's concept of praxis can be found in, *The Nichomachean Ethics*, trans. J. E. C. Welldon (New York: Promethian Books, 1987), 192 (bk. 6, chap. 5)

[36] Lewis Smedes, *Mere Morality* (Grand Rapids: Eerdmans, 1985), 85

[37] *The War Over the Family*, 166-167

[38] Smedes, *Mere Morality*, 72

[39] Rollo May, *Power and Innocence--a Search for the Sources of Violence* (New York: Norton, 1972)

[40] Smedes, *Mere Morality*, 86

[41] Maurice Friedman, *The Confirmation of Otherness--In Family, Community and Society* (New York: The Pilgrim Press, 1983), 20-21

[42] Brigette and Peter Berger, *The War Over the Family*, 146

[43] Ibid., 147

[44] Roszak, *Person/Planet*, 139

[45] *A Community of Character*, 172

[46] Roszak, *Person/Planet*, 142

[47] Some of what follows is taken from "The Role of Parenting in the Development of Persons," by Dennis Guernsey, in *On Being Family: A Social Theology of the Family* (Grand Rapids: Eerdmans, 1985), 74-82

[48] Karl Barth, *Church Dogmatics*, 111/4, 189

[49] Craig Dykstra, "Family Promises: Faith and Families in the Context of the Church", in *Faith and Families*, edited by Lindell Sawyers (Philadelphia: The Geneva Press, 1986), 137, 143

[50] Jürgen Moltmann, *God in Creation: A New Theology of Creation and the Spirit of God* (Harper and Row, 1985), 262-3

[51] *A Community of Character*, 190

[52] *Love and Marriage* (London, Fontana: Collins, 1970), 183

[53] Ibid., 195

[54] *Church Dogmatics*, III, 4, 118, 140

[55] Ibid., 132

[56] *Church Dogmatics*, III/4, 131-132

[57] Ibid., 133

[58] *Church Dogmatics*, III/4, 221

[59] Ibid., 215

[60] Brunner, *Love and Marriage*, 189

[61] *Church Dogmatics*, III / 4, 200-211, 198
[62] *Church Dogmatics*, III / 4, 239-240
[63] *A Community of Character*, 172
[64] Diana and Richard Garland, *Beyond Companionship* (Philadelphia: Westminster, 1986), 82ff
[65] *Church Dogmatics*, III / 4, 225
[66] Ibid., 226
[67] Ibid., 228
[68] Portions of this chapter were taken from, "Spiritual Formation as Family Therapy: A Social Ecology of the Family Revisited," Ray S. Anderson, " *Journal of Family Ministries*, Vol. II, No. 4, Winter 1997
[69] Robert, Bellah, et al. *Habits of the Heart* (San Francisco: Harper and Row, 1985), 144
[70] Dietrich Bonhoeffer, *Communion of Saints* (New York: Harper and Row, 1963), 43-44
[71] Jürgen Moltmann, *God in Creation: A New Theology of Creation and the Spirit of God* (San Francisco: Harper and Row, 1985), 263
[72] Bonheffer, *Communion of Saints*, 65,73, 80
[73] Ibid., 36-37
[74] Ibid., 65
[75] Ibid., 75
[76] Ibid., 82
[77] Ibid., 82-83
[78] Urie Bronfenbrenner, *The Ecology of Human Development* (Cambridge: Harvard University Press, 1979); Allen Wicker, *Introduction to Ecological Psychology* (Monterey, CA: Brooks-Cole Publishing Company, 1979)
[79] W. W. Meissner, *Life and Faith: Psychological Perspectives on Religious Experience* (Washington, D. C.: Georgetown University Press, 1987), 78
[80] Thomas Moore, *Care of the Soul: A Guide for Cultivating Depth and Sacredness in Everyday Life* (New York: Harper Collins, 1992)
[81] Donald Winnecott, *The Child, the Family and the Outside World* (New York: Penguin Books, 1975); Cameron Lee, "The Good Enough Family," *Journal of Psychology and Theology*, 1985, 13, no. 3,. 182-189
[82] Eugene O'Neil, "The Great God Brown," *The Plays of Eugene O'Neil* (New York: Modern Library, 1982), 318
[83] The study was conducted by the General Social Survey (GSS) of the National Opinion Research Center at the University of Chicago.
[84] Source: http://www.blendedfamilies.net/research-statistics-for-blended-families.htm
[85] Jean Seligmann, "Variations on a Theme," *Newsweek*, Winter / Spring

1990. See also, Howard V. Hayghe, "Family Members in the Work Place," *Monthly Labor Review*, March 1990, 14

[86] The above is taken from, *Equality and the Family: A Fundamental, Practical Theology of Children, Mothers and Fathers in Modern Societies*, by Don Browning (Grand Rapids: Eerdmans, 2007), 247-256

[87] Geoffrey Bromiley, *God and Marriage* (Grand Rapids: Eerdmans, 1989), Introduction

[88] Wayne E. Oates, "The Care of 'Living Together' Couples," in *Family Ministry* Vol. 12, No. 3, Fall, 1998, 57-69

[89] Don Browning, *Equality and the Family*, 262

[90] Statistics gathered in an unofficial survey of 55 pastors in the state of Illinois for presentation to the Consultation on Pastor Care with Couples, by David Bugh and Judigh Bugh, October 1984

[91] Paul Hiebert, "Conversion, Culture and Cognitive Categories," *Gospel in Context*, Vol. 1, No. 4, October, 1978, 24-29

[92] Hauerwas, *A Community of Character*, 148

[93] Ibid.

[94] *A Community of Character*, 131

[95] This is a case that I have developed for class discussion based on an incident that actually occurred. Names have been changed to protect the identity of the participants.

[96] *Time Magazine*, June 29, 1992, 57

[97] Richard J. Gelles and Murray A. Straus, *Intimate Violence: The Causes and Consequences of Abuse in the American Family* (New York: A Touchstone Book, Simon and Schuster, Inc., 1988), 18, 20-21

[98] Ibid., 51

[99] Ibid., 43

[100] Gelles and Cornell, *Intimate Violence in Families*, 128

[101] Gelles and Cornell distinguish between normal and abusive violence: "Normal violence is the commonplace pushes, shoves, and spankings that frequently are considered a normal or accepted part of raising children or interacting with a spouse. . . . The more dangerous acts of violence we shall refer to as 'abusive violence.' These acts are defined as acts that have the high potential for injuring the person being hit." Gelles, Richard J. and Cornell, Claire Pedrick. *Intimate Violence in Families--Family Study Series # 2.* (Newbury Park, CA: Sage Publications, 1985), 22-3. However, Gelles and Strauss, in a later book, appear to abandon this distinction: "Our view is that it is impossible to distinguish between force and violence. Rather, all violent acts--from pushing and shoving to shooting and stabbing--properly belong under a single definition of violence. . . .

In reality, true insight into the nature of violence requires us to shed our stereotypes and blinders about routine spankings, normal pushings, and seemingly harmless grabbings, and to see these acts as part of the problem of intimate violence." *Intimate Violence* (1988), 54-55

[102] Gelles and Cornell, *Intimate Violence in Families*, 76

[103] W. W. Meissner, *Life and Faith--Psychological Perspectives on Religious Experience* (Washington, D.C.: Georgetown University Press, 1987), 252

[104] Ibid., 249

[105] Gelles and Cornell, *Intimate Violence in Families*, 76

[106] *Intimate Violence in Families*, 32, 33-34

[107] Karl Barth, *Church Dogmatics*, III/4, 182

[108] Ibid., 140

[109] Geoffrey Bromiley, *God and Marriage* (Grand Rapids: Eerdmans, 1980), Introduction

[110] Ibid.

[111] Karl Barth, *Church Dogmatics* III/4, 154

[112] Ibid., 181,

[113] *Church Dogmatics*, III/1, 312

[114] *Church Dogmatics*, III/4, 143

[115] Ibid., 165

[116] See also Barth, *Church Dogmatics*, III/4, 296ff

[117] Ibid., 208-209

[118] Ibid., 209

[119] Ibid., 211

[120] Emil Brunner, *Love and Marriage* (London: Collins, 1970), 189

[121] Lisa Sowle Cahill, "Homosexuality: A Case Study in Moral Argument." *Homosexuality in the Church--Both Sides of the Debate*, Jeffrey S. Siker, editor (Louisville: Westminster/John Knox, 1994), 61-75

[122] See V. P. Furnish, "The Bible and Homosexuality: Reading the Texts in Context," *Homosexuality in the Church--Both Sides of the Debate*, Jeffrey S. Siker, editor (Louisville: Westminster/John Knox, 1994) 18-35

[123] P. Pronk, *Against Nature? Types of Moral Argumentation Regarding Homosexuality* (Grand Rapids: Eerdmans, 1993)

[124] D. F. Wright, "Homosexuality: The Relevance of the Bible." *The Evangelical Quarterly*, 1989, 61: 291-300

[125] G. Grant, *Unnatural Affection: The Impuritan Ethic of Homosexuality in the Modern Church* (Franklin, TN: Legacy Communication, 1991)

[126] V. P. Furnish, "The Bible and Homosexuality: Reading the Texts in Context." *Homosexuality in the Church--Both Sides of the Debate*, Jeffrey S. Siker, editor (Louisville: Westminster/John Knox, 1994), 20

[127] Cardinal Joseph Ratzinger, "Letter to the Bishops of the Catholic Church on the Pastoral Care of Homosexual Persons" (1986). *Homosexuality in the Church--Both Sides of the Debate*, Jeffrey S. Siker, editor (Louisville: Westminster/John Knox, 1994), 39-48. A. Comiskey, *Pursuing Sexual Wholeness* (Santa Monica: Desert Streams Ministries. 1988). G. Grant, *Unnatural Affection: The Impuritan Ethic of Homosexuality in the Modern Church*, (Franklin, TN: Legacy Communication. 1991)

[128] V. P. Furnish, "The Bible and Homosexuality: Reading the Texts in Context." *Homosexuality in the Church--Both Sides of the Debate*, Jeffrey S. Siker, editor (Louisville: Westminster/John Knox, 1994), 18-35

[129] See for example: James B. Nelson, "Sources for Body Theology: Homosexuality as a Test Case." *Homosexuality in the Church--Both Sides of the Debate*. Jeffrey S. Siker, editor (Louisville: Westminster/John Knox, 1994), 76-90. J. S. Siker, "Homosexual Christians, The Bible and Gentile Inclusion: Confessions of a Repenting Heterosexist." *Homosexuality in the Church--Both Sides of the Debate*, Jeffrey S. Siker, editor (Louisville: Westminster/John Knox, 1994), 178-194. R. Scroggs. *The New Testament and Homosexuality* (Philadelphia: Fortress Press, 1984). G. R. Edwards,. *Gay/Lesbian Liberation: A Biblical Perspective* (New York: Pilgrim Press, 1984). J. Boswell, *Christianity and Social Tolerance: Gay People in Western Europe from the Beginning of the Christian era to the Fourteenth Century* (Chicago: University of Chicago Press, 1980)

[130] D. F. Wright, "Homosexuality: The Relevance of the Bible," *The Evangelical Quarterly.*, 1989, 61: 291-300

[131] R.B. Hays, "Awaiting the Redemption of our Bodies: The Witness of Scripture Concerning Homosexuality," in *Homosexuality in the Church--both Sides of the Debate*..Jeffrey S. Siker. (ed) (Louisville: Westminster/John Knox, 1994), 3-17

[132] E. Brunner, *Love and Marriage* (London: Collins. Fontana Books. 1970)

[133] Karl Barth, *Church Dogmatics*, III/1 (Edinburgh: T & T Clark, 1958), 186

[134] Karl Barth, *Church Dogmatics*, III/4 (Edinburgh: T & T Clark, 1961), 166

[135] Karl. Barth, *Church Dogmatics*, III/1 (Edinburgh: T & T Clark, 1958), 195

[136] C. Burr, "Homosexuality and Biology," *Homosexuality in the Church--Both Sides of the Debate*, Jeffrey S. Siker, editor (Louisville: Westminster/John Knox, 1994), 116-134

[137] S. L. Jones, and D. E. Workman, "Homosexuality: The Behavioral

Sciences and the Church." *Homosexuality in the Church--Both Sides of the Debate,* Jeffrey S. Siker, editor (Louisville: Westminster / John Knox, 1994), 93-115

[138] C. Burr, "Homosexuality and Biology," *Homosexuality in the Church--Both Sides of the Debate,* Jeffrey S. Siker, editor (Louisville: Westminster / John Knox, 1994), 116-134. P. Pronk, *Against Nature? Types of Moral Argumentation Regarding Homosexuality* (Grand Rapids: Eerdmans, 1993). S. L. Jones and E. E. Workman, "Homosexuality: The Behavioral Sciences and the Church." *Homosexuality in the Church--Both Sides of the Debate,* Jeffrey S. Siker, editor (Louisville: Westminster / John Knox, 1994), 93-115

[139] C. Burr, "Homosexuality and Biology," *Homosexuality in the Church--Both Sides of the Debate,* Jeffrey S. Siker, editor (Louisville: Westminster / John Knox, 1994), 116-134

[140] J. J. McNeill, *The Church and the Homosexual* (Kansas City: Sheed and Ward. 1976). J. J. McNeill, "Homosexuality: Challenging the Church to Grow." *Homosexuality in the Church--Both Sides of the Debate,* Jeffrey S. Siker, editor (Louisville: Westminster / John Knox, 1994),. 49-58

[141] James B. Nelson, "Sources for Body Theology: Homosexuality as a Test Case." *Homosexuality in the Church--Both Sides of the Debate,* Jeffrey S. Siker, editor (Louisville: Westminster / John Knox, 1994), 76-90. L. Q. Scanzoni, and V. R. Mollenkott, *Is the Homosexual my Neighbor? A Positive Christian Response: Revised and Updated* (San Francisco: HarperSanFrancisco. 1994). J. Boswell, *Christianity and Social Tolerance: Gay People in Western Europe from the Beginning of the Christian era to the Fourteenth Century* (Chicago: University of Chicago Press, 1980)

[142] Some additional sources for study and discussion are: *Gay Children, Straight Parents: A Plan for Family Healing,* Richard Cohen (InterVarsity, 2007); *Parents of the Homosexual,* David and Shirley Switzer (Philadelphia: Westminster, 1980). A helpful source for family members; provides practical guidelines and biblical principles for compassion and understanding. *Coming Out as Parents: You and Your Homosexual Child.* David Switzer, (Westminster John Knox, 1997). *Understanding Gay Relatives and Friends* (New York: Seabury Press, 1978). *Compassionate and Understanding. Pursuing Sexual Wholeness,* Andrew Comiskey (Santa Monica: Desert Streams Ministries, 1988). Offers strategies for ministry to recovering homosexuals. *Against Nature? Types of Moral Argumentation Regarding Homosexuality.* Pim Pronk (Eerdmans, 1993). He argues that biological nature cannot be used to distinguish between hetero and homosexuality. Only moral considerations apply, he concludes, and suggests a Christian and moral basis for homosexual relations. *Unnatural Affection: The Impuritan Ethic of*

Homosexuality in the Modern Church. George Grant (Franklin, TN: Legacy Communication, 1991). He takes a strong stand against homosexuality. *The Homosexual Person: Ne Thinking in Pastoral Care.* John Francis Harvey (San Francisco: Ignatious Press, 1987). Helpful guidance for pastoral care to homosexual persons, from a Roman Catholic perspective. *Gay Christians: A Moral Dilemma.* Peter Edward Coleman (London: SCM Press, 1989). Surveys the various positions, attempts balance between rejection and compassion. *Homosexuality in the Church--Both Sides of the Debate,* Jeffrey S. Siker, J Editor. Westminster/John Knox, 1994. *Straight and Narrow? Compassion and Clarity in the Homosexuality Debate.* Thomas E. Schmidt (Downers Grove: InterVarsity Press, 1995). Presents a biblical and theological critique from an evangelical perspective; balanced and informative on medical and psychological issues. "Concerning Homosexuality," *Our Dignity as Human.* P. K. Jewett/M. Shuster (Eerdmans, 1996), 290-350. "Homosexuality and the Ministry of the Church: Theological and Pastoral Considerations," in, *More Than a Single Issue: Theological Considerations Concerning the Ordination of Practicing Homosexuals,* edited by Murray Rae and Graham Redding (Hindmarsh: SA. Australian Theological Forum, 2000), 49-76. "Homosexuality: Theological and Pastoral Considerations," in *Journal of Psychology and Christianity,* Vol. 15, #4, Winter, 1996. "Homosexuality: Theological and Pastoral Considerations," in *The Shape of Practical Theology — Empowering Ministry with Theological Praxis,* Ray S. Anderson (InterVarsity Press, 2001), 266-283

[143] Claudia Wallis, "Faith and Healing." In *TIME Magazine,* 24 June, 1996 Volume 147, No. 26. Reported by Jeanne McDowell/Los Angeles, Alice Park/ New York and Lisa H. Towle/Raleigh

[144] Arthur C. McGill, *Suffering: A Test of Theological Method* (Philadelphia: Westminster, 1982), 116

[145] J. Christian Beker. *Suffering and Hope* (Philadelphia: Fortress Press, 1987), 21. For additional resources on suffering from a Christian perspective see, Randy Becton, *Does God Care When We Suffer and Will He Do Anything About It?* (Grand Rapids: Baker, 1988); D. A. Carson, *How Long, O Lord? Reflections on Suffering and Evil* (Grand Rapids: Baker, 1990); John Timmer, *God of Weakness* (Grand Rapids: Zondervan, 1988); W. Sibley Towner, *How God Deals with Evil* (Philadelphia: Westminster Press, (1976); James Walsh, and P. G Walsh. *Divine Providence and Human Suffering: Message of the Fathers of the Church* (Wilmington, Delaware: Michael Glazer, 1985)

[146] Otto Weber, *Foundations of Dogmatics,* Vol I. (Grand Rapids: Eerdmans, 1981), 560

[147] W. Eichrodt, *Theology of the Old Testament*, Vol. 2. (Philadelphia: Westminster Press, 1975), 120-121

[148] Robert Nelson, *Human Life--A Biblical Perspective for Bioethics* (Philadelphia: Fortress Press, 1984), 107ff

[149] *Los Angeles Times*, Saturday, April 21, 1984

[150] See the discussion in my book, *Theology, Death and Dying* (Blackwell, 1986), Chapter Seven, "Christian Perspectives on Death and Dying," 124-142; also, see "When Does Human Life Begin and End," in *Dancing with Wolves While Feeding the Sheep: The Musings of a Maverick Theologian*, Ray S. Anderson (Eugene, Or: Wipf & Stock, 2002), 111-122

[151] Otto Weber, *Foundations of Dogmatics*, Vol I, 560

[152] Viktor Emil Frankl, *Man's Search for Meaning; An Introduction to Logotherapy. A Newly Revised and Enlarged Edition of From Death-Camp to Existentialism*, translated by Ilse Lasch. Pref. by Gordon W. Allport (Boston: Beacon Press, 1963)

[153] Otto Weber, *Foundations of Dogmatics*, Vol I., 547

[154] Web site: http://www.growthhouse.org/educate/flash/mortals/mor0.html

[155] http://www. Elca.org/dcs/endoflife.html

[156] Herbert Anderson, *The Family and Pastoral Care* (Philadelphia: Fortress Press), 1984, 31

[157] Peter and Brigette Berger, *The War Over the Family*, 146

[158] *The Family and Pastoral Care*, 15-16

[159] Phyllis Trible, *God and the Rhetoric of Sexuality* (Philadelphia: Fortress Press, 1978), 80; 99

[160] Martin Buber, *Between Man and Man* (London: Collins, Fontana, 1961), 109

[161] Clara Mayo, "Man: Not Only an Individual, But a Member," *Zygon* 3 (March 1968). 21

[162] Dietrich Bonhoeffer, *Sanctorum Communio* (London: Collins, 1967), 44. 45. "It will appear that all Christian and moral content, as well as the entire spirituality of [persons], is possible and real only in sociality. . . . Here we have to show that [a person's] entire so-called spirituality, . . . is so constituted that it can only be seen as possible in sociality."

[163] See his chapter, "What Kind of Family is the Church?" in *On Being Family: A Social Theology of the Family*, Ray S. Anderson and Dennis B. Guernsey (Grand Rapids: Eerdmans, 1985), 155-159

[164] Henrika Vande Kemp and G. Peter Schreck, "The Church's Ministry to Singles: A Family Model," *Journal of Religion and Health* 20 (1981): 141-55

[165] *A Community of Character,* 168

[166] *Lumen Gentium II,* cited by David M. Thomas in, *Family Life and the Church* (New York: Paulist Press, 1979), 2

[167] Ibid., 36-37

[168] Ibid., 109

[169] Ibid.

[170] Eugene O'Neill, 'The Great God Brown.' *The Plays of Eugene O'Neill,* Vol 1 (New York: Modern Library, 1982), 318

[171] Portions of this chapter have appeared earlier in "The Tasks of Grandparents in Families," by Ray S. Anderson, *The Family Handbook,* Herbert Anderson, et al, editors (Louisville: Westminster John Knox, 1998), 83-88

[172] http://www.census.gov/population/www/socdemo/childcare.html

[173] Selected References for further reading: Ray S. Anderson, *Unspoken Wisdom--Truths My Father Taught Me* (Minneapolis: Augsburg Publishing House, 1995); Lillian Carson, *The Essential Grandparent: A Guide to Making a Difference* (Deerfield Beach, FL: Health Communications, 1996); Carolyn Gutowski, *Grandparents are Forever* (New York: Paulist Press, 1994); Arthur Kornhaber, with Sondra Forsyth. *Grandparent Power!: How to Strengthen the Vital Connection Among Grandparents, Parents, and Children* (New York: Crown, 1994); Karen O'Connor, *Innovative Grandparenting: How Today's Grandparents Build Personal Relationships with their Grandkids* (St. Louis, MO: Concordia Publishing. House, 1995)

[174] *The Journals of Kierkegaard* (New York: Harper Torchbook, 1958), 89

[175] "J. G. Hamann and the Princess Gallitrzi," *Philomathes,* Robert Palmer and Robert Hamerton-Kelley, editors (The Hague: Martinus Nijhoff), 339

[176] Kay S. Hymowitz, "The Daddy Dilemma," *Los Angeles Times,* Monday, April 16, 2007, A15

[177] Dietrich Bonhoeffer, *Letters From Prison,* New Greatly Enlarged Edition (New York; Macmillan Company, 1971), 360, 366

[178] For example, consider the Traditional Values Coalition campaign against the progressive secular culture's so-called anti-family agenda: http://www.traditionalvalues.org

[179] *Habits of the Heart,* Robert Bellah, et al (Harper and Row, 1985), 144

[180] Thomas Wolfe, *Look Homeward, Angel* (New York Charles Scribners and Sons, 1930), from the Frontispiece

[181] Ibid.

[182] Michael Polanyi, *Personal Knowledge* (London: Routledge and Kegan Paul, 1958), 322

[183] Ronald Gregor Smith, "History is Personal," Collected Papers of Ronald Gregor Smith, University of Glasgow Library, Scotland, unpublished (ca 1940-1944), 11

[184] The traditional model of a hierarchical order in a marriage where the husband has authority over his wife continues to have support by some as 'ordained of God.' For example. A. D. Litfin argues "that the universe should be ordered around a series of over / under hierarchical relations is His idea, a part of His original design. He delegates His authority to His own pleasure to those whom He places in appropriate positions and it is to Him that His creatures submit when they acknowledge that authority." "Evangelical Feminism--why Traditionalists Reject it", *Bibliotheca Sacra* 136:258-271; cited by Diana S. and David E. Garland, *Beyond Companionship--Christians in Marriage* (Louisville: Westminster, 1986), 53. The Roman Catholic lay theologian, Stephen Clark, presents a view of male and female role relationships based on a natural theology grounded in a metaphysical, or essentialist view of reality. For example, Clark argues that ordination of women in the church violates the essential order of creation. "The evidence solidly verifies the existence of differences between men and women that are not merely the product of culture or socialization. The evidence also solidly demonstrates that these differences are related to a structure of society and set of role differences common to the entire human species. To be sure, these differences can be expressed in many ways and, in fact, this variety can be observed in the cultures of the world. But beneath this variety is a common pattern or fundamental structure which is rooted in human biology. One might say that a role difference between men and women was 'created into' the human race. . . [I]n a time when the scriptural teaching is dismissed as culturally relative and outmoded, it is helpful to observe that God's purposes indeed seem to have been 'created into' the human race." Stephen Clark, *Man and Woman in Christ* (Ann Arbor: Servant Books, 1980), 440, 441, 447

[185] Diana S. and David E. Garland, *Beyond Companionship--Christians in Marriage*, 58-59

[186] Ibid., 59

[187] Ibid., 57, 72

[188] *A Community of Character*, 172

[189] *Beyond Companionship—Christians in Marriage*, 82

[190] Ibid., 82-83

[191] Craig Dykstra, "Family Promises: Faith and Families in the Context of the Church", in *Faith and Families*, edited by Lindell Sawyers (Philadelphia: The Geneva Press, 1986), 144

[192] *A Community of Character*, 190

[193] "There is no instinct for marriage, but it does organize a wide range of our natural tendencies by elevating some and de-emphasizing others. A variety of natural inclinations are order by marriage--the desire for sexual union, the desire Aristotle believed humans share with the animals 'to leave behind them a copy of themselves,' and following Aristotle again, the need to 'supply' humans with their 'everyday wants.'" Don Browning, *Equality and the Family*, 210

[194] Dietrich Bonhoeffer, *The Communion of Saints* (New York: Harper and Row, 1963) 146

[195] Martin Luther, "The Babylonian Captivity of the Church," in *Luther's Works* 36 (Philadelphia: Muhlenberg Press, 1959), 92-96

Index

Bibliography of Sources Cited

Anderson, Herbert, *The Family and Pastoral Care*, Philadelphia: Fortress, 1984

Anderson, Ray S. and Guernsey, Dennis B. *On Being Family: A Social Theology of the Family*, Grand Rapids: Eerdmans, 1985

Anderson, Ray S. "Spiritual Formation as Family Therapy: A Social Ecology of the Family Revisited," in *Journal of Family Ministries*. Vol. II, No. 4, Winter 1997, 10-27

_____, "Homosexuality and the Ministry of the Church: Theological and Pastoral Considerations," in, *More Than a Single Issue: Theological Considerations Concerning the Ordination of Practicing Homosexuals*, edited by Murray Rae and Graham Redding, Hindmarsh: SA. Australian Theological Forum, 2000, 49-76.

_____, "Homosexuality: Theological and Pastoral Considerations," in *Journal of Psychology and Christianity*, Vol. 15, #4, Winter, 1996, 301-312

_____, "Homosexuality: Theological and Pastoral Considerations," in *The Shape of Practical Theology—Empowering Ministry with Theological Praxis*, InterVarsity Press, 2001, 266-283

_____, *Theology, Death and Dying*, Blackwell, 1986

_____, *Dancing with Wolves While Feeding the Sheep: The Musings of a Maverick Theologian*, Eugene, Or: Wipf & Stock, 2002

_____, "The Tasks of Grandparents in Families," *The Family Handbook*, Herbert Anderson, et al, editors, Louisville: Westminster John Knox, 1998, 83-88

_____, *Unspoken Wisdom--Truths My Father Taught Me*, Minneapolis: Augsburg Publishing House, 1995

Aristotle, *The Nichomachean Ethics*, trans. J. E. C. Welldon, New York: Promethian Books, 1987

Barth, Karl, *Church Dogmatics, III/1*, Edinburgh: T & T Clark, 1958

_____, *Church Dogmatics, III/2*, Edinburgh: T & T Clark, 1960

_____, *Church Dogmatics, III/4*, Edinburgh: T & T Clark, 1961

Becton, Randy, *Does God Care When We Suffer and Will He Do Anything About It?*, Grand Rapids: Baker, 1988

Beker. J. Christian, *Suffering and Hope*, Philadelphia: Fortress Press, 1987

Bellah, Robert, et al, *Habits of the Heart*, San Francisco: Harper and Row, 1985

Berger, Brigette and Peter, *The War Over the Family*, Anchor Press, 1983

Bonhoeffer, Dietrich, *Communion of Saints*, New York: Harper and Row, 1963

_____, *Letters From Prison*. New Greatly Enlarged Edition, New York; Macmillan Company, 1971

Boswell, J., *Christianity and Social Tolerance: Gay People in Western Europe from the*

Beginning of the Christian era to the Fourteenth Century, Chicago: University of Chicago Press, 1980

Bromiley, Geoffrey, *God and Marriage*, Grand Rapids: Eerdmans, 1989

Browning, Don, *Equality and the Family: A Fundamental, Practical Theology of Children, Mothers and Fathers in Modern Societies*, Grand Rapids: Eerdmans, 2007

Bronfenbrenner, Urie, *The Ecology of Human Development*, Cambridge: Harvard University Press, 1979

Brunner, Emil, *Love and Marriage*, London, Fontana: Collins, 1970

Buber, Martin, *Between Man and Man*, London: Collins, Fontana, 1961

Burr, C., "Homosexuality and Biology," *Homosexuality in the Church--Both Sides of the Debate*. Jeffrey S. Siker, editor, Louisville: Westminster / John Knox, 1994, 116-134

Cahill, Lisa Sowle, "Homosexuality: A Case Study in Moral *Argument." Homosexuality in the Church--Both Sides of the Debate*. Jeffrey S. Siker, editor, Louisville: Westminster / John Knox, 1994, 61-75

Carson, D. A., *How Long, O Lord? Reflections on Suffering and Evil*, Grand Rapids: Baker, 1990

Carson, Lillian, *The Essential Grandparent: A Guide to Making a Difference*, Deerfield Beach, FL: Health Communications, 1996

Cohen, Richad, *Gay Children, Straight Parents: A Plan for Family Healing*, InterVarsity, 2007

Clark, Stephen. *Man and Woman in Christ*, Ann Arbor: Servant Books, 1980

Coleman, Peter Edward, *Gay Christians: A Moral Dilemma*, London: SCM Press, 1989

Comiskey, Andy, *Compassionate and Understanding: Pursuing Sexual Wholeness*, Santa Monica: Desert Streams Ministries. 1988

Covey, Stephen R. *Principle Centered Leadership*, New York: Simon and Schuster, 1990

Dykstra, Craig "Family Promises: Faith and Families in the Context of the Church," in *Faith and Families*, edited by Lindell Sawyers, Philadelphia: The Geneva Press, 1986

Edwards, G. R., *Gay/Lesbian Liberation: A Biblical Perspective*, New York: Pilgrim Press, 1984

Eichrodt, W. *Theology of the Old Testament*, Vol. 2., Philadelphia: Westminster Press, 1975

Frankl, Viktor Emil, *Man's Search for Meaning; An Introduction to Logotherapy*. A newly revised. and enlarged edition of From Death-Camp to Existentialism. Translated by Ilse Lasch. Preface by Gordon W. Allport, Boston: Beacon Press, 1963

Friedman, Maurice, *The Confirmation of Otherness--In Family, Community and Society*, New York: The Pilgrim Press, 1983

Furnish, V. P. "The Bible and Homosexuality: Reading the Texts in Context," *Homosexuality in the Church--Both Sides of the Debate. Jeffrey S. Siker, editor*, Louisville: Westminster / John Knox, 1994, 18-35

Garland, Diana and Richard, *Beyond Companionship*, Philadelphia: Westminster, 1986

Gelles, Richard J. and Murray A. Straus, *Intimate Violence: The Causes and Conse-*

quences of Abuse in the American Family, New York: A Touchstone Book, Simon and Schuster, Inc., 1988

Gelles, Richard J. and Cornell, Claire Pedrick. *Intimate Violence in Families-Family Study Series # 2.* Newbury Park, CA: Sage Publications, 1985

Grant, G., *Unnatural Affection: The Impuritan Ethic of Homosexuality in the Modern Church,* Franklin, TN: Legacy Communication, 1991

Gutowski, Carolyn, *Grandparents are Forever,* New York: Paulist Press, 1994

Harvey, John Francis,*The Homosexual Person: New Thinking in Pastoral Care,* San Francisco: Ignatious Press, 1987

Hauerwas, Stanley, *A Community of Character,* Notre Dame: University of Notre Dame Press, 1981

Hayghe, Howard V., "Family Members in the Work Place," *Monthly Labor Review,* March 1990

Hays, R. B., "Awaiting the Redemption of our Bodies: The Witness of Scripture Concerning Homosexuality," in *Homosexuality in the Church--both Sides of the Debate.* Jeffrey S. Siker, editor, Louisville: Westminster/John Knox, 1994, 3-17

Hiebert, Paul ,"Conversion, Culture and Cognitive Categories," *Gospel in Context,* Vol. 1, No. 4, October, 1978, 24-29

Jewett, P. K. and M. Shuster, "Concerning Homosexuality," *Our Dignity as Human,* Eerdmans, 1996, 290-350

Jones, S. L. and D. E. Workman, "Homosexuality: The Behavioral Sciences and the Church." *Homosexuality in the Church--Both Sides of the Debate.* Jeffrey S. Siker, editor, Louisville: Westminster/John Knox, 1994, 93-115

Kierkegaard, Søren, *The Journals of Kierkegaard,* New York: Harper Torchbook, 1958

Kornhaber, Arthur with Sondra Forsyth, *Grandparent Power!: How to Strengthen the Vital Connection Among Grandparents, Parents, and Children,* New York: Crown, 1994

Kynes, William, "Postmodernism: A Primer For Pastors, **The Ministerial Forum,** Evangelical Free Church of America, Fall, 1977, Vol. 8, No. 1

Lee, Cameron, "The Good Enough Family," *Journal of Psychology and Theology.* 1985, 13, no. 3, 182-189

Lowe, C. Marshall, *Value Orientation in Counseling and Psychotherapy.* Cranston, R. I.: The Carroll Press, 1976; second edition, 1969

Luther, Martin, "The Babylonian Captivity of the Church," in *Luther's Works* 36, Philadelphia: Muhlenberg Press, 1959, 92-96

McGill, Arthur C., *Suffering: A Test of Theological Method,* Philadelphia: Westminster, 1982

Macmurray, John, *Persons in Relation,* London: Faber and Faber, 1961

McNeill, J. J., *The Church and the Homosexual,* Kansas City: Sheed and Ward. 1976

_____, "Homosexuality: Challenging the Church to Grow." *Homosexuality in the Church--Both Sides of the Debate,* Jeffrey S. Siker, editor, Louisville: Westminster/John Knox, 1994, 49-58

May, Rollo, *Power and Innocence--a Search for the Sources of Violence,* New York: Norton, 1972

Mayo, Clara, "Man: Not Only an Individual, But a Member," *Zygon* 3 (March

1968)

Meissner, W. W., *Life and Faith: Psychological Perspectives on Religious Experience*, Washington, D. C.: Georgetown University Press, 1987

Moltmann, Jürgen, *God in Creation: A New Theology of Creation and the Spirit of God*, Harper and Row, 1985

Moore, Thomas, *Care of the Soul: A Guide for Cultivating Depth and Sacredness in Everyday Life*, New York: Harper Collins, 1992

Nelson, James B., "Sources for Body Theology: Homosexuality as a Test Case," in *Homosexuality in the Church--Both Sides of the Debate*. Jeffrey S. Siker, editor, Louisville: Westminster/John Knox, 1994, 76-90

Oates, Wayne E., "The Care of 'Living Together' Couples," in *Family Ministry* Vol. 12, No. 3, Fall, 1998, 57-60

O'Connor, Karen, *Innovative Grandparenting: How Today's Grandparents Build Personal Relationships with their Grandkids*, St. Louis, MO: Concordia Publishing. House, 1995

O'Neil, Eugene, "The Great God Brown," *The Plays of Eugene O'Neil*, New York: Modern Library, 1982

Palmer, Robert and Robert Hamerton-Kelley, editors "J. G. Hamann and the Princess Gallitrzi," *Philomathes*, The Hague: Martinus Nijhoff

Polanyi, Michael, *Personal Knowledge*, London: Routledge and Kegan Paul, 1958

Pronk, Prim. *Against Nature? Types of Moral Argumentation Regarding Homosexuality*, Grand Rapids: Eerdmans, 1993

Ratzinger, Cardinal Joseph, "Letter to the Bishops of the Catholic Church on the Pastoral Care of Homosexual Persons" (1986) in *Homosexuality in the Church--Both Sides of the Debate*. Jeffrey S. Siker, editor, Louisville: Westminster/John Knox, 1994, 39-48.

Roszak, Theodore, *Person/Planet*, New York: Anchor Press, 1979

Scanzoni, L. Q. and V. R. Mollenkott, *Is the Homosexual my Neighbor? A Positive Christian Response: Revised and Updated*, San Francisco: HarperSanFrancisco. 1994

Schmidt, Thomas E., *Straight and Narrow? Compassion and Clarity in the Homosexuality Debate* Downers Grove: InterVarsity Press, 1995

Scroggs. R., *The New Testament and Homosexuality*, Philadelphia: Fortress Press, 1984

Seligmann,Jean, "Variations on a Theme," *Newsweek*, Winter/Spring 1990

Siker, Jeffrey, S. "Homosexual Christians, The Bible and Gentile Inclusion: Confessions of a Repenting Heterosexist." *Homosexuality in the Church--Both Sides of the Debate*. Jeffrey S. Siker, editor, Louisville: Westminster/John Knox, 1994, 178-194

Smedes, Lewis, *Mere Morality*, Grand Rapids: Eerdmans, 1985

Smith, Ronald Gregor, "History is Personal," Collected Papers of Ronald Gregor Smith, University of Glasgow Library, Scotland, unpublished (ca 1940-1944)

Switzer, David and Shirley, *Parents of the Homosexual*, Philadelphia: Westminster, 1980

Switzer, David, *Coming Out as Parents: You and Your Homosexual Child*, Westminster John Knox, 1997

_____.*Understanding Gay Relatives and Friends*, New York: Seabury Press,

1978

Thatcher, Adrian and Elizabeth Stuart eds., *Christian Perspectives on Sexuality and Gender*, Eerdmans, 1996

Thomas David M., *Family Life and the Church*, New York: Paulist Press, 1979

Timmer, John, *God of Weakness*, Grand Rapids: Zondervan, 1988

Towner, W. Sibley, *How God Deals with Evil*, Philadelphia: Westminster Press, 1976

Trible, Phyllis, *God and the Rhetoric of Sexuality*, Philadelphia: Fortress, 1978

Vande Kemp Henrika, and G. Peter Schreck, "The Church's Ministry to Singles: A Family Model," *Journal of Religion and Health* 20 (1981): 141-55

von Balthasar, Hans Urs, *A Theological Anthropology*, New York: Sheed and Ward. 1967

Wallis, Claudia, "Faith and Healing," In *TIME Magazine*, 24 June, 1996 Volume 147, No. 26.

Walsh, James and P. G Walsh, *Divine Providence and Human Suffering: Message of the Fathers of the Church*, Wilmington, Delaware: Michael Glazer, 1985

Weber, Otto, *Foundation of Dogmatics*, Eerdmans, Vol I, 1981

Wicker, Allen *Introduction to Ecological Psychology*, Monterey, CA: Brooks-Cole Publishing Company, 1979

Winnecott, Donald, *The Child, the Family and the Outside World*, New York: Penguin Books, 1975

Wolfe, Thomas, *Look Homeward, Angel*, New York Charles Scribners and Sons, 1930

Wright, D. F., "Homosexuality: The Relevance of the Bible." *The Evangelical Quarterly*, 1989, 61: 291-300